VALUE CHANGE AND GOVERNANCE IN CANADA

Edited by Neil Nevitte

Over the past forty years, citizens of most Western industrialized coun-tries have become increasingly alienated from, and mistrustful of, their elected officials. In this study, scholars of political science and psy-chology argue that significant changes in values, the result of several cross-societal transformations – such as the increase of wealth in west-ern countries, a change in the source of that wealth, a rapid growth in the level of education among the general population, and the resulting growth of the middle class – are responsible for these shifts in attitude. Consequently, they argue, the institutions of democratic governance now operate in a profoundly different environment than that in which they were founded.

Among the issues discussed are how these value changes affect citi-zens' views of democracy, government, and legislation, and how these changes have affected modern democracy. The contributors consider the impact value changes will have on future governments, and the impli-cation for this shift in citizen–state relations for the course of further policy making, as well as look at ways governments can address emerg-ing issues important to today's citizens. As part of the Trends Series to examine Canadian public policy from the point of view of academia, this book is part of an effort seeking to strengthen government policy development on long-term issues.

(The Trends Project Series)

NEIL NEVITTE is Professor in the Department of Political Science at the University of Toronto

Policy Research: The Trends Project Series

The Trends Project is a result of the Government of Canada's Policy Research Initiative, an undertaking that seeks to strengthen the Government of Canada's policy capacity and ensure that policy development benefits from the work of researchers and academics. The Policy Research Initiative, in cooperation with the Social Sciences and Humanities Research Council, developed a new model for academics and government to collaborate on policy research. Teams of academics examined the forces that are driving change in Canada and identified the potential implications for public policy. This collaboration came to be known as the Trends Project. Under the project, academics, research institutes, and government officials worked in partnership to build a better knowledge base on longer-term issues to support policy development and identify knowledge gaps requiring further research. The Trends Project will result in the following books:

Gordon Smith and Daniel Wolfish, editors,
Who Is Afraid of the State?: Canada in a World of Multiple Centres of Power

Edward A. Parson, editor,
Governing the Environment: Persistent Challenges, Uncertain Innovations

Neil Nevitte, editor,
Value Change and Governance in Canada

George Hoberg, editor,
Capacity for Choice: Canada in a New North America

David Cheal, editor,
Aging and Demographic Change in Canadian Context

Danielle Juteau, editor,
Social Differentiation: Patterns and Processes

VALUE CHANGE AND GOVERNANCE IN CANADA

Edited by Neil Nevitte

UNIVERSITY OF TORONTO PRESS
Toronto Buffalo London

© University of Toronto Press Incorporated 2002
Toronto Buffalo London
Printed in Canada

ISBN 0-8020-8405-2

Printed on acid-free paper

National Library of Canada Cataloguing in Publication Data

Main entry under title:

Value change and governance in Canada

(Trends series)
ISBN 0-8020-8405-2

1. Canada – Politics and government – 1933–   2. Social values –
Canada.   3. Political participation – Canada.   4. Representative
government and representation – Canada.   I. Nevitte, Neil
II. Series: Trends series (Toronto, Ont.)

JL186.5.V34 2001   320.971'09'049   C2001-903467-9

The University of Toronto Press acknowledges the financial assistance
to its publishing program of the Canada Council for the Arts and the
Ontario Arts Council.

University of Toronto Press acknowledges the financial support for
its publishing activities of the Government of Canada through the
Book Publishing Industry Development Program (BPIDP).

Contents

Tables

Figures

Preface

Exchanging ideas, perspectives, frameworks, and data between academics and government is, at once, necessary for the development of innovative and effective public policy and difficult to accomplish in time of constant change. The Trends Project, a collaborative effort of the Policy Research Initiative and the Social Sciences and Humanities Research Council, was conceived as a means of addressing this difficulty by providing a new model for academics and government to collaborate on policy research that informs the policy-development process.

Three goals lie at the heart of the Policy Research Initiative and the Trends Project:

- Supporting the creation, sharing, and use of policy research knowledge;
- Strengthening departments by recruitment, development, and retention of people; and
- Building a policy research community through networks and concrete vehicles and venues.

In the past, either the government has commissioned research to address government-identified knowledge gaps or the federal granting councils have funded an academic-led research agenda. Under the Trends Project, academics, think tanks, and government officials worked in partnership to identify the knowledge gaps requiring further research. This collaboration sought to identify opportunities for research and scholarship to inform longer-term policy and societal choice.

The make-up of the teams themselves was unique. Led by some of Canada's leading academics, the project's eight teams involved more than fifty researchers from universities across the country, chosen through a call for proposals administered by the Social Sciences and Humanities Research Council. These multidisciplinary teams of participants from across Canada brought people together who would not normally have the opportunity to collaborate. The result of this multidisciplinary and cross-Canada approach has been that we now have a greater depth and breadth of understanding on the emergent policy areas Canada is likely to confront in the coming years.

The Trends Project research papers were presented on several occasions at workshops and conferences across the country where Canadian researchers and government officials provided insight and feedback. Finally, each of the papers published under the Trends Project underwent anonymous peer review.

The Trends Project was also innovative because it provided a means for academics to have their ideas and research circulated widely throughout government. The project was concerned not only with producing papers, but also with the continued process of dialogue and collaboration between thoughtful people engaged in these issues from multiple disciplines and professions, and from the university, government, private, and non-profit sectors. The second annual National Policy Research Conference in November 1999 offered an opportunity for researchers to showcase their work to over 800 policy developers and experts in the federal and provincial governments. Commentaries and research excerpts have been featured regularly in *Horizons*, the Policy Research Initiative's newsletter. *Horizons* targets a broad policy audience from throughout the Canadian policy research community, both inside and outside of government, reaching more than 8,000 people.

By bringing government and academic communities together on an ongoing basis, the Trends Project exposed these groups to each other's research needs, perspectives, and constraints. The Trends Project has been one part of a larger effort to build Canada-wide policy research capacity. It is a model that we would like to build on in the future.

Laura A. Chapman
Executive Director
Policy Research Initiative
February 2002

Contributors

David C. Docherty, Department of Political Science, Wilfrid Laurier University

Mebs Kanji, Department of Political Science, University of Calgary

Richard Nadeau, Département de science politique, Université de Montréal

Neil Nevitte, Department of Political Science, University of Toronto

Neal J. Roese, Department of Psychology, Simon Fraser University

Lisa Young, Department of Political Science, University of Calgary

VALUE CHANGE AND GOVERNANCE IN CANADA

1. Introduction: Value Change and Reorientation in Citizen–State Relations

Neil Nevitte

Significant shifts in the dynamics of citizen–state relations have taken place throughout the advanced industrial world over the last two decades or so, and a growing body of evidence suggests that these reorientations have been shaped by value changes among publics. On these two broad themes there is a consensus.[1] But this consensus fragments when it comes to providing answers to second-order questions, such as What are the causes of these transformations? What are the most important dimensions of these value changes? What are their implications? and How can the consequences of some of these shifts be addressed?

The aim of this chapter is to assemble some of the core empirical findings and interpretations concerning Canadian value shifts and to analyse how these shifts mediate citizens' relations with the state. Relations between citizens and the state are bilateral: they can be altered from either direction. The prevailing view is that these relations have been fundamentally modified not because the nature of the state has changed, but because citizens have changed.[2] There is a new political culture.

Neither values nor institutions exist in a vacuum – we must begin by situating them in context and by considering the structural factors that must be the foundation for interpreting broad shifts in citizenship values. Values, sometimes referred to as core beliefs, are related to conceptions of what is desirable and form the basis of judgments that citizens make about their social, economic, and political worlds.[3] Our next task is to examine the available strands of evidence that tell us something about Canadian values and their relationship to governance in this setting. Two kinds of evidence are especially relevant here: the first concerns indications of cross-time shifts in core citizenship values, and the second elaborates how these particular values are related to each other. Finally, we must evaluate the evidence and consider some of the policy implications of these findings.

Structural Change

Nearly forty years ago, Gabriel Almond and Sidney Verba launched a pioneering study examining civic culture in five countries. That project emphatically made the point that to understand variations in the success of democratic political systems it is necessary to move beyond an exclusive preoccupation with their institutional features to incorporate an explicit understanding of the political orientations of citizens.[4] By placing the notion of 'political culture' at the centre of their analysis, Almond and Verba built a conceptual bridge linking the micro-worlds of individual citizens to the macro-world of the institutions that perform the tasks of governance. And, in the process of building that conceptual bridge, they drew a distinction between 'culture' in general and 'political culture.' According to Almond and Verba, 'culture' refers to 'psychological orientations towards social objects,'[5] while 'political culture' refers more specifically to 'the particular distribution of patterns of orientations towards political objects.'[6]

With the advantage of hindsight, and the benefit of forty years' worth of empirical research, it is not difficult to find fault with Almond and Verba's original project. But the fundamental contribution of their path-breaking work remains intact: most analysts now accept the premise that citizens' values matter to the successful functioning of democratic societies because, at a very fundamental level, values have to do with what people want out of life. The values, or core beliefs, of citizens have important practical consequences because they shape preferences and guide expectations, and because citizens in democratic societies have regular opportunities – elections – for expressing these preferences and for evaluating whether the performance of governments has met public expectations.[7]

Most advanced industrial states have experienced significant structural transformations since the early 1960s, and these transformations have profoundly reshaped the setting in which representative democratic institutions work. The pace of these changes has varied from one country to the next, but the essential point is that the basic character of these structural changes is replicated again and again in the post-1945 histories of virtually all western European states, as well as in Canada and the United States. The core features of these shifts have been documented elsewhere,[8] but it is useful to summarize their major contours because they provide a vital context for interpreting the shape, scope, and implications of value change.

First, all advanced industrial states have experienced dramatic increases in wealth during the latter half of the twentieth century.[9] The trajectories towards greater wealth have not been entirely smooth, however; for example, most states experienced temporary economic reversals during the oil crisis of the mid-1970s, and there have been periods of stagnation in both the 1970s and the 1980s. Nevertheless, these economic reversals have been relatively short-lived – from the late 1940s to the end of the 1990s the overall trend has been one of economic expansion. To be sure, this sustained economic growth has not eradicated poverty, but the vast majority of citizens in advanced industrial states are far wealthier than their compatriots of preceding generations.

A second significant structural change concerns shifts in the sources of wealth. In the immediate postwar period, much of the economic growth in the Western world came from increased efficiencies in, and the expansion of, the industrial sector. By the late 1960s, however, the balance of wealth-generating activities began to shift from the industrial sector to the tertiary, or service and technology, sector of these economies. The major benchmark separating industrial from advanced industrial states concerns the proportion of the labour force working in the tertiary sector; economies qualify as 'advanced industrial' when more than 50 per cent of the paid workforce is employed in the tertiary sector.[10] Most western European countries, as well as Canada and the United States, had crossed this threshold by the early 1980s. Simply put, what the vast majority of people now do for a living is substantially different from the work world of previous generations.

The remarkably rapid expansion of the technology and service sectors of these economies would not have been possible had it not been for yet another structural change – the dramatic expansion of access to post-secondary education. Knowledge-based economies are unthinkable without a supply of knowledge workers. Once again, regardless of the variations in the rates at which this 'education revolution' took place,[11] its consequences have startlingly similar effects – the rapid expansion of the middle classes and greater occupational and geographic mobility. The impacts of these kinds of transformations reverberate throughout society. For example, the dramatic rise in the number of women entering post-secondary educational institutions has produced profound changes in the gender composition of the paid workforce. And these two shifts, in turn, have had a significant impact on family incomes and family structures.[12]

Other related structural transformations have taken place in the areas of communications and information. Modern means of communications – computers, satellites, cable – have massively reduced the cost of gaining access to information. Information from around the world is now immediately and directly accessible to larger and larger segments of the population in advanced industrial states. Parallel shifts have taken place in transportation. The ever-broadening accessibility to modern modes of transportation, coupled with dramatic advances in electronic communications, means that hardly any corner of the world now qualifies as 'remote.'

The combined effects of these changes mean that the institutions of democratic governance, designed and shaped during the industrial era, now operate in a profoundly different environment. Much of the available evidence indicates that citizens' values, as well as their skills and expectations of government, underwent significant changes alongside these structural shifts. And given the permeability of economic, social, and political dynamics, it would be remarkable indeed if the structural transformations that have reshaped society and the economy over the last twenty-five years were to have no impact whatever on the political dynamics of citizens' connections' to the state.

Structural Change and Value Change

The linkages between the structural shift from deep industrialism to advanced industrialism and value change have been specified in a variety of ways. Daniel Bell provides an arresting account of some of the essential themes. The transitions from pre-industrial to industrial society, and from industrial to advanced industrial society, produced fundamental changes not only in people's daily life experiences but also in prevailing world views.[13] Bell characterizes pre-industrial life as a 'game against nature' in which one's 'sense of the world is conditioned by the vicissitudes of the elements – the seasons, the storms, the fertility of the soil, the amount of water, the depth of the mine seams, the droughts and the floods.'[14] Industrialization provided greater control over the natural environment. And with its consolidation, life became a 'game against fabricated nature,'[15] a technical, mechanical, rationalized, and bureaucratic existence directed toward creating and dominating the made environment. With the emergence of postindustrial societies, world views evolved yet again, becoming a 'game between persons.'[16] Most people spend their productive hours dealing with other people and symbols; less effort is focused on producing material objects and more is focused on communicating and processing information. For Bell, the hallmark value shift associated with this final transition is the increased salience of 'individual autonomy.' One observer characterizes the transition to advanced industrialism as a shift away from 'solidarity toward self-affirmation.'[17] Another associates it with the emergence of 'individualization.'[18] Still others focus on the rise of 'expressivism' or 'self expression.'[19] The precise language used to describe the central axis of value change varies, but these differences are of degree rather than kind; the perspectives are congenial.

One of the most influential accounts of how value change is linked to the emergence of late advanced industrialism is supplied by Ronald Inglehart.[20] This value-change thesis contends that the economic security produced in advanced industrial societies has gradually changed the goal orientations of its citizens. In the process, 'an emphasis on economic security gradually fades, and universal but often latent needs for belonging, esteem, and the realization of intellectual potential become increasingly prominent.'[21] Individuals continue to place value on 'materialist' concerns of economic and physical security, but 'post-materialist' or higher-order concerns, such as the need for self-expression, freedom, and quality of life, become increasingly prominent.[22]

This particular explanation of value change has not been universally accepted, but it presents a number of significant strengths. One is its strong regard for context – it acknowledges the importance of the kinds of structural changes outlined above. For example, Inglehart's claim that value change is gradual is grounded in both socialization theory and a recognition of the timing of the onset of widespread prosperity. From the standpoint of socialization theory, formative conditions and experiences matter. Those who grew up during periods of scarcity and physical insecurity, the Depression and the Second World War, tend to retain materialist orientations; in contrast, those socialized during the era of post-war prosperity tend to be more inclined toward post-material values. And clearly, the latter are gradually replacing the former.[23]

A second strength of this account is that it produces clear expectations about the socio-demographic distribution of value changes. Huge volumes of data from multiple countries over several decades indicate not only that the values associated with the new political culture do seem to be becoming more widespread among publics in advanced industrial states, but also that these transformations are associated with generational change. As expected, post-material values are most pronounced among the younger generations.[24] There is also compelling evidence that these shifting value orientations have consequences for changing the public's agenda. For example, it appears that those segments of the public that have internalized 'new values' are less supportive of the redistributive policies that were once central to the agendas of traditional political parties. More salient for them are issue orientations that reflect a pre-occupation with the quality of life, such as concern for the environment.

The particulars of Inglehart's explanation for value change may be challenged on a variety of grounds.[25] Nevertheless, there is reliable evidence from independent researchers indicating that significant value changes have indeed taken place among citizens in advanced industrial states.[26] Data from the World Values Survey suggest that there have been systematic shifts in a host of political, social, and economic orientations since the 1980s. These findings, summarized in table 1.1, illustrate the cross-national consistency of these shifts. The directions of these changes are strikingly similar country by country, and the changes in Canada are almost precisely equivalent to those taking place among publics in eleven other advanced industrial states. What is also striking is the extent to which these cross-national shifts are consistently and systematically related to age, education, and post-materialist value type. The changes do not appear to be random; they conform to similar patterns in multiple settings.[27] It is possible, of course, that Inglehart's explanation for these changes is not satisfactory in every respect. But discounting that explanation does not change the fundamentals: the cumulative evidence indicates coherent changes in the basic value orientations of publics in advanced industrial states.

Signs of Stress

In the 1970s a number of observers began to notice that the political systems of many advanced industrial states seemed to be exhibiting signs of stress. Diagnoses of the problem varied. Some interpreted these stresses as evidence of government overload;[28] others argued that they

TABLE 1.1
Shifting orientations in 12 advanced industrial countries including Canada, 1981–1990

Dimensions	Direction of change in all 12 advanced industrial countries*	Direction of change in Canada	Correlated with		
			Age	Education	Post-materialist value type
Political orientations					
Interest in politics	rising 12/12	rising	yes (+)	yes (+)	yes (∧)
Confidence in government institutions	falling 10/12	falling	yes (+)	yes (−)	yes (−)
Confidence in non-government institutions	falling 10/12	falling	yes (+)	yes (+)	yes (−)
Protest potential	rising 11/12	rising	yes (∧)	yes (+)	yes (+)
Civil permissiveness	rising 9/12	rising	yes (−)	yes (+)	yes (+)
General deference	falling 10/12	falling	yes (+)	yes (−)	yes (−)
National pride	rising 7/12	falling	yes (+)	yes (−)	yes (−)
Cosmopolitanism	rising 8/12	rising	yes (−)	yes (+)	yes (+)
Economic orientations					
Importance of work	falling 9/11	falling	yes (+)	yes (−)	yes (−)
Support for meritocracy	rising 12/12	rising	yes (+)	yes (+)	yes (+)
Pride in work	rising 12/12	rising	yes (+)	yes (∨)	yes (−)
Worker expressiveness	falling 7/12	falling	yes (−)	yes (+)	yes (+)
Workplace obedience	falling 6/12	falling	yes (+)	yes (−)	yes (−)
Worker participation	rising 6/12	rising	yes (−)	yes (+)	yes (+)
Job satisfaction	falling 8/12	falling	yes (+)	yes (+)	yes (−)
Financial satisfaction	falling 7/12	falling	yes (+)	yes (+)	yes (−)

TABLE 1.1 – concluded
Shifting orientations in 12 advanced industrial countries including Canada, 1981–1990

Dimensions	Direction of change in all 12 advanced industrial countries*	Direction of change in Canada	Correlated with		
			Age	Education	Post-materialist value type
Social orientations					
Importance of God	falling 10/12	falling	yes (+)	yes (−)	yes (−)
Church attendance	falling 10/12	falling	yes (+)	yes (−)	yes (−)
Moral permissiveness	rising 10/12	rising	yes (−)	yes (+)	yes (+)
Principle of tolerance	rising 12/12	rising	weak	yes (+)	yes (+)
Social intolerance	rising 11/12	rising	yes (+)	yes (−)	yes (−)
Racial intolerance	rising 9/12	rising	yes (+)	yes (−)	yes (−)
Political intolerance	rising 11/12	rising	yes (+)	yes (−)	yes (−)
Egalitarian spousal relations	rising 12/12	rising	yes (−)	yes (+)	yes (+)
Egalitarian parent–child relations	rising 12/12	rising	yes (−)	yes (+)	yes (+)

Source: 1981 and 1990 World Values Surveys.

*Countries include France, Britain, West Germany, Italy, Netherlands, Denmark, Belgium, Spain, Ireland, Northern Ireland, United States, and Canada.

signified a legitimacy crisis;[29] still others suggested that these stresses reflected a problem of 'governability.'[30] Regardless of the particulars, however, there is a significant degree of agreement about the symptoms. One point of agreement involves evidence of important shifts in the electoral landscape of most advanced industrial states.[31] Citizens seem to have become both more fickle and less compliant. While some data point to a gradual erosion in the rates of electoral participation, most of these shifts would have to be characterized as glacial, and there are significant cross-national variations.[32] A more significant sign of stress, perhaps, are the indications that citizen attachments to political parties have become progressively weaker: the proportion of voting publics declaring themselves to be 'strong' party identifiers, for example, has been on the decline in nearly every advanced industrial state for which there are comparable data. Moreover, there has been a decline in party memberships among these publics. One consequence of these shifts has been a rising level of voter volatility.[33] More broadly still, long-standing party systems seemed to be in a state of flux.

Until the middle of the 1960s, navigating the electoral landscape was a comparatively easy task; political cleavages were widely characterized as relatively few, and voting decisions were correspondingly simple.[34] By the 1970s, however, the capacity of such cleavages as region and class – cleavages that had for generations underpinned the bases of support for traditional parties – seemed to be weakening. By the middle of the 1980s, the trend toward de-alignment was well established in many advanced industrial states.[35] Alongside this trend appears evidence that indicates the advent of new parties with non-traditional agendas emerging to challenge the old.[36]

Declining party memberships, shifting patterns of partisan behaviour, and the emergence of new axes of electoral mobilization represent three important indications of possible 'stress,' and these dynamics deserve attention not least of all because in most representative democracies political parties carry the unique responsibility of connecting citizens to the state by aggregating, representing, and responding to citizens' interests. But, to focus only on the shifting foundations of political parties and rising levels of voter volatility captures only a narrow slice of what counts as 'political.' Moreover, to rely exclusively on these indicators as signs of stress may falsely invite the conclusion that citizens in advanced industrial states are simply becoming more disengaged from, and less interested in, their political worlds.

In fact, systematic comparative evidence embracing a much wider range of political behaviours among these very same publics leads to quite different conclusions. In *Political Action*, Barnes and Kaase and their collaborators[37] clearly demonstrate that citizens in advanced industrial states are becoming neither less participatory nor more disengaged from their political worlds. Indeed, the data point to the opposite conclusion: citizens are becoming *more* interested in political matters and *more* inclined to participate in public life. Participation in such conventional political activities as voting may be flat, or declining modestly, but citizen engagement in unconventional forms of political behaviour is clearly on the rise.[38] Since the middle of the 1970s, citizens have become more inclined to sign petitions, attend lawful demonstrations, engage in boycotts, and participate in new social movements. Citizen involvement in such alternative forms of political action may be construed as yet another sign of stress.[39] The increased popularity of these kinds of elite-challenging behaviours may also signify a qualitative shift in how citizens choose to relate to the state or at least to those state institutions that continue to work from traditional hierarchical assumptions.

Value shifts have a lot to do with why these changes are taking place. But a more compelling and complete interpretation, perhaps, is that the shifting axes of citizen–state relations are a consequence of the interaction of value shifts with the kinds of structural changes outlined above. Consider the case of education. Recall that the 'education explosion,' the surge in post-secondary educational opportunities, was characterized as one aspect of structural change associated with the transition to advanced industrialism. Expanding educational opportunities may well have been driven primarily by rising demand for a larger supply of knowledge workers, but growing levels of formal education can reshape citizen–state relations. The basic idea that education is conducive to the development of citizens' characteristics is rarely contested. More nuanced accounts, however, suggest that expanded educational opportunities can have an impact on citizen–state relations along two distinct dimensions. One concerns the connection between levels of formal education and what has been called 'democratic enlightenment,' and the other concerns political engagement.[40] Education promotes democratic enlightenment in the sense that it encourages citizens to understand the long-term trade-offs necessary to sustain democratic life; it encourages tolerance and an understanding of, as well as adherence to, the norms and principles of democracy. On this dimension, the indications are that the effects of growing levels of education within a population are cumulative: the higher the levels of formal education within a public, the greater the adherence to democratic norms.

The second dimension, the link between expanding educational opportunities and political engagements, is more complex, involving a resorting process. Engagement includes the capacity to formulate considered policy preferences and to act on one's own behalf to seek political goals.[41] The ways in which higher education promotes these capacities are well documented. People with higher levels of formal education have a greater capacity to organize and comprehend politically relevant information. The better educated are also more interested in their political worlds, which means that they have a stronger motivation to seek out politically relevant information, and this in an environment where the costs of gaining access to information have been dramatically lowered. Further, a high level of education is associated with such politically relevant attributes as higher levels of efficacy and an increased capacity to articulate interests. It is for this combination of reasons that higher levels of education better equip citizens to be actively engaged. The effects of education apply not only to values – encouraging stronger adherence to democratic norms – but also to citizens' political capacities. The expansion of education produces a more articulate, better informed, more engaged, and more sophisticated citizenry. It is also a more demanding citizenry.

Growing access to higher education, then, is a structural change that has had a profound effect on the redistribution of politically relevant skills.[42] It is the timing of the educational revolution that provides a clue as to how structural and value shifts interact. The expansion of post-secondary education coincided, approximately, with the shift toward those world views associated with advanced industrialism, and so those generations socialized in an environment of post-war material security are not only equipped with a new set of participatory skills but they also carry a new set of preferences and expectations.

Shifts in Citizens' Values: Conceptualizing Citizen–State Relations

The indications are that Canada has experienced the same kinds of political-system stress as that documented in other advanced industrial states. For instance, average levels of voter turnout in Canadian federal elections have tended to be slightly lower than those found in other comparable industrial democracies: since 1945, voter participation rates in Canada average around 74 per cent compared to 77 per cent for all other democracies.[43] And voter turnout in the 2000 Canadian federal election dropped to 67 per cent, the lowest since 1925.[44] There is also evidence in the Canadian setting of high levels of electoral volatility and of rising levels of disenchantment with mainstream political parties.[45] Moreover, there are clear indications of increased fluidity in the Canadian federal party system. The 1993 election was a watershed as far as the party system is concerned: one long-standing 'traditional' party suffered a crushing defeat and two entirely new parties emerged. The party system appears to be in transition.[46] Alongside these changes appears evidence of rising levels of unconventional forms of political behaviour on a scale comparable to that documented in other advanced industrial states.[47] As in other states, these shifts may be interpreted as a consequence of the interplay of structural and value changes among citizens. This kind of system-level evidence and interpretation is certainly plausible, but the evidence is nonetheless indirect. What is required is direct evidence.

The point of distinguishing between political culture and culture in general, according to Almond and Verba,[48] is to draw attention to the importance of 'political objects' in mediating citizen–state relations. Political objects, however, are not all of a kind. The notion of political support, for example, is multidimensional and so levels of support are likely to vary depending upon which particular political objects or orientations are under consideration. What kinds of political objects and values are central? There are several and they can be organized conceptually in at least two ways. Building on the work of others,[49] Norris identifies five different kinds of political objects, or orientations, as basic to effective democratic governance;[50] as table 1.2 illustrates, these orientations can be distributed according to their generality or specificity.

At the most abstract level are attachments to the larger political community and to identities. In settings where the boundaries of the state and nation coincide, attachments to 'the country' are less problematic than in settings where loyalties are more fractured along regional, linguistic, or religious lines. Most data indicate that citizen attachments to their political community are relatively high and stable. There is evidence that there have been shifts in people's communal horizons; publics throughout most advanced industrial states have gradually become less parochial and more cosmopolitan, but, significantly, these shifts have yet to have had much impact on aggregate levels of national

TABLE 1.2
Political objects: levels of support and trends

		Level and trend for advanced industrial states	
Most general	Political object	Level of support	Trend
	Political community (e.g., country)	High	Stable
	Regime principles (e.g., democracy)	High	Relatively stable
	Regime performance (e.g., satisfaction with the way democracy works)	Moderate	Relatively stable
	Institutions (parliament, courts, civil service, police)	Moderate	Declining
Most specific	Political actors (leaders, elected representatives)	Low	Variable

Source: Adapted from P. Norris, *Critical Citizens* (New York: Oxford University Press, 1999).

pride.[51] And in the broader context of the twenty-two countries for which directly comparable data are available, levels of national pride in Canada rank third highest, behind only the United States and Ireland.

Support for regime principles also operate at a relatively high level of abstraction. There is no consensus about which particular regime principle is pre-eminent. Rather, support for such principles typically envelope a cluster of values that include such ideas as freedom, participation, tolerance and moderation, and respect for rights and the rule of law. According to Norris, it is the conjunction of these orientations that sets the operational structure for the democratic regime.[52]

Regime *performance* is less abstract; it concerns citizens' evaluations of how well their own democracy performs in the light of their expectations about how democracy should work. The most widely used indicator of citizens' views about regime performance comes from responses to the question 'How satisfied are you with the way democracy works in your country?'

The fourth level of political objects is more grounded still; it concerns the levels of citizen confidence in an array of regime institutions –

parliament, the courts, the civil service, and the police. Confidence in institutions serves as a middle-range indicator, one that lies between support for such overarching regime principles as 'democracy,' and support for such specific political actors as elected government officials.[53] Evaluations of public confidence in institutions is most informative when understood comparatively because there are no agreed-upon meaningful standards for what qualifies as 'high' or 'low' levels of confidence in institutions.[54] As will become apparent in the Canadian case, when making their evaluations of these kinds of institutional objects citizens do distinguish between different regime institutions, and it turns out that citizen confidence in parliament has eroded most of all.

The most concrete political objects that citizens evaluate are political actors. Here, the focus is upon these actors as a class of office holders, not as particular individuals. The available evidence is that elected public officials are not, typically, held in very high esteem, but there are wide cross-national variations as well as significant cross-time fluctuations in these kinds of public evaluations.[55]

The conceptual scheme outlined by Norris provides a very useful starting point: it identifies which kinds of political objects are central and it makes the important point that there are significant variations in the generality and specificity of these objects. Norris's guidelines can also be extended in directions that are even more helpful for understanding the underlying dynamics of citizen–state relations. That is, it is important not only to know how citizens' orientations have changed along each of the dimensions that Norris identifies, but also to understand if, and how, each of these orientations are related to each other. And to what extent are these orientations also linked to such dispositions as trust, to knowledge and associational life, dimensions that are also viewed as contributing to a vibrant democracy?[56] Moreover, given the interaction of structural and value shifts, it is important to know how these new political-cultural orientations are distributed throughout the population. Then there is the question of how these orientations are connected to citizen behaviour, to how citizens view their representatives, and to how elected representatives, in turn, understand their roles. These are the central research questions that guide the investigation of value change in the Canadian setting. This extension of Norris's schema is summarized in figure 1.1, in which these relevant dimensions are organized around two nodes. The dimensions clustering around the 'state' in the upper part of the figure are concerned with

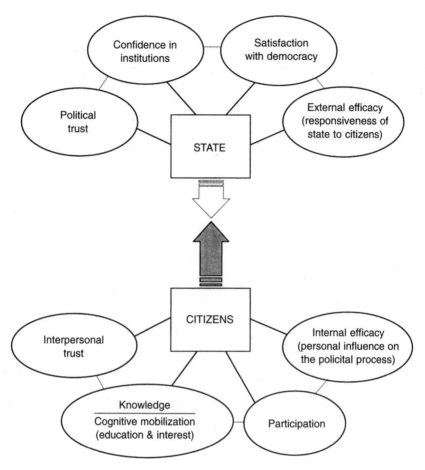

Figure 1.1 Value change and citizen–state relations

how citizens evaluate the state, its institutions, and legislators; the lower cluster refers to the attributes of citizens themselves – their capacities, orientations, and behaviours.

The Evidence

The ideal data for mapping value change would be those coming from longitudinal panel studies in which the same individuals are repeatedly asked the same questions about their values at different interludes. With these kinds of data it would be possible not only to track individual value change, but also to determine quite precisely the extent to which any detected value shift is attributable to life-cycle or generational effects. The limitation in this instance is a practical one: there is no single longitudinal panel study in Canada that explores cross-time changes in these particular citizens' orientations.

Absent such data, the next best alternative is to turn to reliable cross-sectional data that contain relevant and comparable indicators and that have been collected from random samples of the same population at different intervals. Publicly available Canadian data sources of this variety are scarce. The challenge is to make the most of those data that are available. Before presenting the core findings, it is important to explicitly identify what combination of strategies the value-trend researchers used to address these limitations.

One strategy is to seek out longitudinal evidence wherever it is available. For example, when it comes to evidence of some specific political orientations toward the Canadian political system, the Canadian Election Studies are an invaluable source not least of all because they contain data on political orientations across a thirty-five-year time span. These kinds of data tell us about value change within the Canadian setting, but they can also be difficult to interpret. The point is a straightforward one: to be able to say anything meaningful about whether the level of support for the political community rates as 'high' or 'low,' for example, there needs to be some base of comparison. The question is, high or low compared to what? The most relevant points of comparison, for the reasons already outlined, are other countries that exhibit similar characteristics, namely, other advanced industrial states. And so a second research strategy is to seek out comparable cross-national data wherever possible.

Cross-time cross-sectional data are valuable, but secondary data sets of this variety are often designed to address research questions that are somewhat different from those that are of primary interest to secondary-data users. In these circumstances, a reasonable alternative, and one followed in this project, is to rely on specialized data sets that allow for a systematic analysis of the linkages between key indicators (Lisa Young, chapter 4) or of key segments of the population (David C. Docherty, chapter 6). Lisa Young's investigation sheds light on the connections between civic engagement, trust, and democracy using data from a single province, and David Docherty's analysis, using data from a survey of legislators, sheds light on how elected legislators view their roles as representatives.

All data are limited in one way or another, and these limitations have to be acknowledged. Certainly, there are reasons to be cautious when drawing conclusions about value change on the basis of cross-sectional data collected at a single point in time. Nonetheless, it is possible to make informed inferences. For example, if we know on the basis of one study using cross-time data that public confidence in institutions, or trust, reflects generational effects, then it is reasonable to suppose that a correlation between age and trust found in another set of data collected from the same population at a single time point might also be plausibly interpreted as indicating generational effects. Nor is it unreasonable to draw inferences across populations. For example, Nie and colleagues[57] detail the impact of higher education on citizen enlightenment and participation in the American setting. Absent data indicating otherwise, it is reasonable to suppose that the spread of higher education would likely have similar enlightenment and participation effects in the Canadian setting.

The Core Findings

Satisfaction with Democracy

One widely used benchmark for tapping citizens' evaluations of their political system comes from responses to the question 'How satisfied are you with the way democracy works in your country?' There are strong reasons for expecting Canadians to express very high levels of satisfaction. As Richard Nadeau points out in chapter 2, the United Nations Human Development report, 1994–8, ranks Canada first among all countries on the quality of life; the country is at peace, it is affluent, and by most standards the rights and liberties of citizens are well entrenched and widely respected. Here, it is the cross-national benchmarks for comparison that are vital for interpretation. Certainly, when compared with citizens of India, Taiwan, or Mexico, Canadian levels of satisfaction do indeed look very high. But when compared with the responses from citizens in other similarly affluent, old, established liberal democracies, the results are less gratifying. Canadian levels of satisfaction with democracy are on a par with those found among publics in Ireland and the Netherlands, but they are significantly lower than those found in Norway, Denmark, Luxembourg, and pre-unification West Germany. Just one in ten Canadians say they are 'very satisfied' and a substantial one in three expresses 'little satisfaction' with the way democracy works in the country.

What explains these findings? Why are Canadians less satisfied than might be expected? Who is least satisfied? And are these variations in levels of satisfaction related to those orientations and citizen attributes that are outlined in figure 1.1?

In answering those questions in chapter 2, Nadeau delves into Canadian Election Study data and finds that some of the pillars that prop up citizens' satisfaction with democracy are relatively fragile. As Norris[58] predicts, part of the answer has to do with people's attachment to their political community, Canada. Attachment to Canada, confidence in the federal government and the courts, identification with a federal political party, and a positive evaluation of politicians are all significant and positive predictors of higher levels of satisfaction with the workings of Canadian democracy. Moreover, there are significant socio-demographic markers. Predictably, wealthier and better-educated Canadians, along with those born outside of the country, all express higher levels of satisfaction with democracy.

These initial findings are relatively straightforward, but a deeper investigation of indirect effects yields a slightly more revealing and nuanced picture, one that identifies clear pockets of discontent. First, there is a very substantial gap between francophones in Quebec and others when it comes to attachments to Canada. While this finding is not particularly surprising, the additional relevant point is that these orientations spill over into negative views of the federal government, the courts, and politicians. Second, there is also evidence of age-related effects. The young are significantly more weakly attached to Canada, and they evaluate the federal government, political parties, and politicians significantly more negatively than do their older counterparts. And there is a third important finding: a very substantial proportion of Canadians, some 53 per cent, indicates that they feel they have little say in what the government does. It turns out that these feelings of voicelessness are not related to people's attachments to their broader political community; feeling voiceless does not make citizens less attached to Canada. But this voicelessness does have a powerful and negative effect on their level of satisfaction with the way democracy works, and on their evaluations of the federal government, the courts, politicians, and political parties.

Human Capital

The importance of the interactions between value change and structural change is brought into clear focus by Mebs Kanji's analysis in chapter 3, which builds on, and fills out, some of Nadeau's findings. In general, Canadian Election Study data gathered since 1965 show that Canadians' confidence in their political institutions is low, their trust in elected officials is low and declining, and there is a downward trend in external efficacy; that is, Canadians are increasingly likely to believe both that 'government doesn't care much about what people like me think' and that 'elected officials soon lose touch with the people.' These cross-time shifts are not always smooth; but there is an aggregate trend. As citizens' evaluations of government responsiveness are becoming harsher, there is evidence of growing citizen competence, or what Kanji and others refer to as 'human capital.' Human capital has to do with a cluster of attributes – such as greater knowledge, more attentiveness to politically relevant information, greater interest in the political world, reduced reliance on political parties for information and cues – that along with rising levels of education make citizens more autonomous. These findings mirror changes that have been documented in other advanced industrial states, and at one level they seem to signify a narrowing of the 'skill gap' between citizens and elected officials, a phenomenon that appears to be accompanied by other dynamics.

The research findings regarding 'efficacy' provide a graphic illustration of the changing relationship between citizens and their political system. External efficacy refers to how responsive citizens believe the political system is to their demands. Internal efficacy, the other side of that same conceptual coin, refers to subjective competence, which has to do with how much influence an individual citizen feels she or he can have on the political process. The data summarized in figure 1.2, drawn from the Canadian Election Studies, point to an intriguing and arguably important trend, namely, the emergence of an 'efficacy gap.'

According to these data, levels of internal efficacy have increased slightly over the twenty-three years reported; Canadians have become somewhat *less* inclined to believe that politics is 'so complicated that a person like me can't really understand what's going on,' and *less* likely to think that 'people like me don't have any say about what the government does.' This finding is consistent with what one would expect to find given that higher internal efficacy is positively related to higher education and larger segments of the Canadian public have experi-

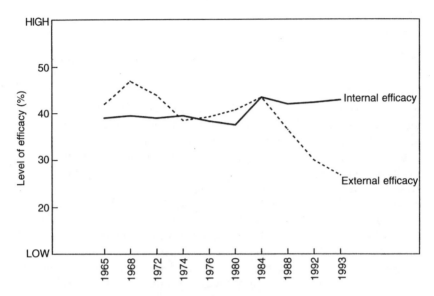

Source: Canadian Election Studies, 1965–93.

Notes: The percentages reported in the figure are the average scores from the two items in the internal and external efficacy indices. Only the 'disagree' and 'strongly disagree' responses are used in the calculation of the averages. 'No opinion' responses are excluded from the analysis.

External efficacy: 1. 'Generally, those elected to Parliament soon lose touch with the people.' 2. 'I don't think the government cares much what people like me think.' (Strongly Agree, Agree, Disagree, Strongly Disagree, and No Opinion)

Internal efficacy: 1. 'Sometimes, politics and government seem so complicated that a person like me can't really understand what's going on.' 2. 'People like me don't have any say about what the government does.' (Strongly Agree, Agree, Disagree, Strongly Disagree, and No Opinion.)

Figure 1.2 The efficacy gap

enced higher education over the course of the last two decades. But over the same period, levels of external efficacy have eroded: Canadians became significantly more inclined to believe that those who are elected to parliament 'soon lose touch with the people' and that government doesn't 'care much about what people like me think.' In effect, as peoples' sense of their own subjective political competence has been sustained, their evaluations of the responsiveness of their own political system have been declining; this 'efficacy gap' has widened quite sharply since 1988. Furthermore, a detailed investigation of these data clearly shows that low levels of external efficacy are linked to low confidence in governmental institutions and mistrust of politicians.[59] The findings are statistically significant.

Social Capital

Like efficacy, trust is a fundamental social and political orientation that has been theoretically and empirically linked to the effective performance of democratic systems. In Robert Putnam's scheme of things,[60] civic engagement is a precondition for the accumulation of social capital (norms of reciprocity and trust), which are conducive to the effective functioning of democratic governments. Consequently, the civil society / social capital explanation asserts that declining levels of civic engagement lead to a decline in 'social capital,' which ultimately 'erodes the basis on which democratic governance flourishes.'[61]

Using individual-level data from the 1999 Alberta Civil Society Survey, Lisa Young develops three measures of engagement: (1) *civic* engagement – participation in non-political, non-market civic organizations; (2) *professional* engagement – involvement in unions and professional or business organizations; and (3) *political* engagement – membership in a political party and membership in a political action group other than a political party. Social capital is measured by gauging levels of interpersonal trust and democratic governance is measured by probing people's trust in government and confidence in political institutions.

Here, the data show that civic engagement is a strong predictor of interpersonal trust, a finding that lends support to Putnam's civil society / social capital explanation. Citizens who are active by being involved within the community are much more likely to express greater levels of interpersonal trust. Other predictors of interpersonal trust include fear of walking in one's neighbourhood at night (the strongest predictor), general life satisfaction, age (positive effect), and education (also a positive effect).

But what explains citizens' trust in government and confidence in governmental institutions? It turns out that interpersonal trust is a strong predictor of trust in government and confidence in political institutions. However, civic engagement is not.[62] The implication is that any meaningful effect that civic engagement might have on trust and confidence in governmental institutions is indirect; it works mainly through interpersonal trust and then indirectly from interpersonal trust to confidence and trust in governmental institutions.

Political efficacy turns out to be *positively* linked to confidence in the federal government, the provincial government, and political parties.[63]

Young's analysis supports Neal Roese's finding (chapter 5) that political activism is positively related to distrust in government, and the evidence is consistent with the cognitive-mobilization hypothesis; individuals who are more closely involved with the political system are dissatisfied with what they see.

What about age effects? Albertans under the age of thirty-five are the least trusting of others in general, but have the highest trust and confidence in governments and political institutions, respectively. Baby boomers (ages 35 to 44) are the least confident in political institutions. If these age variants are really driven by generational rather than life-cycle effects, then the expectation would be that confidence in government would increase over time as new generations replace the cynical baby boomers in the population. But it is difficult, on the basis of cross-sectional data, to demonstrate whether these age-related dynamics reflect generational or life-cycle effects.

Trust

Roese's analysis probes the issue of trust in greater detail and shows that Canadians' trust in the federal government is on the decline, a trend that is consistent with data from other Western industrial states. Evidence to support this conclusion comes from the Canadian Election Studies between 1965 and 1993, the 1981 and 1990 World Values Surveys, and the American National Election Surveys since 1958. But, as Roese argues, these findings can be interpreted in two ways: a negative interpretation that focuses on 'individual political disengagement' and a positive interpretation that stresses the 'value of healthy skepticism born of increasing individual cognitive sophistication.'[64] Findings drawn from the data lend support to the positive notion of trust to demonstrate that scepticism toward the government may, in fact, be associated with greater levels of political engagement.

Is the decline in trust toward the Canadian government attributable to a general decline in interpersonal trust among citizens? The data suggest not. In fact, as Roese notes, World Values data from 1981 and 1990 show that interpersonal trust has been on the rise in Canada.

It is possible that people's decreasing trust of their government is connected to a more widespread cynicism about large institutions. Once again, however, the data do not support this line of speculation. Canadians' trust in 'major companies' has fallen between 1981 and 1990, but this decrease is marginal compared to the decline in trust in the federal government.[65]

There are also some substantively important non-findings that emerge. Declining trust in government is *not* associated with any shifts in the economic status of Canadians. Negative psychological factors unleashed as a result of unemployment, such as feelings of reduced empower- ment, reduced satisfaction, or reduced happiness, have no impact on people's perception of trust in their government. The same applies to general life satisfaction, job satisfaction, household financial satisfac- tion, and home-life satisfaction: none has any significant impact on people's trust in government. Levels of satisfaction for each of the above items have remained constant between 1981 and 1990.

What does help to explain declining levels of trust in government is internal efficacy and political activism. Out of the five variables entered into a regression analysis (internal efficacy, political activism, proselytization – i.e., how often an individual attempts to persuade friends, relatives, or fellow workers to share his or her view – interest in politics, and left-right political ideology), only political activism (beta = −.12) and internal efficacy (beta = −.08) have significant independent effects on declining trust. In other words, the more empowered Canadi- ans feel, the less they trust government. The American data are similar to Canada's except that, in the United States, interest in politics also appears to be linked to trust. In Western Europe, all five predictors help to explain declining trust, with the strongest predictor being interest in politics (beta = .17).

There may well be other factors that help to explain the decline in trust among Canadians. These shifts might be partly determined by the media's more active role in news coverage, especially regarding scan- dals involving politicians, and by greater use of negative campaign ads that help to build an image of a 'bad government.' Another possible explanation could be that the government has failed to meet the height- ened expectations of citizens in the age of postmaterialism.

The Representation 'Gap'

Independent analyses produce converging conclusions about citizen evaluations of their political environment. A clear majority of Canadians believe that governments are non-responsive to them, confidence in parliament and political parties is low, and people do not trust their elected officials. These findings, the data suggest, are at least partly attributable to the structural and value changes documented earlier: citizens are more critical, less deferential, and perhaps more cynical. But these same findings also suggest a second set of questions: Why do citizens hold these particular actors and institutions in such low esteem? What is it about the MP's role or behaviour that elicits these kinds of evaluations? Why do an increasing number of Canadians, regardless of income or education levels, believe that politicians soon 'lose touch' with the people who elected them?

Docherty's analysis in chapter 6 provides some important insights into these questions. He argues that there are two parallel developments taking place. One concerns the changing attitudes and capacities of citizens themselves; the new political culture encourages publics to be more articulate and critical. The other concerns the perceptions that MPs and citizens have about what priorities elected representatives should have. There is a 'gap' in their respective views of representation.

Relying on a combination of surveys of members of the 34th Parliament of Canada, candidates for office in the 1993 federal election, and rookie members of the 35th Parliament, along with Canadian Election Study surveys and Gallup data, Docherty demonstrates, first, that the belief that politicians 'lose touch' is broadening and deepening throughout Canadian society. Second, he shows that the public believes that the first priority of MPs should be to 'keep in touch with constituents about what government is doing,' whereas MPs in the 34th Parliament (1988–93) say that 'helping people who have personal problems with government' is their first priority. And there is a third significant finding: it appears that the priorities of MPs shift during the course of their career cycle as elected officials. The priorities of rookie MPs are much closer to those of citizens; the longer an MP holds office, the further his or her priorities drift away from the expectations of the public.[66] These data suggest that the public perception of MPs 'losing touch' is an accurate one. And this drift from one modality of representation to another may well, Docherty suggests, have to do with the shift in the political centre of gravity toward cabinet and the increased difficulties MPs face in influencing policy direction. In that environment, MPs have a greater incentive to give priority to issues whose outcomes they can influence rather than those they cannot.

Conclusions and Implications

Demonstrating causality with any kind of empirical data is a treacherous business, and for that reason the usual practice is to steer well clear of language suggesting that data 'demonstrate,' or 'prove,' causal direction. Nonetheless, speculating about the most likely causal directions can be constructive, particularly when considering the possible policy implications of the findings. In considering the various policy implications suggested by the authors, it is also useful to consider the larger contextual issue set out here.

If the stresses experienced by the Canadian state are attributable to value change, then it might well be argued that policy prescriptions are necessarily uncertain because values are in a state of continual evolution. A reversal of economic fortunes, to return to Inglehart's account of advanced industrial value change, might be accompanied by a resurgence of materialist orientations. And, indeed, there is some evidence indicating that such short-term reversals have taken place.[67] Values are uncertain, but when they do change they do so slowly. Nonetheless, if the stresses are attributable to the interaction of such structural factors as the spread of post-secondary education along with value change, then the policy implications are rather different. Economic reversals may induce citizens to become less post-materialist in their orientations, but they do not make citizens less educated, less attentive, less interested, or less informed about their political world. Nor do they diminish citizens' capacities. The combined effects of the changes associated with late industrialism have made it easier for citizens to make demands on those who govern them. But, it is not at all clear that those same changes have made it any easier for governments to respond to citizen demands.

We began with the observation that in the bilateral relationship between citizens and the state, the weight of the evidence suggests that perturbations in citizen–state relations may be mostly attributable to the changing values and capacities of citizens. But this should not rule out considering the possibilities of institutional adaptation. What measures can institutions take to address some of the problem areas that the research identifies? One such area concerns the perception on the part of citizens that elected representatives are not responsive. Labelling the 'efficacy gap' a 'crisis' probably overstates the case. But it is a worrying trend plainly identified in the research data. Evidently one reason why citizens think that governments are not responsive is that office holders do not give a high priority to 'keeping in touch with constituents about what the government is doing.' The policy implication is that elected officials should develop a much clearer appreciation of what citizens expect of them.

A second recurring theme concerns the connection between low levels of trust in elected officials and confidence in governmental institutions. Once again, the direction of causality is not entirely certain; the relationship between these orientations is likely to be reciprocal. Citizens expect their elected officials to have high standards of conduct.[68] Regardless of the reasonableness of that expectation, the evidence is that citizens' confidence in public officials declines when those high standards are not seen to be met. The same seems to apply to election campaign promises. For example, confidence in the federal government is much lower among Canadians who believed that the governing Liberals did not really try to keep their 1993 election promise to abolish the GST. Because citizens are increasingly interested in politics, they are more attentive, and there is greater media exposure, the chances are that the behaviours of elected officials will continue to be scrutinized very closely. Aside from representatives exercising caution when making campaign promises, there may also be complementary institutional strategies such as reforming, and making public, tougher guidelines concerning codes of conduct for elected officials.

Do these two broad sets of findings mean that the Westminister system of representative government is flawed and in need of fundamental reform? There are three considerations that might temper calls for radical institutional surgery. First, there is no indication that dissatisfaction with the way democracy works in this country is broad and deep. Certainly, there are important pockets of discontent that deserve attention and serious policy consideration. Young Canadians, for example, have the weakest attachments to the political community and the lowest confidence in political institutions. Canada's youth are more sceptical about politicians and political parties. And so there are reasons to try to understand better why this is so and to look for strategies that will strengthen young people's connections to the political system. But the general point is that the broad swath of the population is not deeply dissatisfied with the way democracy works in Canada. Nor is there any indication that Canadians' attachments to democratic principles have weakened. From these standpoints the malaise has not yet reached a profoundly troubling level.

Second, the comparative context is instructive. The Canadian evidence concerning citizens' orientations to the state is broadly consistent with, and similar to, evidence coming from citizens in other states, including states that do not operate under the Westminster parliamentary system. Put more sharply, declining levels of confidence in political institutions, trust in government, and distrust of political elites are not unique features of the Westminster rules of the game. Nor does it seem that those living under Westminster rules are less satisfied with the way democracy works than those who do not. It is difficult, then, to pin all of the blame for the malaise on the Westminster system.

The third consideration has to do with political participation. Citizens' *levels* of political participation, broadly conceived, are rising not falling. Moreover, interest in politics is on the rise not declining. Rising levels of political participation and interest are signs of democratic health not sickness. What is at issue is the *style* of political participation: citizens are turning *less* to political parties, and relying *more* on direct-action strategies of participation. Once again, it is instructive to note that these same trends are evident in the United States and western Europe;[69] they are not unique to Westminster-style regimes.

These considerations do not mean that the Westminster system of representation is faultless or that institutional design does not matter. Instead, they bring into clear focus the important role that political parties play. The challenge facing political parties is how to harness, or respond to, the rising participatory instincts of citizens. One immediate possibility to consider is electoral reform. Electoral rules do have an impact on voter turnout and the indications are that if we moved to proportional representation, voter turnout might increase by as much as 3 per cent.[70] And electoral reforms undertaken in Italy, Japan, and New Zealand, in fact, were inspired by perceptions of public dissatisfaction with electoral procedures.[71] But as one country moved toward proportional representation as a solution, another moved in the opposite direction. Moreover, there is no indication in Canada of much public dissatisfaction with the present electoral rules.[72] The indications are, then, that the source of the malaise lies deeper than the matter of electoral procedures.

The basic structures for citizen participation in this country were set out in the nineteenth century: citizens get to vote once every four or five years depending upon the electoral cycle. The opportunities for meaningful citizen participation at other times are limited. It seems that the rising levels of non-traditional forms of political participation are a consequence of the redistribution of political skills and greater public interest in more frequent opportunities to participate.

Canadian political parties face a challenge and some dilemmas. Their challenge is to lead the search for ways to accommodate, and respond to, the public's interest in more meaningful participation during the long intervals between elections.[73] If political parties do not lead this search, take the issue seriously, and define themselves as part of the solution, the threat is that citizens with strong participatory instincts will continue to avoid participation through political parties.

There are at least three areas of research that deserve further investigation. The first is comparative in scope. As has already been indicated, a number of countries have experimented with institutional reforms aimed at re-engaging citizens. In some cases, such as Italy, Japan, and New Zealand, these efforts have focused on the electoral system. In other cases, such as Germany, the reforms have allowed for greater citizen participation in local administration. What needs to be determined is which, if any, of these strategies work to satisfy citizens' participatory demands.

The second area concerns the representation gap. The research has detected the presence of this gap. What needs now to be determined is the explanation for the gap and why it is that legislators' priorities change the longer they hold office.

The third area concerns the status of political parties. Given the themes outlined in this chapter, and given the responsibility that parties have for connecting citizens to the state, it is truly striking that we know so little about what citizens expect of their political parties. Where do political parties fall short of public expectations? Why are they held in such low esteem? And what can political parties do to reconnect themselves to citizens?

Notes

I extend my thanks to my colleagues in the Trends Project, 'Value Change,' for their insights and willing collaboration, and to the insightful commentary of the reviewers of the initial draft of this chapter. I also thank Amanda Ng for her valuable research assistance.

1 Hans-Dieter Klingemann and Dieter Fuchs, eds, *Citizens and the State* (New York: Oxford University Press, 1995); Paul Abramson and Ronald Inglehart, *Value Change in Global Perspective* (Ann Arbor: University of Michigan Press, 1995).

2 Klingemann and Fuchs, *Citizens and the State*.
3 Values are referred to as core beliefs because they are more stable than either attitudes or opinions. For empirical purposes, values are typically identified as stable patterns of interconnected attitudes. For a discussion of these distinctions, see Jan van Deth and Elinor Scarbrough, 'The Concept of Values,' in van Deth and Scarbrough, eds, *The Impact of Values* (New York: Oxford University Press, 1995), 21–47.
4 Gabriel Almond and Sidney Verba, *The Civic Culture* (Princeton: Princeton University Press, 1963).
5 Ibid., 13.
6 Ibid.
7 van Deth and Scarborough, *The Impact of Values*.
8 Russell J. Dalton, *Citizen Politics in Western Democracies: Public Opinion and Political Parties in the United States, Great Britain, West Germany and France.* 1st, edition (Chatham, NJ: Chatham House Publishers, Inc., 1988); Klinge-mann and Fuchs, *Citizens and the State*; Abramson and Inglehart, *Value Change*.
9 J.E. Lane, D. McKay, and K. Newton, *Political Data Handbook: OECD Countries* (Oxford: Oxford University Press, 1991).
10 Samuel Huntington, 'Post-Industrial Politics: How Benign Will It Be?' *Comparative Politics* 6 (1974): 147–77.
11 Typically, the increases in the number of people entering post-secondary institutions took place earlier and expanded more rapidly in Canada and the United States than in some of the more class-bound societies of Western Europe.
12 Ron Lesthauge and Guy Moors, 'Living Arrangements and Parenthood: Do Values Matter?' in Ruud de Moor, ed., *Values in Western Societies* (Tilburg, The Netherlands: Tilburg University Press, 1995); J. Simons, 'Europe's Aging Population: Demographic Trends,' in J. Bailey, ed., *Social Europe* (London: Longman, 1992).
13 Daniel Bell, *The Cultural Contradictions of Capitalism* (New York: Basic Books, 1976).
14 Ibid., 147.
15 Ibid., 147.
16 Daniel Bell, *The Coming of Post-Industrial Society* (New York: Basic Books, 1973), 148–9.
17 Pierro Ignazi, 'The Silent Counter-Revolution: Hypotheses on the Emergence of Extreme Right-Wing Parties in Europe,' *European Journal of Political Research* 22 (1992): 3–34.
18 Peter Ester, Loek Halman, and Ruud de Moor, 'Value Shift in Western Societies,' in Ester, Halman, and de Moor, eds, *The Individualizing Society:*

Value Change in Europe and North America (Tilburg, The Netherlands: Tilburg University Press, 1993).

19 John R. Gibbins and Bo Reimer, 'Postmodernism,' in van Deth and Scarborough, *The Impact of Values*. Ronald Inglehart, *The Silent Revolution* (Princeton: Princeton University Press, 1977) and *Modernization and Postmodernization: Cultural, Economic and Political Change in 43 Societies* (Princeton: Princeton University Press, 1997).

20 Inglehart, *The Silent Revolution; Modernization and Postmodernization*; and *Culture Shift in Advanced Industrial Society* (Princeton: Princeton University Press, 1990).

21 Abramson and Inglehart, *Value Change*, 9.

22 Ibid., 9.

23 Ibid.

24 Terry Nichols Clark and Michael Rempel, eds, *Citizen Politics in Post-Industrial Societies* (Boulder, CO: Westview Press, 1997); Terry Nichols Clark and Vincent Hoffman-Martinot, eds, *The New Political Culture* (Boulder: Westview Press, 1998).

25 Some argue that the materialist/post-materialist scale used by Inglehart is a problematic one, on the grounds that items within the scale may be sensitive to short-term economic considerations. See, for example, Harold D. Clarke and Nittish Dutt, 'Measuring Value Change in Western Industrialized Societies: The Impact of Unemployment,' *American Political Science Review* 85(3) (1991): 905–20. See also Harold D. Clarke, Nittish Dutt, and Jonathon Rapkin, 'Conversations in Context: The (Mis)measurement of Value Change in Advanced Industrial Societies,' *Political Behavior* 19(1) (1997): 19–39. The debate is a vigorous one, and some of Inglehart's responses to the measurement issue are found in Abramson and Inglehart, *Value Change*.

26 Pippa Norris, ed., *Critical Citizens: Global Support for Democratic Governance* (Oxford: Oxford University Press, 1999); Ester, Halman, and de Moor, *The Individualizing Society*; Dalton, *Citizen Politics*.

27 For a more detailed discussion of these findings, see Neil Nevitte, *The Decline of Deference* (Peterborough, ON: Broadview Press, 1996).

28 Michael Crozier, Samuel Huntington, and Joji Watanuki, *The Crisis of Democracy: Report on the Governability of Democracies to the Trilateral Commission* (New York: New York University Press, 1975).

29 Jürgen Habermas, *Legitimation Crisis* (Boston: Beacon Press, 1975).

30 Anthony King, 'Overload: Problems of Governing in the 1970's,' *Political Studies* 23 (1975): 284–96.

31 Russell J. Dalton, Scott Flanagan, and Paul Allen Beck, eds, *Electoral*

Change in Advanced Industrial Democracies: Realignment on Dealignment? (Princeton: Princeton University Press, 1984).

32 Richard Topf, 'Beyond Electoral Participation,' in Klingemann and Fuchs, *Citizens and the State.*

33 Herman Schmitt and Soren Holmberg, 'Political Parties in Decline?' in Klingemann and Fuchs, *Citizens and the State.*

34 Seymour Martin Lipset and Stein Rokkan, 'Cleavage Structures, Party Systems, and Voter Alignments: An Introduction,' in Lipset and Rokkan, eds, *Party Systems and Voter Alignments: Cross-National Perspectives* (New York: Free Press, 1967); Max Kaase and Kenneth Newton, *Beliefs in Government* (Oxford: Oxford University Press, 1995).

35 See, in Dalton, Flanagan, and Beck, *Electoral Change*: James Alt, 'Dealignment and the Dynamics of Partisanship in Britain'; Paul Allen Beck, 'The Dealignment Era in the United States'; Ole Borre, 'Critical Electoral Change in Scandinavia'; and Galen Irwin and Karl Dittrich, 'And the Walls Came Tumbling Down.'

36 S. Bartolini and P. Mair, *Identity, Competition and Electoral Availability: The Stabilization of European Electorates 1885–1985* (Cambridge: Cambridge University Press, 1990); Dalton, *Citizen Politics.*

37 Samuel Barnes, Max Kaase, et al., *Political Action: Mass Participation in Five Western Democracies* (Beverly Hills and London: Sage Publications, 1979).

38 Ibid.

39 Herbert Kitschelt, 'Resource Mobilization Theory: A Critique,' in Dieter Rucht, ed., *Research on Social Movements: The State of the Art in Western Europe and the USA* (Boulder: Westview Press, 1991); Bert Klandermans, 'New Social Movements and Resource Mobilization: The European and American Approach Revisited,' in Rucht, *Research on Social Movements.*

40 Norman H. Nie, Jane Junn, and Kenneth Stehlik-Barry, *Education and Democratic Citizenship in America* (Chicago: University of Chicago Press, 1996).

41 Ibid.

42 Sidney Verba, Kay Lehman Schlozman and Henry E. Brady, *Voice and Equality: Civic Voluntarism in American Politics* (Cambridge, MA: Harvard University Press, 1995).

43 André Blais and Agnieszka Dobrzynska, 'Turnout in Electoral Democracies,' *European Journal of Political Research* 33 (1998): 239–62.

44 Neil Nevitte et al., *Unsteady State: The 1997 Canadian Federal Election* (Toronto and New York: Oxford University Press, 2000).

45 Harold D. Clarke and Nittish Dutt, 'Measuring Value Change in Western

Industrialized Societies: The Impact of Unemployment,' *American Political Science Review* 85(3) (1991): 905–20; Harold D. Clarke and Allan Kornberg, 'Evaluations and Evolution: Public Attitudes toward Canada's Federal Political Parties 1965–1991,' *Canadian Journal of Political Science* 26 (1993): 287–311; Elisabeth Gidengil et al., 'Exit, Voice and Loyalty: Anti-Party Parties,' Paper presented at annual meeting of Atlantic Provinces Political Science Association, Sackville, NB, 15–17 October 1999.
46 Nevitte et al., *Unsteady State*.
47 Russell J. Dalton, 'Cognitive Mobilization and Partisan Dealignment in Advanced Industrial Democracies,' *Journal of Politics* 46 (February) (1984): 264–84; Barnes et al., *Political Participation*; Nevitte, *Decline of Deference*.
48 Almond and Verba, *The Civic Culture*.
49 Dieter Fuchs and Hans-Dieter Klingemann, 'Citizens and the State: A Changing Relationship?' in Klingemann and Fuchs, *Citizens and the State*; Seymour Martin Lipset and William C. Schneider, *The Confidence Gap: Business, Labor, and Government in the Public Mind*, rev. ed. (Baltimore: Johns Hopkins University, 1987); Richard Rose, *Survey Measures of Democracy* (Glasgow: University of Strathclyde Studies in Public Policy no. 294, 1997).
50 Norris, *Critical Citizens*.
51 Nevitte, *Decline of Deference*; Inglehart, *Modernization and Post-modernization*.
52 Norris, *Critical Citizens*.
53 Norman Nie, J. Mueller, and T.W. Smith, *Trends in Public Opinion* (New York: Greenwood, 1989), 93.
54 Ola Listhaug and Matti Wiberg, 'Confidence in Political and Private Institutions,' in Klingemann and Fuchs, *Citizens and the State*.
55 Ola Listhaug, 'The Dynamics of Trust in Politicians,' in Klingemann and Fuchs, *Citizens and the State*.
56 Robert Putnam, 'Bowling Alone,' *Journal of Democracy* 6(1) (1995): 65–78.
57 Nie, Junn, and Stehlik-Barry, *Education and Democratic Citizenship*.
58 Norris, *Critical Citizens*.
59 Kanji, chapter 3; see also Mattei Dogan, 'Erosion of Confidence in Advanced Democracies,' *Studies in Comparative International Development* 32(3) (1997): 3–29.
60 'Bowling Alone' and 'Tuning In, Tuning Out: The Strange Disappearance of Social Capital in America,' *PS: Political Science and Politics* 28 (December 1995): 664–83.
61 Young, chapter 4.
62 Ibid.

63 Young notes that this finding seems to contradict Neal Roese's finding (chapter 5) that high self-efficacy contributes to *less* confidence in government. In fact, the measures used in the two studies are not directly comparable. Roese uses a general measure of efficacy, while Young employs a political measure of efficacy. As Young states, 'It is a rather different thing to conclude that those who believe they can influence political outcomes have the greatest confidence in the political process than to conclude that those who believe they can control their surroundings have greater confidence' (chapter 4).

64 Chapter 5.

65 Ibid. This finding is unique to Canada; no similar trend emerges in the U.S.

66 David C. Docherty, *Mr. Smith Goes to Ottawa* (Vancouver: UBC Press, 1997).

67 The clearest evidence of these period effects come from the impact of the oil crisis on people's sense of material security. The most impressive feature of these data concerns the cross-generational impact of the period effect. See Abramson and Inglehart, *Value Change*, 29.

68 Maureen Mancuso et al., *A Question of Ethics: Canadians Speak Out* (Toronto and London: Oxford University Press, 1998).

69 Verba, Lehman Schlozman, and Brady, *Voice and Equality*; M. Kent Jennings and Jan van Deth, *Continuities in Political Action* (New York: de Gruyter, 1989).

70 Blais and Dobrzynska, 'Turnout in Electoral Democracies.'

71 Russell J. Dalton, 'Political Support in Advanced Industrial Democracies,' in Norris, *Critical Citizens*.

72 André Blais and Elisabeth Gidengil, *Making Representative Democracy Work: The Views of Canadians*, vol. 17 of the Research Studies, Royal Commission on Electoral Reform and Party Financing (Toronto and Oxford: Dundurn Press, 1991).

73 The use of referendums is an increasingly popular option in several advanced industrial states, and it is significant, perhaps, that it is the young and the better educated who support referenda the most.

2. Satisfaction with Democracy: The Canadian Paradox

Richard Nadeau

In the mid-1970s, many political scientists thought the Western democracies were on the verge of a profound legitimacy crisis.[1] There is less pessimism today, but for many, the current conjuncture does not evoke much optimism. The dissolution of the communist world deprives the democracies of a favourable comparison,[2] the tone of the media's coverage of governmental activity is increasingly negative,[3] and the citizens of Western democracies now show less confidence and respect towards political institutions and actors than in the past.[4]

This chapter seeks to determine whether the citizens of Western democracies, under today's circumstances, remain satisfied with the performance of their political institutions. This question is examined using a measure of the overall evaluation of these institutions, namely, citizens' degree of satisfaction with the working of democracy. This study deals principally with the Canadian case, which is examined in a comparative perspective.

The study of Canadians' perceptions of their democracy is of both general and particular interest. Canada is one of the oldest and most stable democracies in the Western world. The numerous similarities between Canada's culture and political institutions and those of the majority of the other well-established democracies[5] make it a sort of test case. It sits as a representative case of the way in which, at the end of the century, the political institutions of the developed countries might adjust to meet their citizens' new demands. But Canada also has its own specific problems and its own political dynamic. The examination of satisfaction with Canadian democracy provides a glance at the extent to

which Canada's political institutions respond to these particular problems as well as to the more global problems shared by all Western
democracies.

This chapter has three main sections. First, we consider the existing
work on the principal tendencies in public opinion concerning democracy and on the institutions and actors it involves. The Canadian case
will then be considered more specifically. This examination allows us to
observe that the level of support for democracy in Canada is not as high
and stable as one might otherwise believe. The study of determinants of
this support finally allows us to explain this relative deficit and to
suggest some means by which it can be overcome.

Old Institutions and New Values

The diagnosis of the functioning of Western democracies has evolved
greatly over the last quarter-century. In the mid-1970s, many political
scientists believed that a chronic deficit was being established between
citizens' expectations and the capacity of democratic systems to fulfil
them. In feeding citizens' dissatisfaction, this deficit or overload was
seen as having the long-term potential of significantly eroding support
for democratic institutions.[6]

This pessimism rapidly appeared as excessive.[7] By the end of the
1970s, the focus of work on democracy had shifted. The crisis theories
gave way to the much less radical notion of challenges for democracy,
with the challenges being posed by changes in the political culture and
values of citizens in the Western countries.[8]

The work of Ronald Inglehart greatly inspired this new approach.[9]
According to him, the Western electorates had undergone two fundamental transformations. The first was cognitive. Being better educated
and informed, the 'new' voters would be better equipped to understand and actively participate in political debates.[10] The priorities of
voters also had changed. 'Materialist' preoccupations and values such
as the maintenance of law and order or of economic stability gradually
gave way to 'post-materialist' priorities like protecting freedom of expression or wishing to be consulted in the making of significant governmental decisions.[11]

Inglehart's approach and conclusions have fed many debates. The
role of values as the factor determining democratic stability and performance has been questioned,[12] while the concept of cognitive mobilization has raised certain challenges[13] (see Mebs Kanji's account in this

volume, chapter 3, of this evolution in the Canadian context). Some have even held that the apparent progression of post-materialist values results from a construction flaw in Inglehart's way of measuring values.[14] However, these debates do not remove the heuristic value of Inglehart's approach. At the heart of the approach and the studies it has inspired is a fundamental questioning of the consequences of the growing chasm between the political institutions of the Western democracies and the political culture of their citizens.

A New Citizen?

Inglehart summarizes the change that has occurred in the political culture of Western voters as the passage from a fundamentally 'elite-directed' attitude to an 'elite-directing' attitude. Deference towards political authorities has been displaced by an attitude of defiance. He argues that 'publics [are now] less amenable to doing what they are told and more adept at telling government what to do.'[15] This new spirit is evident not only in the expression of greater demands for participation in political debates, but also, and more fundamentally, in the desire to participate in a more direct, active, and systematic manner in the making of important political decisions. This attitude opens the way to a 'more participatory, issue-oriented democracy.'[16]

Do the available studies allow the inference that Inglehart's new citizen has emerged in the Western democracies? Three important studies have addressed this question. Inglehart studied the changes in political values in forty-three countries during the 1980s, [17] a European collective did the same for Western Europe since the 1960s,[18] and Nevitte studied the Canadian case in detail.[19]

The conclusions of these studies do not converge on all points. The conclusions on the decline of traditional forms of participation (like voting) are mitigated. The decline of traditional organizations of interest representation (political parties, unions) to the benefit of new collective actors (pressure groups, environmentalists, etc.) is not yet very pronounced. Meanwhile, citizen disaffection with politicians and governmental and non-governmental institutions varies by country and circumstance.[20]

Despite these divergences, the observed trends remain relatively clear and signal significant changes in Western societies on two accounts. First, an impressive number of studies confirm that the citizens of Western democracies are in fact more and more interested in politics and more and more inclined to participate in non-conventional political action.[21] The portrait drawn by these studies is thus very different from what common sense might suggest. Interest in politics is on the increase, apathy is declining, the desire to be consulted on important political decision is more and more rooted, and the desire to participate beyond passive and institutionalized activities like the vote and political-party membership is increasingly manifest.

The more active and autonomous citizen suggested by this portrait is also more critical of political actors and institutions.[22] A revealing manifestation of this phenomenon may well be the sharp decline of confidence in the American federal government: 'Confidence in government has declined. In 1964, three-quarters of the American public said they trusted the federal government to do the right thing most of the time. Today only a quarter of Americans admit the same trust.'[23]

Do the changes in citizens' political culture in the developed countries present a threat, at least in the long term, to the stability of the Western democracies? Fuchs and Klingemann's typology of changes provoked by 'individual modernisation' provides a frame of reference to answer this question.[24] According to these authors, the new citizen, more sophisticated than before, and more concerned with making his or her rights respected and voice heard, would jettison traditional forms of political participation (the vote), would cease to privilege institutional channels of interest representation (political parties, unions), and would question his or her allegiance to elites (politicians), institutions (parliament, courts, army, etc.) and the political community of belonging (decline of exclusive sense of identification with country of origin). These would be replaced by new forms of participation (petitions, demonstrations, etc), new forms of defending interests (new political parties, new social movements, etc.) and new social relations (decline of sense of authority, emergence of individual values, etc.). A possible but not inevitable consequence of these changes would be the questioning of the democratic system of government itself by a significant proportion of the population. According to Fuchs and Klingemann, only at this point could we speak of a genuine crisis of democracy.[25]

Neal Roese's chapter in this book provides an interesting perspective about the gap between citizens' political culture and institutions with the reminder that citizens' degree of confidence in institutions lies on a continuum between an unconditional adherence, or blind trust, and a generalized mistrust that can lead to cynicism and disengagement. This characterization of political support highlights that a certain amount of scepticism towards democratic institutions is not only inevitable, but also desirable. The question is then one of knowing whether citizens' healthy scepticism of their political institutions is in danger of intensifying to the extent that it is transformed into a simple cynicism. In the long run, such a change would corrode popular support for democratic ideals. In other words, and using Pippa Norris's terms, will 'dissatisfied democrats,' namely, 'citizens who adhere strongly to democratic values [but] find the existing structures ... to be wanting'[26] be transformed over time into a core of 'cynical democrats'? One way to examine this issue is to see, in an overall manner, whether citizens in the Western democracies, and particularly in Canada, seem satisfied with the way in which democracy works in their respective countries.

A Declining Satisfaction with Democracy?

The most commonly used indicator for measuring the state of opinion on the functioning of a country's democracy is satisfaction with democracy.[27] In operational terms, satisfaction with democracy results from the aggregation of answers obtained to the following question: 'On the whole, are you very satisfied, fairly satisfied, not very satisfied, or not satisfied at all with the way democracy works in [country]?' This variable's theoretical status has raised numerous debates, but most researchers recognize the intellectual affiliation between the concept of satisfaction with democracy and David Easton's work on political support.[28] Kornberg and Clarke underline that satisfaction with democracy is 'positively related to but not coterminous with, what Easton has termed the authorities, regime and community support.'[29] Meanwhile, Fuchs suggests that this measure could be considered as an amalgam reflecting the general support for the idea of democracy and a specific support for the performance of a democratic system of government at a moment in time.[30] This second definition, which underlines that satisfaction with democracy must not be confounded with the evaluation of the government in place, mirrors Kuechler's perspective, which holds that this measure 'reflects a sort of emotionally-biased running tally that citizens keep on the performance of a system.'[31]

An indicator of a state of crisis in the democracies would be the progressive decline of citizens' satisfaction levels with the working of democracy in their respective countries. This hypothesis, advanced by Inglehart, has been tested using measures of satisfaction with democracy administered in the Eurobarometer, which are biannual surveys administered in the countries of the European Economic Communities since the mid-1970s.[32]

The results do not seem to support the notion of a long-term downward tendency of satisfaction with democracy. Most researchers have yet to uncover a tendency to support the belief in a secular decline in satisfaction levels with democracy in western Europe (see table 2.2). Indeed, these levels have remained more or less stable over the past two decades[33] and more particular and partial findings on other democracies (Canada, the United States, and Australia for instance; see the next section) confirm this conclusion.[34]

How can one explain the stability of support for political institutions as measured by the indicator of satisfaction with democracy? A first explanation rests on a parallel between the pessimism of the 1970s and the 1990s. In the same way that theories of 'the crisis of democracy' amplified government overload and its consequences a quarter-century ago, approaches inspired by Inglehart have exaggerated both the extent of changes of citizens' political culture in the Western democracies and the significance of the challenges posed by these changes to the stability of democratic systems. A second explanation, compatible with Inglehart's views on the secular decline in support for democratic institutions, rests on the idea that the transformation of political culture is not yet complete and thus has not made its full weight felt. In this explanation, the Western democracies are currently benefiting from a reprieve. However, with time, the new political culture will extend and deepen itself, eventually undermining the very legitimacy of the democratic process.

The two explanations listed above presume an institutional rigidity and a relative incapacity to adapt to a changing environment. This perspective is not unanimously held. For some authors like Dahl, the stability of support for democracies over the last decades is explained by their flexibility and their capacity to adjust to changes.[35] Fuchs and Klingemann take this perspective, arguing that democracies possess adaptive mechanisms allowing them to adjust in response to changes in the values and expectation of citizens.[36] In the European context, for instance, the most explicit manifestations of this adaptive capacity are seen in the growing place occupied by new issues on the political agenda, by the emergence of new collective actors, and by a series of changes in the party system.

A rich and nuanced picture thus emerges from this overview of the literature concerning the state of, and tendencies in, opinions regarding diverse facets of democratic functioning. The citizens of Western democracies have evolved over the last decades, and Canadians have not escaped this change.[37] The political culture of these new citizens thus involves increased demands for participation and consultation and a growing scepticism of political actors and institutions. At least to date, this scepticism does not seem to have touched the evaluation of the working of their democratic institutions. For some, this is only a matter of time.[38] For others, by contrast, the stability of democracies is assured by their adaptive capacity,[39] their performance,[40] the absence of alternatives,[41] and the realism of their citizens.[42] At any rate, the tension between citizens' growing interest in politics and their growing scepticism towards its actors and institutions has put the democracies perhaps 'not so much in crisis as in a state of transition,'[43] a transition that might be facilitated by appropriate institutional changes.

Satisfaction with Democracy: The Canadian Paradox

The notion of satisfaction with the working of democracy refers to the issue of performance. As the tree is judged by its fruit, so democracy is judged by its results. This perspective is held by researchers who have studied the determinants of satisfaction with democracy. Kornberg and Clarke[44] cite Sartori in the inscription to their text on political support in Canada: 'What democracy is cannot be separated from what democracy should be.'[45] Likewise, Anderson and Guillory justify the use of this measure because it reflects the reality of democracy, [46] a notion well captured in their view by formulations such as those of Lane and Ersson on the 'constitution in operation'[47] or of Fuchs, Guidorossi, and Svensson on 'constitutional reality.'[48]

The principle behind this discussion is that satisfaction with the functioning of democracy must be particularly elevated in countries where the electoral process is equitable, where rights and liberties are adequately protected, and where the quality of life is high. In this respect, one might believe that the level of satisfaction with democracy in Canada should be among the highest (if not the highest) in the world. Many United Nations studies have shown that Canada places first with respect to the quality of life enjoyed by its citizens[49] and that its democratic institutions respond entirely to the usual criteria of a liberal democracy.[50]

The findings in table 2.1, which deal with a 1995 study led by Gallup in seventeen countries, seem to confirm this view, at least at first sight.

TABLE 2.1
Satisfaction with democracy, 1995

Country	% Satisfied	% Dissatisfied	% Net satisfied
Canada	62	24	38
United States	64	27	37
Iceland	54	23	31
Germany	55	27	28
Costa Rica	52	25	27
Thailand	54	27	27
Chile	43	31	12
France	43	32	11
Taiwan	42	32	10
Japan	35	32	3
Dominican Republic	40	38	2
Spain	31	30	1
United Kingdom	40	43	-3
India	32	43	-11
Venezuela	28	59	-31
Hungary	17	50	-33
Mexico	17	67	-50

Question wording: 'How satisfied are you with the way democracy works in this country: very satisfied, somewhat satisfied, neither satisfied nor dissatisfied, somewhat dissatisfied, or very dissatisfied?' (Answers 'Neither satisfied nor dissatisfied' and 'No opinion' are omitted in the table).

Source: CNN/USA Today/Gallup poll conducted 21–24 April 1995 (18 countries), in The Gallup Poll, *Public Opinion 1995*, Washington, Delaware: Scholarly Resources Inc. (Sample sizes are about 1000 per country.)

In this study, Canada sits second to the United States in terms of the gross level of satisfaction with democracy (62%) and is in first place in terms of net satisfaction (+38%).[51] Satisfaction with democracy in Canada is not only higher than in developing countries like India (–11%), Venezuela (–31), or Mexico (–50%), but is also significantly higher than in other well-established democracies like Great Britain (–3%), France (+11%), and Germany (+28%).

Is this portrait believable? Can one regard Canada as effectively the best country in the world as much in terms of its quality of life as in terms of its citizens' satisfaction with the working of their democracy? Table 2.2, which enlarges the comparison to several European countries, shows that this idyllic picture does not correspond with reality. Satisfaction with democracy in Canada is more or less the same as in

TABLE 2.2
Satisfaction with democracy in Europe and Canada, various years

Country	1990	1993	1995
Norway	86	N/A	82
Germany (west)	84	57	68
Luxembourg	76	78	80
Denmark	71	78	83
Netherlands	70	69	70
Canada	69	67	62*
Ireland	64	64	73
Belgium	60	51	57
Great Britain	54	49	50
France	48	48	48
Italy	22	13	20

Question wording: 'On the whole, are you very satisfied, fairly satisfied, not very satisfied, or not at all satisfied with the way democracy works in [country]?'

Source: Eurobarometer, various years (sample sizes are about 1000 per country).

*Different wording (see table 2.1). Excluding the category 'neither satisfied nor dissatisfied' would result in a satisfaction level slightly higher than 70 per cent.

Ireland and the Netherlands, and remains clearly below the level registered in Norway, Denmark, Luxembourg, and pre-unification Germany. Moreover, recent results show levels of satisfaction with democracy of 81 per cent in the United States and 78 per cent in Australia.[52] It is therefore clear that despite favourable circumstances, Canada trails in terms of its citizens' satisfaction with the working of their democratic institutions.[53] The fact that one Canadian in three is little satisfied with the functioning of democracy in his or her country and that barely one in ten feels very satisfied underlines the importance of examining the causes of this rather disappointing performance.

The Global Picture

Does satisfaction with democracy vary in a significant fashion according to the respondent's region and socio-demographic characteristics? In other words, are there identifiable sectors of unhappiness with the working of Canadian democracy? Table 2.3 shows that evaluations are

TABLE 2.3
Satisfaction with democracy in Canada, 1993

	% Satisfied
All	67
Male	67
Female	67
Less than high school	62
More than high school	71
Income: lowest third	60
medium third	66
highest third	72
Age: 18–34	66
35–54	67
55+	68
Foreign born	72
Born in Canada	66
Maritimes	72
French Quebec	59
English Quebec	75
Ontario	68
Prairies	72
Alberta/BC	68

Source: Canadian Election Study, 1993.

slightly higher among foreign-born Canadians and vary little as a function of the individuals' sex or age. If the absence of a generational cleavage may appear surprising, the higher satisfaction of Canada's most wealthy and best educated is compatible with theoretical perspectives stressing that the most positive evaluations of a system come from those whom it benefits the most, or from those who have most internalized its values.[54]

Regional and linguistic cleavages play an important role in Canada's political dynamics.[55] In the case of support for Canadian political institutions, the available work shows that the dominant cleavage is that opposing Quebec francophones to other Canadians.[56] The findings in table 2.3 confirm this analysis. The regional variations in the evaluation of Canadian democracy are slight outside of Quebec, and within Quebec the chasm between francophones and non-francophones is considerable. Overall, one group stands out, namely Quebec francophones, whose level of satisfaction with Canadian democracy is about ten points below that of other Canadians.

The diagnosis offered by table 2.3 on the existence of sectors of relative unhappiness with Canadian democracy is useful but limited. It is necessary to extend this examination to more explicitly political determinants. We will now proceed to this examination using a multivariate model of satisfaction with democracy.[57]

A Model of Satisfaction with Democracy

The objective of this section is to account for the specific contribution of a series of factors in the explanation of the level of satisfaction with democracy. The model's dependent variable, whose different components we will now consider, is the measure of satisfaction with democracy that we have been discussing up to this point.[58] For the sake of presentation, the model's different components correspond to a series of variables that are grouped together in function of their theoretical similarity. We first present the model's socio-demographic variables, followed by the respondent's economic perceptions, measures of interest, and political participation, and finally measures judging the respondent's level of support for a certain number of political institutions and actors.

A. Socio-demographic Variables
These variables include age, sex, schooling, income, place of birth, and membership in Quebec's francophone group. These variables are included as controls, and help to determine the impact of group belonging on the perception of the functioning of democracy. Previous studies suggest that satisfaction with democracy should be less strong among the younger, less-fortunate, and less-educated citizens, as well as among the Quebec francophone group.[59]

The factors explaining Quebec francophones' lower satisfaction with Canadian democracy are no doubt numerous and complex. An interesting approach to the question is suggested by Easton's theories on political support, whose principal objects are the regime, the elites, and the community. [60] It was mentioned above that satisfaction with democracy derives in part from this type of support. In the case of Quebec francophones, it is likely that a significantly weaker support for the political community is the basis for their lower level of satisfaction with democracy in this country. In 1993, the average attachment of Quebec francophones to Canada, placed on a scale of 0 to 100, was 66 (where 0 is the expression of an absence of attachment and 100 is a very profound attachment). The average sat at 86 for non-francophone Québécois and 89 for Canadians from other provinces.[61] Given that this variable measuring support for the Canadian political community is an integral part of the model (see section E below), it is possible that the effect of belonging to the Quebec francophone group on satisfaction with democracy does not manifest itself directly in the multivariate analysis. Rather, it may express itself in an indirect manner through reduced attachment to Canada. The possibility that certain variables exert indirect rather than direct effects on democratic satisfaction is also plausible in the case of age given the numerous studies that demonstrate a generational effect on the level of support for political actors and institutions.

B. Economic Perceptions

Economic perceptions play a considerable role in evaluating the performance of governments[62] and should also influence citizens' overall evaluation of their democracy's performance.[63] Two variables are included in the model. The first measures the respondent's evaluation (positive, negative, or neutral) of the Canadian economy's performance over the past year. The second measures his or her expectations (optimistic, pessimistic, neutral) for the next twelve months. Positive evaluations and optimistic expectations should be positively linked to satisfaction with democracy.

C. Participation

Two variables are used to measure two aspects of individuals' cognitive engagement in politics: interest in the 1993 campaign, which is used as a 'proxy' for a general interest in politics; and the degree of support for the statement 'People like me don't have any say about what government does.' The theoretical interpretation of these two variables is very different. Interest in politics reveals a positive evaluation of the channels of consultation and participation, while, in contrast, agreement with the statement cited above underlines their insufficiency. Interest in politics thus should be positively linked with satisfaction with democracy, while the feeling of lacking a voice should be negatively linked.

D. The Loser's Status

Anderson and Guillory's work reveals that voters belonging to the losing side are generally less satisfied with the working of democracy, with the unhappiness of losers being particularly vivid in 'majoritarian' systems where the winners usually govern without sharing power.[64] Canada belongs to this majoritarian category, such that the effect of the variable distinguishing the losers from the winners should be relatively important.

E. The Objects of Political Support

Borrowing from David Easton's typology on political support[65] and from Inglehart's model of value change[66] in Western democracies, the model employs five indicators to measure the effect of support for democracy's principal incarnations on the overall evaluation of democracy's performance in and of itself. A first dimension is support for the community, measured using the previously mentioned thermometer variable (0 to 100) gauging attachment to Canada. Support for the regime is measured using two variables measuring the respondent's degree of confidence in the federal government and the courts. Confidence in political elites is measured using a statement on the corruption of politicians since, according to Orren, perceptions concerning corruption are an essential factor in the maintenance of public confidence in the political class.[67] Finally, individuals' support for the party system, the traditional mechanism of interest representation, is measured by a variable distinguishing respondents identifying with a party from those who do not see themselves in any party. The theoretical expectations, for these variables are fairly clear. Satisfaction with democracy should be highest among those who show a marked support for the Canadian political community, its elites, its institutions, and its mechanisms of interest representation.

The Results

The results of the regression analysis are presented in table 2.4.[68] The block of socio-demographic variables shows that richer and better-educated individuals, as well as those born outside of Canada, show more satisfaction with the working of Canadian democracy.[69] The positive effect of education and income conforms to our expectations and denotes the greater satisfaction of those who benefit the most from the Canadian political system.[70] The higher satisfaction of citizens born outside of Canada is compatible with Black's results[71] and seems in part to reflect the greater enthusiasm of those who have 'discovered' certain virtues of democracy in their new country. From a dynamic perspective, this result implies that the growing place of immigration in

TABLE 2.4
Satisfaction with democracy in Canada, 1993: regression analysis

Independent variables	B	Std error	Beta
Age	.03	(.12)	.01
Gender	.01	(.03)	.01
School	.16	(.07)*	.05
Income	.14	(.05)**	.07
Foreign-born	.09	(.05)*	.04
French Quebec	.06	(.05)	.03
Retrospective evaluation of Canadian economy	.01	(.03)	.01
Prospective evaluation of Canadian economy	.05	(.03)*	.04
Political interest	.17	(.07)*	.06
People like me don't have any say	−.13	(.06)*	−.06
Loser	−.15	(.04)**	−.10
Feelings toward Canada	.46	(.11)**	.12
Confidence in the federal government	.41	(.08)**	.13
Confidence in the courts	.34	(.07)**	.11
Party identification	.18	(.04)**	.10
Politicians are no more corrupt than anybody else	.20	(.05)**	.09
Intercept	1.62	(.14)**	
Adjusted R^2		.15	
N		1693	

Source: Canadian Election Study, 1993.

Ordinary least squares estimates. See the appendix for variable descriptions.

*p < .05; **p < .01

Canada's demographic profile could have a positive impact on levels of democratic satisfaction in the future.

The two less-intuitive results that arise from the examination of the socio-demographic variables are the absence of an age effect (a result that confirms the data in table 2.3) and, more surprisingly, the absence of an effect from belonging to the francophone group. We will examine in the next section if the effect of these two variables will manifest itself in an indirect manner through reduced attachment to Canada and lower support for political actors and institutions (see section A above).

The results on participation conform to our expectations. Interest in politics, interpreted as a measure of satisfaction with traditional channels of participation in politics, involves more positive evaluations. The inverse is true for individuals having the impression of not being able to make themselves heard, a group composed of no less than 53 per cent of Canadians. This said, the impact on participation remains relatively weak. We will also consider these results in the next section by examining the indirect effect of the variables concerning satisfaction with democracy in terms of their impact on support for the regime, for elites, and for the community.

If the direct effect of the participation measures seems weaker than predicted, this is not the case for the variable accounting for the voter's 'loser' status, as attested by the value of the standardized (.10) and non-standardized (–.15) coefficients that are associated with it. The fact that losers are in general a little less satisfied with the working of democracy is not in itself surprising, reflecting a natural unhappiness with the turn of events.[72] The distance between winners and losers in 1993, where 77 per cent of Liberal party voters (the victorious party) claimed to be satisfied with Canadian democracy, as opposed to only 61 per cent among supporters of other parties, seems to give weight to Anderson and Guillory's argument that 'winning and losing mean different things in different political systems' and that losing is more bitter in winner-takes-all electoral systems like Canada's.[73]

Variables measuring support for the 'pillars' of democracy all exert a significant and roughly equal impact, as the standardized regression coefficients for these variables of between .09 and .13 demonstrate. Attachment to Canada, a marked confidence in the federal government and the courts, identification with a federal political party, and a positive evaluation of politicians all exert an important impact on satisfaction with the working of Canadian democracy.

The results for the variables measuring support for the political community and its institutions and actors offers a nuanced portrait of support for democracy. On the one hand, this support seems sufficiently high to assure a fairly high, while not exceptional, level of satisfaction with the working of Canadian democracy. On the other hand, certain pillars underlying this support remain shaky. Attachment to Canada is weak among Quebec francophones, while confidence in the federal government (31%),[74] the courts (46%), and politicians remains divided,[75] and the number of Canadians identifying with a political party is in decline.[76] These results demand an examination of the dynamic linked to support for democracy's pillars.

Support for the Regime, the Elites, and the Community

To examine the determinants of support for the 'pillars' of Canadian democracy, we have used variables measuring support for the regime, the elites, and the community as dependent (or explained) variables. To attempt to discern the different sources of support for these different political objects, a series of explanatory variables have been included in five regression analyses having the dependent variables of attachment to Canada, confidence in the federal government, confidence in the courts, opinions concerning politicians, and partisan identification. These explanatory variables include the respondents' socio-demographic characteristics (age, sex, education, income, country of origin, place of residency) as well as the measures of participation used in table 2.4. To account for possible regional variations, we have enlarged the variable dealing with the place of residence to include the Maritimes, francophone Quebec, non-francophone Quebec, Ontario (which constitutes the reference category), the Prairies (Manitoba and Saskatchewan), and the West (Alberta and British Columbia; for a similar division, see Kornberg and Clarke[77]).

The results of the analysis are presented in table 2.5. To facilitate the reading of this table, the results are limited to the standardized coefficients for the six variables having a relatively systematic impact on the measures of political support, such as age, country of origin, means of participation, belonging to the group of Quebec francophones, and the fact of residing in Alberta or British Columbia.

The overall conclusion that comes from these tables is that certain pillars of Canadian democracy remain relatively fragile. The case of attachment to Canada is particularly revealing in this regard. This attachment is significantly less strong among Quebec francophones (standardized coefficient of –.45), which helps to explain this variable's lack of impact on satisfaction with democracy observed in table 2.4. Younger voters' less-pronounced attachment to Canada is also quite clear (the coefficient of .13 signals that this attachment grows with age). This result confirms Nevitte's conclusion that Canadians are becoming less parochial in their attitudes[78] and conforms with Inglehart's model in showing that the effect of generational replacement is to progressively undermine support for the political community, which is one of the foundations of democratic satisfaction.

This same erosion effect of generational replacement is very visible in the case of confidence in the federal government. Older voters express

TABLE 2.5
Determinants of political support in Canada

	Canada	Federal government	Courts	Politicians	Parties
Age	.14**	.13**	.02	.05*	.04*
Foreign-born	.05**	.08**	.03	.02	.04
Political interest	.06*	.10**	.00	.01	.15**
No say	.02	−.20**	−.15**	−.12**	−.03
French Quebec	−.45**	−.11**	−.07**	−.09**	.08**
Alberta/BC	.01	−.08**	.01	−.11**	.03

Source: Canadian Election Study, 1993.

Ordinary least squares estimates, standardized coefficients. See the appendix for variable descriptions.

*p < .05; **p < .01

the highest support for the political institutions, while the youngest voters show the most reservations. The scepticism of Quebec francophones and of residents of Alberta and British Columbia is clearly highlighted, a result that again helps to understand the absence of a direct effect for the first variable in table 2.4 and that is not at all surprising given the electoral behaviour of these two groups in the 1993 and 1997 federal elections.

Another notable result is the contrast between the impact of variables measuring interest in politics and the feeling of having a say. If voters who are more interested in politics are also more likely to be confident in the federal government, citizens with the impression of not having a genuine voice in governmental decisions express the opposite feelings. It is revealing that this last variable is the one that has the greatest impact on confidence not only in the federal government, but also in the courts (see the third column) and in politicians (column 4). It is also significant that interest in politics is the principal determinant of partisan attachment (column 5). Other results also arise, namely, the greater scepticism shown by Western residents towards politicians (column 4) and, again, by the youngest towards politicians and parties (columns 4 and 5).

The nature of support for the Canadian political community and its actors and institutions has numerous implications on the level and the evolution of satisfaction with the working of Canadian democracy. The chronic dissatisfaction of certain groups, the erosion of support for the Canadian political community and its institutions shown by younger citizens (which is but partially compensated for by the more positive attitudes of Canadians born abroad; see particularly columns 1 and 2), and the generalized expression of greater demands for participation and consultation are questions that must be addressed if Canada wishes to gain and maintain high levels of citizen satisfaction with the working of democracy.

Discussion: The Political Implications of the Results

The political culture of citizens in the Western democracies is in mutation. Being better educated, more conscious of their competence, and more interested in politics, voters now wish to take a more active and determining role in government decisions that affect them. These new demands for participation seem unlikely to be met through traditional channels of democratic participation and interest representation. This situation creates a frustration that has largely manifested itself to date through declining support for political institutions and actors.

The will to enhance the role of individuals in political decision-making in order to attenuate this frustration is not new[79] and the practical difficulties of alternatives have often been underlined.[80] Sartori has been particularly critical of participationist prescriptions, doubting the competence of voters, questioning the feasibility of increasing their participation ('how, what, why, and where?'), and concluding on the impossibility of plans not only to involve all citizens in all political decisions but even to involve them in all important ones.[81] Even authors favourable to the idea of greater citizen participation have stressed the potentially perverse effects of efforts promoting the principle. Kaase and Newton have, for instance, underlined that 'to go beyond the vote [poses] a major problem [because] different strata or groups are not equally inclined to participate ... which brings back the old issue of political equality.'[82] Mansbridge, in turn, has rightfully observed that 'active forms of political participation could produce more non-governmental resources for solving problems, but if they are directed primarily at increasing demands on government, they may contribute indirectly to distrust.'[83]

These observations clearly highlight the difficulties, and to a certain extent the dangers, of policies seeking to increase citizen participation. The implication of a greater number of citizens being involved in a greater number of important decisions poses the problems of feasibility raised by Sartori. This said, what our study of satisfaction with democracy and support for political institutions illuminates is, first and foremost, the negative effect cast on both by a feeling of voicelessness in important government decisions – a feeling that is shared by a large number of Canadians. In other words, before considering increased participation, whose forms have yet to be determined, Canadians are more interested in being able to express themselves and, more importantly, in being listened to more attentively by political decision-makers.

A necessary condition for giving citizens the impression of being listened to is to ensure a greater linkage between the message transmitted by voting and the parliamentary representation that results. In this sense, the first step to reconciling Canadian political culture and political institutions involves reforming the electoral system. This idea mirrors that of Nevitte, who claims that 'electoral reform is one strategy for reconnecting citizens with such traditional representative institutions as parties.'[84] The spirit in which this reform should be undertaken is eloquently expressed in a study by Britain's Constitution Unit for which 'the intention behind the new voting systems is to strengthen the representative link between voters and government and thus create a more sophisticated and participatory political culture.'[85] In the Canadian case, one can in fact argue that the goal of reform would be as much to respond to an emergent participatory political culture as to aid and encourage its development.

The reasons justifying some changes to Canada's current electoral system are numerous. First, the system presents the double disadvantage of both deforming and limiting voters' choices. The Report of the Independent Commission on the Voting System in Great Britain is eloquent on this point: 'Fairness to the voters is the first essential. A primary duty of an electoral system is to represent the wishes of the electorate as effectively as possible. The main "fairness" count against First past the Post is that it distorts the desires of the voters.'[86] Farrell's study, showing Canada ranking as 35th out of 37 studied cases in terms of adequately translating votes into parliamentary seats,[87] highlights the amplitude of distortion produced by the Canadian electoral system and signals the extent to which the results it produces fail to meet this equity objective.

The other problem of the Canadian electoral system, at least in the eyes of Canadian voters, is the limited range of choices offered. Blais and Gidengil have shown that the vast majority of Canadians (81%) believe that their electoral system makes it difficult for new parties to elect candidates because some voters will abstain from supporting them for fear of wasting their vote.[88] For these authors, this situation has created frustration over time. In light of the Norwegian case where the arrival of new parties led to increased voter satisfaction with the working of democracy,[89] they are led to conclude that 'Canadians are cynical towards politics, in part because they feel that their choices are too limited.'[90]

While it may seem paradoxical in light of what was just said, the arrival of the Bloc Québécois and the Reform Party on the federal scene points out another limit of the Canadian electoral system. To the extent that the only way to overcome political marginality involves building regional electoral support, one can argue that the current system tends to exacerbate Canadian regionalism. Among other gains, reforming the Canadian electoral system would have the merit of not requiring new parties to be regionalist, even while assuring a more balanced regional representation of already established parties.

A final limitation of the Canadian electoral system also deserves mention. The current system has the double drawback of maximizing the number of losers and, as our analysis confirmed, of creating a chasm between winners and losers.[91] This situation relates to the very nature of majoritarian systems. Unlike 'consensual' regimes, they tend to concentrate all executive power in the hands of the winning party. Along with Great Britain, Australia, and pre-electoral-reform New Zealand,[92] Canada constitutes one of the countries where this tendency is most evident.[93] It is also noteworthy that among these four countries, one has already changed its voting system (namely, New Zealand) while another (Britain) is on the verge of doing so.

What elements should be part of a reformed Canadian electoral system? The principles enunciated by the Independent Commission on the Voting System in Great Britain provide a useful foundation: 'Our proposition for this country stems essentially from the British constituency tradition and proceeded by limited modification to render it less haphazard, less unfair to minority parties and less nationally divisive in the sense of avoiding large areas of electoral desert for the two major parties.'[94]

Based on these principles, we propose that 25 per cent of Canada's Members of the House of Commons be elected by proportional representation from candidate lists established by the parties in each province. For voters, this type of electoral reform would combine the advantage of maintaining a 'direct link in each constituency between voters and their representatives'[95] while producing a more equitable and representative parliamentary representation. Being more equitable, this method of voting would also be more inclusive. Farrell's work showing that PR systems increase the chance for women to gain adequate representation in parliament[96] illustrates the type of potential benefits to be expected from the introduction of a dose of proportional representation in the Canadian electoral system. While the nature of majoritarian regimes is to confide all power to a party with a minority of the votes but a majority of parliamentary seats, a consensual system enlarges the governmental coalition 'to as many people as possible.'[97]

The more adequate parliamentary representation of Canadians' values and interests that a new voting system would provide would likely increase the pertinence of political debates for many voters. It would also facilitate the development of a political culture more clearly concerned with the values of responsibility, participation, and consensus. This new voting system is therefore arguably more in keeping with Canadians' political culture. In this respect, it seems clear that the most profound and no doubt dysfunctional split between Canadians' new political culture and their political institutions exists in the method of nominating members to the current Canadian senate. It follows that the second element of electoral and institutional reform in Canada should be the transformation of the Senate into a House of the Regions whose members would be elected through universal suffrage.

A senate chosen by universal suffrage would answer Canadians' new demands for participation and consultation. Its transformation into a House of the Regions would more specifically address the expressed desire for a more adequate representation of the interests and views of the Western and Atlantic provinces in the Canadian parliament. The election of a House of the Regions through universal suffrage would allow more active and sophisticated citizen participation in Canadian political life, even while enriching Canadian federalism with a new institutional mechanism to assure a better balance between the Canadian regions and a more adequate representation of their interests.[98]

We suggest that the members of the Chambers of Regions should also be elected by proportional representation from candidates lists established by the parties in each province. Considered together, the changes to the electoral system proposed in this chapter would mean that Canadians would make three choices in federal elections. One vote would be for the member in their riding, a second for the quarter of House of Commons members elected through proportional representation, and a third to elect members to the Chamber of Regions. We believe that this system is not excessively complicated for the 'new' Canadian voter. In fact, it responds much better to their capacities and their desire to vote in a nuanced and sophisticated manner.

Another source limiting satisfaction levels with the functioning of Canadian democracy that this study highlights is citizens' widespread and growing scepticism of politicians' honesty and integrity. According to many, this trend is attributable to increasingly negative media coverage of governmental activity in general, and of politicians in particular.[99] While part of this scepticism is explained by conjunctural factors, certain heavy tendencies requiring an institutional response are also in play. This response could mean adopting even stricter party financing laws. Canadians' feelings of powerlessness in the political process often comes from an impression that some voices count for more than others. Strict financial rules for party and electoral activities would attenuate this impression and restore the impression of a more equitable, honest, and transparent electoral process.

This recommendation finds common cause with that of Blais and Gidengil, who concluded several years ago that 'a stricter regulation of election funding would help renew Canadians' confidence.'[100] Their comments on Québec's regulation of election funds, which places firm ceilings on contributions and limits them to individuals, is particularly interesting. They conclude that 'the Québec experience does not seem to be a failure: rather it appears more like a clear success.'[101] Then, having observed that 'political cynicism is less widespread in Québec than elsewhere in the country,' they come to conclude that Québec's 'more stringent electoral laws can be a positive factor' explaining this state of affairs.[102] Given the observations of the preceding paragraphs and Blais and Gidengil's conclusions, we argue that the regulation of electoral funds in federal elections should adopt the Quebec model.

A final factor limiting satisfaction with Canadian democracy is the level of support for the Canadian political community shown by the younger generations in general, and even more strikingly and particularly by Quebec francophones.[103] The support deficit of Quebec francophones on this question, which is even more evident among the younger generations, poses the most complex and difficult question for Canada.[104] The institutional answer to this challenge remains to be found.

Conclusion

> If we had to specify the most important concern about support for government, the cross-national evidence points towards the institutional level.

> If popular pressures lead to institutional reforms this can be understood as a demand-side process which helps resolve tensions between democratic ideals and reality.[105]

Satisfaction with the working of Canadian democracy is not as high or as stable as one might first believe. This situation arises from factors specific to Canada's political dynamics, but also reflects the transformation of citizens' political culture across the Western democracies. Though these changes in political attitudes must not be exaggerated, nor must the tranformative capacity of political institutions be minimized, it seems that Canadian democracy faces several challenges that could be appropriately addressed by a certain number of institutional changes. The above quotations from Norris's important book give even more credence to the idea that these changes, in assuring a better fit between political culture and political institutions, would help reinforce one of the weak links in Canada's democratic process.

This conclusion is in agreement with the older work of the Lortie commission[106] and with Howe and Northrup's recent analysis of Canadians' attitudes towards their political institutions.[107] This agreement seems to give further weight to the idea that strengthening Canadian democracy involves institutional and legislative changes dealing with existing voting and party financing practices. Canadians' persistent disenchantment with their political institutions leads us to believe that the implementation of these reforms would be better realized sooner than later.

Appendix

a) Data source

We use the 1993 Canadian Election Study. Data for this study were collected by the Institute for Social Research at York University, Toronto, for the co-investigators: Richard Johnston, André Blais, Henry E. Brady, Elisabeth Gidengil, and Neil Nevitte. Further details on the sample and technical features of the CES can be found in Northrup and Oram and Johnston et al.[108] This database is available through the Inter-University Consortium for Political and Social Research.

b) Variable descriptions

The dependent variable used in table 2.4 is a 4-point positive scale constructed using the following question: 'On the whole, are you very satisfied, fairly satisfied, not very satisfied, or not satisfied at all with the way democracy works in Canada?'
   The core group of independent variables (see table 2.4) were coded as follows:

- *Age*: actual age of respondent (continuous variable divided by 100)
- *Gender*: female = 1, male = zero
- *School*: a 9-point scale running from zero (no schooling) to 1 (completed university)
- *Income*: a 8-point scale running from zero (less than $20,000) to 1 (more than $80,000)
- *Foreign-born*: coded zero if respondent was born in Canada, coded 1 otherwise
- *French Quebec*: coded 1 if respondent lives in Quebec and speaks French, coded zero otherwise
- *Retrospective evaluations of Canadian economy*: coded 1 if respondent says the national economy has gotten better, coded –1 if respondent says it has gotten worse, coded zero if respondent says it stayed about the same or if he/she doesn't know
- *Prospective evaluations of Canadian economy*: coded 1 if respondent expects the national economy will get better, coded –1 if respondent expects it will get worse, coded zero if respondent expects it will stay the same or doesn't know
- *Political interest*: a 4-point scale running from zero (not at all interested) to 1 (very interested) using a question measuring respondent's interest in the past federal election campaign
- *No say*: a 4-point scale running from zero (strongly disagree) to 1 (strongly agree) using responses to the following statement: 'People like me don't have any say about what the government does.'
- *Loser*: coded zero if respondent voted for the winning party in the past federal election (Liberals), coded 1 otherwise
- *Feelings toward Canada*: a thermometer scale running from zero (very

negative feelings toward Canada) to 100 (very positive feelings), divided by 100
- *Confidence in the federal government*: a 4-point scale running from zero (no confidence at all) to 1 (a great deal of confidence)
- *Confidence in the courts*: a 4-point scale running from zero (no confidence at all) to 1 (a great deal of confidence)
- *Party identification*: coded 1 if respondent identifies her/himself with a federal political party, coded zero otherwise
- *Politicians*: a 4-point scale running from zero (strongly disagree) to 1 (strongly agree) using responses to the following statement: 'Politicians are no more corrupt than anybody else.'

The *dependent variables used in table 2.5* are the last five items just described, coded exactly in the same manner.

Notes

1 Jürgen Habermas, *Legitimation Crisis* (Boston: Beacon Press, 1975); Samuel Brittan, 'The Economic Contradictions of Democracy,' *British Journal of Political Science* 5 (1975): 129–59; Samuel Huntington, 'Postindustrial Politics: How Benign Will It Be?' *Comparative Politics* 6 (1974): 147–77; Michael Crozier, Samuel Huntington, and Joji Watanuki, *The Crisis of Democracy: Report on the Governability of Democracies in the Trilateral Commission* (New York: New York University Press, 1975); Anthony King, 'Overload: Problems of Governing in the 1970's,' *Political Studies* 23 (1975): 284–96.
2 Max Kaase and Kenneth Newton, *Beliefs in Government* (New York: Oxford University Press, 1995); Dieter Fuchs and Hans-Dieter Klingemann, 'Citizens and the State: A Changing Relationship,' in Klingemann and Fuchs, eds, *Citizens and the State* (New York: Oxford University Press, 1995).
3 Thomas E. Patterson, *Out of Order* (New York: Knopf, 1993); Joseph N. Cappella and Kathleen Hall Jamieson, *Spiral of Cynicism: The Press and the Public Good* (New York: Oxford University Press, 1997); Gary R. Orren, 'Fall from Grace: The Public's Loss of Faith in Government,' in Joseph S. Nye, Philip D. Zelikow, and David C. King, eds, *Why People Don't Trust Government* (Cambridge: Cambridge University Press, 1997).
4 Seymour Martin Lipset and William Schneider, *The Confidence Gap: Business, Labor, and Government in the Public Mind* (New York: Free Press, 1983);

Neil Nevitte, *The Decline of Deference: Canadian Value Change in Cross-National Perspective* (Peterborough, ON: Broadview Press, 1996); Ronald Inglehart, *The Silent Revolution: Changing Values and Political Styles among Western Publics* (Princeton: Princeton University Press, 1977); R. Inglehart, *Culture Shift in Advanced Industrial Society* (Princeton: Princeton University Press, 1990); R. Inglehart, *Modernization and Postmodernization: Cultural, Economic and Political Change in 43 Societies* (Princeton: Princeton University Press, 1997).

5 Allan Kornberg and Harold D. Clarke ('Beliefs about Democracy and Satisfaction with Democratic Government: The Canadian Case,' *Political Research Quarterly* 47 [1994]: 540), note that 'Canada resembles other mature Western democracies in several important respects' and Nevitte (*Decline of Deference*, 43) concludes from his work on values that 'there is not a single value dimension along which Canadians qualify as outliers.'

6 Habermas, *Legitimation Crisis*; Brittan, 'Economic Contradictions'; Huntington, 'Postindustrial Politics'; Crozier, Huntington, and Watanuki, *Crisis of Democracy*; King, 'Overload.'

7 Fuchs and Klingemann, 'Citizens and the State.'

8 Kaase and Newton, *Beliefs in Government*.

9 Inglehart, *Silent Revolution*, *Culture Shift*, and *Modernization and Post-modernization*.

10 Inglehart auses the expression 'cognitive mobilization' to account for the expanded competence and sophistication of voters. The link between the voter's 'objective' competence, measurable with indicators like schooling and political information, and this same voter's subjective perception of his or her competence, which refers to the concept of 'internal officacy,' is close, without being absolute. In Inglehart's view, it is ultimately this increased sense of competence felt by the voter that lies at the origin of greater interest in politics and of greater demands for participation in political decisions.

11 The principal measure used by Inglehart to evaluate values consists in asking survey respondents to rank the four following objectives: 1. Maintaining order in the nation; 2. Fighting rising prices; 3. Giving people more say in important governmental decisions; 4. Protecting freedom of speech. An evolution towards post-materialist values (choices 34 and 4) tends to increase at the expense of individuals opting for the materialist values (choices 1 and 2).

12 The role of values in democratic institutions and practices was underlined by Gabriel A. Almond and Sidney Verba (*The Civic Culture: Political Attitudes and Democracy in Five Nations* [Princeton: Princeton University Press,

1963]), Robert A. Dahl (*Polyarchy* [New Haven: Yale University Press, 1971]), Inglehart (*The Silent Revolution; Culture Shift*), and Robert D. Putnam (*Making Democracy Work: Civic Traditions in Modern Italy* [Princeton: Princeton University Press, 1993]), but recently challenged by Edward N. Muller and Mitchell A. Seligson ('Civic Culture and Democracy: The Question of Causal Relationship,' *American Political Science Review* 88 [1994]: 635–52), and especially Robert W. Jackman and Ross A. Miller ('A Renaissance of Political Culture?' *American Journal of Political Science* 40 (1996): 632–59).

13 Work on voter's degree of political information (Russell W. Neuman, *The Paradox of Mass Politics: Knowledge and Opinion in the American Electorate* [Cambridge: Harvard University Press, 1986]; Richard Nadeau, Richard G. Niemi, and Jeffrey Levine, 'Innumeracy about Minority Populations,' *Public Opinion Quarterly* 57 [1993]: 332–47; Richard Nadeau and Richard G. Niemi, 'Educated Guesses: The Process of Answering Factual Knowledge Questions in Surveys,' *Public Opinion Quarterly* 59 [1995]: 323–46; Michael X. Delli Carpini and Scott Keeter, *What Americans Know about Politics and Why It Matters* [New Haven: Yale University Press, 1996]) raises doubts concerning the increase in the quality of voters' factual knowledge over the past few decades.

14 The most incisive critiques in this regard come from Harold Clarke and his collaborators (see Harold D. Clarke, Nitish Dutt, and Jonathon Rapkin, 'Conversations in Context: The (Mis)Measurement of Value Change in Advanced Industrial Societies,' *Political Behavior* 19 [1997]: 19–40; Harold D. Clarke et al., 'The Effect of Economic Priorities on the Measurement of Value Change: New Experimental Evidence,' *American Political Science Review* [forthcoming]); see the reply by Ronald Inglehart and Paul R. Abramson ('Economic Security and Value Change,' *American Political Science Review* 88 [1994]: 336–54; 'Measuring Postmaterialism,' *American Political Science Review* [forthcoming]), who underline that the use of inflation as the economic indicator in the battery seeking to measure voters' priorities (see note 3) entails a systematic underestimation of materialist values.

15 Inglehart, *Modernization and Postmodernization*, 236, and 'Postmaterialism Erodes Respect for Authority, but Increases Support for Democracy,' in Pippa Norris, ed., *Critical Citizens: Global Support for Democratic Governance* (Oxford: Oxford University Press, 1999).

16 Inglehart, *Modernization and Postmodernization*, 233, 236, and 'Postmaterialism Erodes Respect for Authority.' Robert D. Putnam ('Bowling Alone: America's Declining Social Capital,' *Journal of Democracy* 6 [1995]:

65–78; 'Tuning In, Tuning Out: The Strange Disappearance of Social Capital in America,' *PS: Political Science and Politics* 28 [1995]: 664–83) suggests that recent decades are also characterized by significant changes in social interaction, as face-to-face activities within the local community have been falling. Increased individual isolation has entailed a decline in social trust, which in turn produces a decrease in political trust. This thesis, which has stirred many debates (see Kenneth Newton, 'Social and Political Trust in Established Democracies,' in Norris, *Critical Citizens*) receives some backing in Lisa Young's findings in this book (chapter 4).

17 Inglehart, *Modernization and Postmodernizaiton.*

18 See Kaase and Newton, *Beliefs in Government.*

19 Nevitte, *Decline of Deference.*

20 See Orren, 'Fall from Grace'; Ola Listhaug, 'The Dynamics of Trust in Politicians,' in Klingemann and Fuchs, *Citizens and the State*; Ola Listhaug and Matti Wiberg, 'Confidence in Political and Private Institutions,' in Klingemann and Fuchs, *Citizens and the State*; and Arthur H. Miller and Ola Listhaug, 'Political Performance and Institutional Trust,' in Norris, *Critical Citizens.*

21 Samuel Barnes and Max Kaas, eds, *Political Action: Mass Participation in Five Western Democracies* (Beverly Hills, CA: Sage, 1979); M. Kent Jennings and Jan van Deth, eds, *Continuities in Political Action* (New York: de Gruyter, 1989); Paul R. Abramson and Ronald Inglehart, *Value Change in Global Perspective* (Ann Arbor: University of Michigan Press, 1995); Klingemann and Fuchs, *Citizens and the State*, 430; Nevitte, *Decline of Deference*; Inglehart, *Modernization and Postmodernization.*

22 Nevitte, *Decline of Deference*; Inglehart, *Modernization and Postmodernization*; Nye, Zelikow, and King, *Why People Don't Trust Government*; Norris, ed., *Critical Citizens.*

23 Joseph S. Nye, Jr, 'Introduction: The Decline of Confidence in Government,' in Nye, Zelikow, and King, *Why People Don't Trust Government*, 3.

24 Fuchs and Klingemann, 'Citizens and the State,' in Klingemann and Fuchs, *Citizens and the State*, 11, 17.

25 Ibid., 22.

26 Pippa Norris, 'Introduction: The Growth of Critical Citizens?' in Norris, *Critical Citizens*, 21.

27 Christopher J. Anderson and Christine A. Guillory, 'Political Institutions and Satisfaction with Democracy: A Cross-National Analysis of Consensus and Majoritarian Systems,' *American Political Science Review* 91 (1997): 66–81.

28 David Easton, *A Systems Analysis of Political Life* (New York: John Wiley,

1965); 'A Re-Assessment of the Concept of Political Support,' *British Journal of Political Science* 5 (1975): 435–7; and 'Theoretical Approaches to Political Support,' *Canadian Journal of Political Science* 9 (1976): 431–48.

29 Kornberg and Clarke, 'Beliefs about Democracy,' 552. See Easton, *A Systems Analysis of Political Life*, 'A Re-Assessment of the Concept of Political Support,' and 'Theoretical Approaches to Political Support.'

30 Dieter Fuchs, 'Trends of Political Support,' in Dirk Berg-Schlosser and Ralf Rytlewski, eds, *Political Culture in Germany* (New York: St Martin's, 1993).

31 Manfred Kuechler, 'The Dynamics of Mass Political Support in Western Europe: Methodological Problems and Preliminary Findings,' in Karlheinz Reif and Ronald Inglehart, eds, *Eurobarometer: The Dynamics of European Public Opinion – Essays in Honor of Jaques-René Rabier* (New York: St Martin's, 1991), 280.

32 Inglehart, *Modernization and Postmodernization*, 238.

33 See Fuchs and Klingemann, 'Citizens and the State'; Kaase and Newton, *Beliefs in Government*; Kuechler, 'The Dynamics of Mass Political Support in Western Europe'; Fuchs, 'Trends of Political Support'; Dieter Fuchs, Giovanna Guidorossi, and Palle Svensson, 'Support for the Democratic System,' in Klingemann and Fuchs, *Citizens and the State*, table 11.7, p. 351; Nye, Jr, 'The Decline of Confidence in Government.'

34 The results concerning a second, related hypothesis from Inglehart regarding the more pronounced dissatisfaction of the post-materialists are no more conclusive, being either mitigated (Brad Lockerbie, 'Economic Dissatisfaction and Political Alienation in Western Europe,' *European Journal of Political Science* 23 [1993]: 281–93; Kuechler, 'The Dynamics of Mass Support in Western Europe') or entirely negative (Fuchs, Guidorossi, and Svensson, 'Support for the Democratic System'; Kaase and Newton, *Beliefs in Government*).

35 Robert A. Dahl, *Democracy and Its Critics* (New Haven: Yale University Press, 1990).

36 'Citizens and the State.'

37 Nevitte (*Decline of Deference*, chapter 9) provides an exhaustive inventory of recent changes in Canadians' political culture, showing that they have become less attached to politics; less compliant towards political authority; less confident in governmental institutions; more interested in politics; more willing to use unconventional forms of political action; more interested in new issues; and more supportive of new social movements.

38 Inglehart, *Modernization and Postmodernization*.

39 Dahl, *Democracy and Its Critics*.

40 Fuchs and Klingemann, 'Citizens and the State.'

41　Kaase and Newton, *Beliefs in Government*.
42　Paul M. Sniderman, *A Question of Loyalty* (Berkeley: University of California Press, 1981).
43　Nevitte, *Decline of Deference*, 75.
44　Kornberg and Clarke, 'Beliefs about Democracy,' 537.
45　Giovanni Sartori, *The Theory of Democracy Revisited* (Chatham, NJ: Chatham House Publishers, 1987), 7.
46　Anderson and Guillory, 'Political Institutions,' 70.
47　Jan-Erik Lane and Sven Ersson, *Politics and Society in Western Europe*, 2nd ed. (London: Sage Publications, 1991), 194.
48　Fuchs, Guidorossi, and Svensson, 'Support for the Democratic System,' 328.
49　United Nations Development Programme, *Human Development Report* (New York: Oxford University Press, 1994–9).
50　See Kenneth A. Bollen, 'Liberal Democracy: Validity and Method Factors in Cross-National Measures,' *American Journal of Political Science* 37 (1993): 1207–30.
51　The net level of satisfaction corresponds to the difference between the percentage of respondents satisfied and the percentage dissatisfied. Respondents who were neither satisfied nor dissatisfied are excluded from the calculation. It is worth noting that the Gallup question is different from the one used in the Eurobarometers since it uses a supplementary category (neither satisfied nor dissatisfied) in addition to the four habitual categories for measuring satisfaction with democracy (namely, very satisfied, somewhat satisfied, not very satisfied, not at all satisfied).
52　ICORE, *Comparative Study of Electoral Systems, 1996–2000* (Version 1) (Ann Arbor: Center for Political Studies, February 1999).
53　Other measures of political support mirror those in table 2.2. An overall index measuring citizen confidence in five political institutions (the armed forces, the legal system, the police, parliament, and the civil service) shows that in the early 1990s, Canada ranked 8th among the ten countries in table 2.2 for which data are available (Luxembourg is the missing case) in terms of political support for these institutions (see Russell J. Dalton, 'Political Support in Advanced Industrial Democracies,' in Norris, *Critical Citizens*, table 3.4, 68).
54　Anderson and Guillory, 'Political Institutions.'
55　Richard Johnston, André Blais, Henry E. Brady, and Jean Crête, *Letting the People Decide: Dynamics of a Canadian Election* (Montreal: McGill-Queen's University Press, 1992); Neil Nevitte, André Blais, Elisabeth Gidengil, and Richard Nadeau, *Unsteady State: The 1997 Canadian Election* (Toronto: Oxford University Press, 2000).

56 Kornberg and Clarke, *Citizens and Community*; 'Beliefs about Democracy.'
57 A recent study by Paul Howe and David Northrup (*Strengthening Canadian Democracy: The Views of Canadians*, 'Policy Matters' Collection (Montreal: Institute for Research on Public Policy, 2000]) confirms the same patterns for region, income, and education. The relatively high level of satisfaction with democracy among younger voters in their survey will require further examination in the future.
58 See the appendix for the definition of the variables used in the regression analysis.
59 Inglehart, *Modernization and Postmodernization*; Kornberg and Clarke, 'Beliefs about Democracy'; Anderson and Guillory, 'Political Institutions.'
60 Easton, *A Systems Analysis of Political Life*; 'A Re-Assessment of the Concept of Political Support'; and 'Theoretical Approaches to Political Support.'
61 Older and newer surveys (1990, Political Support in Canada; 1997, Canadian Election Study) confirm the persistence of these differences.
62 Michael S. Lewis-Beck, *Economics and Elections: The Major Western Democracies* (Ann Arbor: University of Michigan Press, 1988); Helmut Norpoth, 'The Economy,' in Lawrence LeDuc, Richard G. Niemi, and Pippa Norris, eds, *Comparing Democracies: Elections and Voting in Global Perspective* (Thousand Oaks, CA: Sage Publications, 1996).
63 Anderson and Guillory, 'Political Institutions'; Ian McAllister, 'The Economic Performance of Governments,' in Norris, *Critical Citizens*.
64 Anderson and Guillory, 'Political Institutions.'
65 Easton, *A Systems Analysis of Political Life*; 'A Re-Assessment of the Concept of Political Support.'
66 Inglehart, *The Silent Revolution; Culture Shift*.
67 Orren, 'Fall from Grace,' 91–2.
68 The dependent variable being ordinal, it would have been preferable to use the Ordinal Probit method of estimation. Since this method produced very similar results to those in table 2.3, we hold to the results obtained with the method of Ordinary Least Squares (OLS) in order to facilitate the presentation and discussion of results. The current analysis is based on the data of the 1993 Canadian Election Study. An ongoing study of the 1997 data gives an overall confirmation of the results presented in this paper.
69 The dependent variable goes from 1 to 4, from the least satisfied to the most satisfied with the working of Canadian democracy. The coefficients of the independent variables were re-coded between 0 to 1. Their value reflects the maximal effect of a variable when one moves from the minimum to the maximum value of that variable. Take the case of the variable measuring attachment to Canada, whose coefficient is .40. This coefficient

signifies that, *ceteris paribus*, the fact of being profoundly attached to Canada (score of 100, re-coded as 1), increases the level of satisfaction by nearly half a point (.40 in fact) on the scale of 1 to 4. The standardized coefficients in turn reflect the explanatory capacity of the variables. Two similar coefficients signal an overall contribution to explaining the dependent variable.

70 A variable measuring individuals' factual information (see John R. Zaller, *The Nature and Origins of Mass Opinion* [Cambridge: Cambridge University Press, 1992] for an exposition of the theoretical pertinence of this type of variable) was initially included in the model but was not conserved due to its very weak and statistically insignificant impact.

71 Jerome H. Black, 'The Practice of Politics in Two Settings: Political Transferability among Recent Immigrants to Canada,' *Canadian Journal of Political Science* 20 (1987): 731–53.

72 See Richard Nadeau and André Blais, 'Accepting the Election Outcome: The Effect of Participation on Losers' Consent,' *British Journal of Political Science* 23 (1993): 553–63.

73 Anderson and Guillory, 'Political Institutions,' 68.

74 The weak support for the federal government is partly (but not exclusively) linked to the situation prevailing in 1993. This level nevertheless remained weak in 1990 (43%) and in 1997 (41%).

75 In 1993, 40% of Canadians disagreed with the statement that politicians were no more corrupt than others. Orren ('Fall from Grace') provides other indicators in the U.S. context of voters' increasingly negative perceptions of their politicians' honesty.

76 In this paper, we use a conventional measure of party attachment that includes 'leaners.' According to this measure, about 75% of Canadians have some sort of attachment to a federal political party. For a discussion establishing a much lower level of attachment, see Nevitte et al., *Unsteady State*.

77 Kornberg and Clarke, *Citizens and Community*; 'Beliefs about Democracy.'

78 Nevitte, *Decline of Deference*, 63–7.

79 Carole Pateman, *Participation and Democratic Theory* (Cambridge: Cambridge University Press, 1970); Benjamin R. Barber, *Strong Democracy: Participatory Politics for a New Age* (Berkeley: University of California Press, 1984); David Held, *Models of Democracy* (Cambridge: Polity Press, 1987).

80 See Barnes and Kaase, *Political Action*.

81 Sartori, *Theory of Democracy*, 111–20.

82 Kaase and Newton, *Beliefs in Government*, 159.

83 Jane Mansbridge, 'Social and Cultural Causes of Dissatisfaction with U.S.

Government,' in Nye, Zelikow, and King, *Why People Don't Trust Government*, 147.

84 Nevitte, *Decline of Deference*, 76.

85 Alan Hedges et al., *New Electoral Systems: What Voters Need to Know* (London: The Publications Officer, 1999), 3.

86 Secretary of State for Home Department, *The Report of the Independent Commission on the Voting System* (London: The Stationary Office, 1998), chapter 2, para. 6.

87 David M. Farrell, *Comparing Electoral Systems* (London: Prentice Hall, 1997), table 7.1, 146–7.

88 André Blais and Elisabeth Gidengil, 'La démocratie représentative: perceptions des Canadiens et Canadiennes,' in vol. 17 of the Research Studies of the Royal Commission on Electoral Reform and Party Financing (Toronto: Dundurn Press, 1991).

89 Arthur H. Miller and Ola Listhaug, 'Political Parties and Confidence in Government: A Comparison of Norway, Sweden and the United States,' *British Journal of Political Science* 20 (1990): 357–86.

90 Blais and Gidengil, 'La démocratie représentative,' 167.

91 Anderson and Guillory, 'Political Institutions.'

92 Arend Lijphart analysed a number of institutional characteristics in twenty some democracies for the 1945–90 period. He proceeded to classify these countries from the most majoritarian to the most consensual. At the extremity of the majoritarian pole one finds pre-electoral-reform New Zealand (1.70), Great Britain (1.56), Canada (1.51), and Australia (1.34). At the extreme consensual pole, one finds Finland (–1.39) and Switzerland (–1.44). It is worth noting that the countries where democratic satisfaction is the highest – namely, pre-reunification Germany, Norway, Luxembourg, and Denmark – are found near the middle of the scale with respective scores of –.28, –.19, .34, and –.71. We thank Arend Lijphart for the permission to use these numbers.

93 Arend Lijphart, *Democracies* (New Haven: Yale University Press, 1984); 'Democracies: Forms, Performance, and Constitutional Engineering,' *European Journal of Political Science* 25 (1994): 1–17.

94 Secretary of State for Home Department, *Report of the Independent Commission on the Voting System*, chapter 7, para. 108.

95 Hedges et al., *What Voters Need to Know*, 6, 7. David Docherty's chapter in this book shows that the very idea of a link between electors and elected is not without ambiguity, the former stressing that their representatives should keep in touch with their constituents and voice their concerns, and the latter attaching more importance to their legislative work in parlia-

ment. This schism between the priorities of the electors and the elected is interesting as it seems to reflect the difficulty of adapting the member's function to the citizens' new political culture.

96 Farrell, *Comparing Electoral Systems*, table 7.2, 152.

97 Lijphart, *Democracies*, 4.

98 Transforming the senate into a Chamber of Regions does not necessarily imply modifying its legislative responsibilities. However, one might expect that the fact that members of this chamber would be elected rather than appointed could somewhat modify the relations between Canada's two parliamentary chambers.

99 Frederick J. Fletcher and Robert Everett, 'Mass Media and Elections in Canada,' in vol. 19 of Research Studies of the Royal Commission on Electoral Reform and Party Financing, 200; Thomas E. Patterson, 'Bad News, Bad Governance,' *Annals of the American Academy of Political and Social Science* 546 (1996): 97–108; Cappala and Jamieson, *Spiral of Cynicism*; Orren, 'Fall from Grace'; Matthew Mendelsohn and Richard Nadeau, 'The Rise and Fall of Candidates in Canadian Election Campaigns,' *Harvard International Journal of Press and Politics* 4 (1999): 63–76.

100 Blais and Gidengil, 'La démocratie représentative,' 169.

101 Ibid., 168.

102 Ibid.

103 The decline of youth support for the Canadian community and its political institutions is tied to a complex of factors and it is no doubt unrealistic to believe that the institutional changes proposed above will suffice to counter the trend. However, these changes would seem to represent a step in the right direction, since it has been shown that support for these changes (for example, the reform to the British voting system [see Farrell, *Comparing Electoral Systems*, 31, 33]), is often higher among the younger generations.

104 Kornberg and Clarke, *Citizens and Community*; 'Beliefs about Democracy.'

105 Norris, 'Introduction,' in Norris, *Critical Citizens*, 20, 26.

106 Lortie commission.

107 Howe and Northrup, *Strengthening Canadian Democracy*.

108 David Northrup and Anne Oram, *The 1993 Canadian Election Study, Incorporating the 1992 Referendum Survey on the Charlottetown Accord: Technical Documentation* (Toronto: Institute for Social Research, York University, 1994); Richard Johnston et al., 'The Collapse of a Party System? The 1993 Canadian General Election,' paper presented at 1994 annual meeting of the American Political Science Association, New York.

3. Political Discontent, Human Capital, and Representative Governance in Canada

Mebs Kanji

> [We] must not underestimate the potential for change ... [T]he electorates of advanced industrial democracies have undergone a major transformation during the postwar period. Public opinion reflects a dynamic process, and we should avoid static views of an unchanging (or unchangeable) public ... Democracies need to adapt to present-day politics and the new style of citizen politics.
>
> Dalton, *Citizen Politics*, 38, 283

Evidence from a number of advanced industrial states suggests that attitudes toward representative democracy are in a state of flux: confidence in governmental institutions has declined[1] and mistrust in politicians has become increasingly widespread.[2] Trends such as these threaten to make governing more difficult[3] and could bear serious consequences for the future of political support.[4] Eroding faith in governmental institutions and political authorities may detract from people's satisfaction with representative democracy[5] and could worsen perceptions of system responsiveness,[6] which in turn may further suppress the desire to vote.[7]

On the other hand, growing frustrations with governmental institutions and authorities could also lead to a healthier future for representative democracies and a changing (as opposed to deteriorating) approach to electoral choice.[8] Support for the system of representative government in several countries continues to remain reasonably strong, and in some instances there is even evidence to suggest that it has begun to improve.[9] Advancements in information technology, mass communications, and the education explosion have contributed enormously to developments in human capital.[10] Citizens today not only have greater access to political information, but they are also better educated and more engaged in the political process.[11] Trends such as these could help to further reinforce feelings of personal (or internal) efficacy[12] and may produce a new breed of more 'democratic' and 'critical' citizens,[13] who are more understanding of politics and more inclined to feel as though they have some say or influence in the political process.[14] Improvements in human capital, together with higher levels of internal efficacy, might work to influence voter rationale by weakening attachments to parties and social groups,[15] thereby freeing-up voters to be more independent and calculating in their electoral choice.[16]

The aim of this chapter is to investigate which of these projections is most pertinent to the Canadian case. Part I of this analysis begins by examining the extent to which Canadians have become disenchanted with their current system of representative government. How confident are Canadians in their political institutions? How trusting are they of their elected officials? And how do these factors affect overall evaluations of system performance? Do Canadians see their current political system as being sufficiently responsive to their needs and demands? If not, what explains why?

Part II then turns to look more closely at changes in human capital. Do Canadians have greater access to information? Are they better educated? And are they more engaged in political process? If so, to what extent do such variations affect perceptions of personal efficacy? Are Canadians more understanding of politics? And are they more inclined to feel as though they can influence the political system?

Lastly, Part III examines the process of electoral choice. Are Canadians becoming less inclined to vote? Do they exhibit weaker partisan ties? And if so, what does this imply for the future of electoral decision-making? Does today's voter rationale differ from that in the past? If so, what accounts for the changing approach to electoral choice?

The conclusion of this chapter speculates on the future of representative governance. Does disenchantment with governmental institutions and political authorities pose a serious challenge to Canada's representative democracy? Will Canadians continue to turn out at the polls? In what ways are voters in the twenty-first century likely to differ from voters in the past? And what are some implications for political candidates, parties, and electoral competition more generally?

Declining Confidence in Governmental Institutions and Growing Mistrust in Politicians

In representative democracies, both feelings towards the system[17] and overall legitimacy hinge to a great extent on public perceptions of governmental institutions and elected officials.[18] A key concern stems from the fact that over the latter part of this century evidence from a number of democracies, Canada included, indicates that public confidence in various governmental institutions has declined.[19] The shift appears more than subsidiary: based on an extensive examination of seventeen different advanced industrial states, Dalton finds that within the span of just one decade, citizens worldwide became, on average, 6 per cent less confident in government institutions.[20] Similarly, Nevitte contends that during the 1980s, Canadians became, on average, 7 per cent less confident in parliament, the civil service, the armed forces, and the police.[21]

Also important is another concern relating to how citizens view their politicians. 'By expanding the cross-national and cross-temporal breadth of the empirical data,' Dalton reports, there is also 'clear evidence of a general erosion in support for politicians.'[22] Similarly, Clarke and his colleagues indicate that between 1988 and 1993 trust in Canadian politicians dropped by an astounding 17 per cent.[23] The combined magnitude of these shifts has been such that 'publics of rich democracies [now] show [even] less confidence in their leaders and political institutions than do their counterparts in developing countries.'[24]

A multitude of plausible causes are thought to be at the root of the public's growing discontent, but certain explanations, such as Inglehart's (inter-generational) postmodernization thesis, are consistently found to be more relevant than others.[25] Backed by nearly three decades of research and evidence representing 70 per cent of the world's population, Inglehart contends that a significant part of the problem is that the evolving political cultures within postindustrial societies are no longer compatible with the representative, and highly bureaucratic, government structures that were originally put into place during the industrial age.[26] 'Postmodern society is characterized by the decline of hierarchical institutions and rigid social norms, and the expansion of the realm of individual choice and mass participation.'[27] Evidence from more than thirty-five countries across the globe indicates that, over the last two decades, citizens have become, on average, 6 per cent less respecting of authority.[28] Moreover, in Canada, the so-called 'decline of deference' has been close to two times that amount.[29] The result is that mass publics have become 'increasingly critical of their political leaders, and increasingly likely to engage in elite-challenging activities.'[30]

Should these shifts continue to persist, their long-term effects could be quite significant. In many cases, what may potentially be at stake is support for the broader political system: support for political authorities, according to Kornberg and Clarke, affects support for regime institutions, which in turn influences support for the entire political community.[31] Consequently, it is possible that growing disenchantment with government officials and institutions may eventually detract from support for the system of representative governance. 'Citizens in a democracy must have confidence in their ability to make their leaders and the system itself change direction when, and if, things are going awry.'[32] If voters lack confidence in their governmental institutions and mistrust their politicians, they may feel less assured that their political system will be responsive to their needs and demands, and they may therefore become less inspired to turn out to vote. Only citizens who feel that their political system is responsive to their needs are likely to show their support for the political order by participating in activities that are sanctioned by the regime.[33]

The seriousness of this point is reinforced by Inglehart's[34] data, which suggest that both voter turnout and partisan loyalties among the younger, postmodern generations (Canadians included) have already begun to slide.[34] Newer cohorts are not as likely to accept the 'authority of hierarchical, oligarchical organizations like the old-line political parties.'[35] Barring any changes, Inglehart predicts, support for traditional elite-directed types of political participation, such as voting, are almost certain to progressively diminish, and more direct involvement in protest activities and new social movements is likely to rise.

Yet not everyone interprets the evidence in quite the same way. Klingemann, Fuchs, and others, for instance, take issue with Inglehart's prognosis, suggesting that the data from western Europe show no clear sign of any systematic withdrawal from the current democratic process.[36] The findings from the massive *Beliefs in Government* study provide no consistent evidence of any widespread decline in confidence in governmental institutions, no uniform trend to indicate increasing mistrust of politicians, and no clear support for the declining voter turnout hypothesis.[37] It is difficult to tell, Schmitt and Holmberg argue, whether we are 'witnessing the first signs of a general phenomenon of partisan decline or ... [whether] declining partisanship [is] confined to particular countries under particular circumstances.'[38] Furthermore, there is no conclusive evidence to suggest either a withdrawal of support from, or a challenge to, representative democracy.[39] 'Indeed, in so far as there is a trend, it is toward increasing satisfaction with democracy ... There has been no legitimation problem in representative democracies of Western Europe since the mid-1970s ... There is currently no legitimation crisis in West European polities. And ... there is a high probability that there will be no legitimation crisis in the foreseeable future.'[40]

But even Klingemann and his colleagues do not deny that the political-action repertory of citizens has expanded and that postmodern publics have become more demanding and critical of their politicians and governmental institutions. Advances in information technology, the explosion of mass communications and rising education levels have placed the actions and decisions of politicians under much greater public scrutiny. 'Public opinion generated by mass communication [has] a feedback effect on the opinions and preferences of voters, ... [and it has forced] major political actors to consider, continuously and sys-tematically, the opinions and preferences of voters.'[41] That said, how-ever, Klingemann and others maintain that electoral participation continues to be the only means through which citizens decide who governs. Non-institutionalized (or unconventional) political actions are simply attempts to mobilize public opinion; they may or may not affect people's electoral choice. Furthermore, although the repertoire of po-litical action may have been extended, such actions are very seldom put to use. In other words, there remains a considerable gap between the potential for protest and actual protest. And 'if we disregard the rela-tively non-committal signing of petitions, participation in elections is still by far the most frequent political activity undertaken by citizens in Western democracies.'[42]

The Sharper, More Informed Voter

Whether or not one is more persuaded by what Klingemann and his colleagues suggest, as opposed to what Inglehart claims, their argu-ment is significant in that it illustrates the inconclusiveness of the findings to date. It also brings to bear another important point, namely, that the extent to which citizens can be critical of politicians and governmental institutions depends to a great extent on how much they know about politics and whether or not they have the necessary skills and motivation required to participate.[43] Much of the empirical evidence has suggested that most voters are neither capable of reasoning politically, nor very concerned with political affairs. Historically, studies have shown that the mass citizenry is not interested in, or motivated by, the actions of their governments.[44] Indeed, when it comes to politics, most voters have appeared rather 'muddle-headed [lacking constraint], or empty-headed [lacking genuine attitudes] – or both.'[45] Rarely have citizens seemed to possess the types of 'full' and 'perfect' information required to make independent, calculated, and coherent political choices.[46] And voting, in particular, has conventionally been regarded as being heavily 'conditioned by group loyalties and personality considerations.'[47]

This traditional 'minimalist' point of view, however, has recently come under fire by a new line of evidence pointing to dramatic improvements in human capital. While the growth of the knowledge-based economy has resulted in an expanded middle class, it has also meant that workers have had to equip themselves with different skills: 'whereas the main workplace technologies in industrial society involved heavy manufacturing, the main technologies in post-industrial society are advanced scientific and technical knowledge and information handling tools like computer and telecommunication networks.'[48] More importantly, the changing workplace has significant implications for how citizens conduct themselves in other areas in life. For instance, there is now a long line of evidence showing that what citizens learn at their jobs is generalizable to how they conduct themselves in the political domain.[49] As Inglehart (1997) describes it, '[O]ne's job experience helps develop politically relevant skills ... Accustomed to working in less hierarchical decision-structures in their job life, people in the tertiary, or information service sectors are relatively likely to have both the skills and the inclination to take part in decision-making in the political realm as well.'[50]

Growing proportions of electorates in advanced industrial states, it is argued, now possess the 'political resources and skills necessary to deal with the complexities of politics and make their own political decisions.'[51] Through what is commonly referred to within the literature as the process of 'cognitive mobilization,' postmodern citizens are said to be more informed, better educated, and more engaged politically than were their predecessors during the middle part of this century.[52] Assessments of contemporary electorates tend not to be nearly as bleak as those provided by earlier survey research.[53]

At the heart of this transformation are said to be two main forces.[54] The first is broadly defined as the 'information explosion': advances in information technology and the expansion of mass communications have considerably reduced the costs of participating in politics by significantly improving citizens' access to information.'[55] 'The growth of electronic media, especially television, has been exceptional. Other important sources such as books and magazines are also increasing. Even more revolutionary is the growth of electronic information processing: computers, information and retrieval systems [such as the Internet], word processing, and related technologies. Information is no longer a scarce commodity.'[56]

Furthermore, there is also evidence to show that voters have become more attentive to information: 'Opinion surveys routinely find that large majorities of the public regularly watch television, read newspapers and magazines, and hear news on the radio.'[57] Moreover, recent findings indicate that attentiveness to political news is statistically linked to people's sense of internal efficacy. Semetko and Valkenberg, for instance, demonstrate that, over time, attentiveness to news exerts a positive effect on feelings of personal influence.[58] In fact, the robustness of this relationship is such that it remains significant even after controlling for the effects of gender, age, education, and socio-economic status.

Of course, all things being equal, it is important to bear in mind that the link between the sorts of information that people acquire and its eventual consequences is incredibly complex. Exposure to different information mediums is likely to result in different effects. For example, the impact of TV news is much greater than that of television advertisements.[59] Moreover, newspapers are consistently found to emit mixed messages and local presses are thought to have more of an effect than national ones.[60] Furthermore, while greater exposure to moderate radio programming may lead to being more informed, greater exposure to conservative talk radio is said to contribute to being more misinformed.[61] The main point, therefore, is that even though information may be easier to acquire, and citizens more exposed to political news, there is still the possibility that someone who reads the local newspaper might have a different understanding of politics than someone who listens to talk radio or someone who sees a political ad on TV.

A seccond important factor said to be influencing levels of cognitive mobilization is the 'education explosion.'[62] With higher levels of education comes a heightened sense of political curiosity and an improved ability to receive and process political information.[63] 'An increasingly large portion of the public is coming to have sufficient interest and understanding of national and international politics to participate in decision-making at this level.'[64] Thus not only are postmodern electorates thought to be more informed, they are also said to be more involved in politics, and more frequently engaged in political debate.[65]

This is not to suggest, of course, that all voters possess the necessary wherewithal to make complicated political choices; indeed, there is an extensive literature that painstakingly documents how voters go about using informational short cuts in order to compensate for those resources and skills they continue to lack.[66] Despite having better access to information and being more educated, many citizens still continue to fare poorly when it comes to factual knowledge,[67] although Jennings notes that newer cohorts (i.e., younger generations) tend to be much more politically astute than their older counterparts.[68] The key, it seems, is to carefully counter-balance the public's enhanced abilities with the rising complexity of politics.[69] What the information revolution and the education explosion suggest is that today's mass publics may be less reliant on parties and social groups and more apt to make independent and calculated political choices. But what the future holds – that is, whether or not the public's disenchantment with representative institutions and authorities will detract from perceptions of system responsiveness and possibly suppress the desire to vote, or whether today's more informed and educated voters will be more likely to believe that they can successfully influence the current political system, – has yet to be determined.

Data and Methods

The data for this analysis are drawn from a series of Canadian Election Studies (CES), which have been conducted since the mid-sixties.[70] Though the CES are not panel studies per se, they constitute one of the few Canadian data sources available for conducting longitudinal/secondary analysis. Of course, such an endeavour almost certainly raises the issue of comparability. Over time, the CES have been administered by several different research teams, all of whom have approached their research with different objectives in mind. What this means, therefore, is that although there is no shortage of comparable data, some indicators are better suited for longitudinal analysis than others.[71] Certain survey items are considered to be more or less standard and thus repeatedly probed from one study to the next. Others are less consistent and therefore not as easy to compare. Yet regardless of these differences, the results of this analysis suggest that all the measures employed are quite reliable and that the trends they identify are remarkably stable. Even when exposed to the most rigorous statistical tests, the alleged shifts turn out to be highly significant, thereby adding weight to the overall argument that changes are indeed taking place and that they have important effects.

Analysis

Part I: Support for Representative Governance

To begin, consider the issue of Canadians' disenchantment with representative government. Citizens' assessments of representative governance are not always 'of a piece';[72] publics can, and do, 'distinguish between different levels of the regime, often believing strongly in democratic values [or principles], for example, while proving critical of the way that democratic governments work in practice.'[73]

Figures 3.1 and 3.2 distinguish between the level of confidence that Canadians place in their governmental institutions and the amount of trust they vest in their political authorities. The findings are quite intriguing considering the sorts of claims that have been made in the past.[74] For example, unlike the 1980s, support for governmental institutions during the 1990s seems to have increased: on average, Canadians have become almost 10% more confident in both the federal and provincial governments, 11% more confident in the civil service, and 5% more confident in the police. Still, relatively speaking, confidence in both the federal and provincial governments, as well as in the bureaucracy, remains considerably lower than confidence in the police. Only two in every five citizens say that they have any confidence in either government or the civil service, as compared to the strong majority who express confidence in those who enforce the law. Then again, not all law enforcers are viewed in the same way; confidence in the armed forces, for example, is down by 11 per cent. This finding, however, is not as surprising in light of the devastating embarrassment that the Canadian military has suffered from its numerous problems with aging equipment, the Somalia affair, and various other accusations of military misconduct.

Likewise, since 1965, the percentage of Canadians who concur that the 'people running the government are crooked or dishonest' has virtually doubled to more than 50 per cent.[75] Moreover, according to the most recent figures, nearly three in every four Canadians feels that 'politicians waste taxpayer's money,' although this particular trend appears to have already peaked and might well be interpreted as a

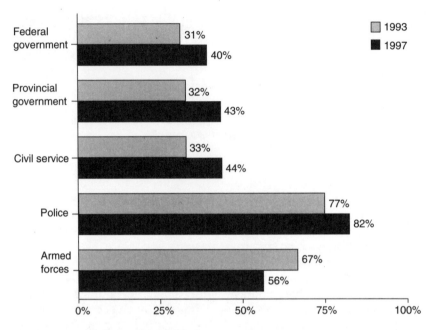

Source: 1993–7 Canadian Election Studies.

Note: The above figures report the percentage of respondents who say that they have either 'a lot' of confidence or 'some' confidence in governmental institutions.

Federal government: Beta = .10**; n = 3,992; provincial government: Beta = .12**; n = 3,986; civil service: Beta = .12**; n = 3,938; police: Beta = .07**; n = 3,998; armed forces: Beta = −.11**; n = 3,997

** significant at p < .01

Figure 3.1 Confidence in governmental institutions

more general ideological shift to the 'right.'[76] That is, this finding may indicate that Canadians have become more demanding of government officials, insisting on greater restraint in the handling of public funds.[77]

The next question, then, becomes: What implications, if any, do these findings have for overall evaluations of representative governance? Are Canadians more or less satisfied with the workings of their current democracy? Nadeau's analysis (this volume) explores this issue in great detail and the results of his investigation project a sense of guarded optimism. Although at face value it may appear as though Canadians are still relatively satisfied with the performance of their current regime

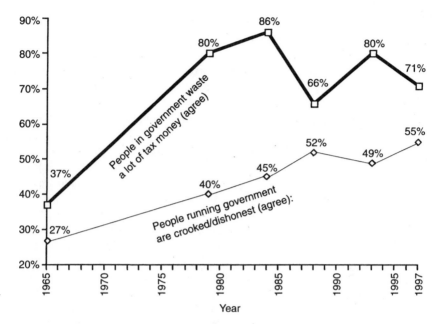

Source: 1965–97 Canadian Election Studies.

People in government waste a lot of tax money (agree): Beta = .22**; *n* = 12,408
People running government are crooked/dishonest (agree): Beta = .18**; *n* = 11,280

** significant at p < .01

Figure 3.2 Trust in politicians

– that is, more than a majority of citizens support the current system, a trend that has remained more or less consistent over several years – when compared to citizens in other European countries, such as Norway, Luxembourg, and Denmark, Canadians, it turns out, are not as satisfied as a recent United Nations report might imply.[78] Furthermore, current levels of political support seem alarmingly fragile: satisfaction with the Canadian political system is heavily contingent upon how citizens feel about government institutions and political authorities (see Nadeau, this volume, table 2.4).[79] Thus, should the public's confidence in governmental institutions begin once again to decline, or mistrust in politicians continue to rise, then it is entirely plausible that such trends may eventually detract from the public's overall support for the system of representative governance.

The same might be said of the public's perceptions toward government responsiveness (or 'external efficacy' as it is sometimes called). While Norris's investigation[80] suggests that there is only a weak link between the public's declining confidence in institutions and their unwillingness to take part in conventional forms of political participation, it may be that both low levels of institutional confidence and growing mistrust in politicians have a more powerful effect on perceptions toward system responsiveness, which in turn may have more serious implications for the future of basic democratic practices such as voting.[81] Consequently, it is equally important to carefully monitor whether Canadians view their government and elected officials as becoming less responsive to their needs and demands.

Figure 3.3 shows that throughout much of the mid to late 1970s, 1980s and early 1990s, perceptions toward government responsiveness became drastically worse. By 1993, more than four in every five Canadians agreed that 'elected officials soon lose touch with the people.' And merely one in every four Canadians disagreed with the claim that 'government doesn't care much about what people like me think.' More recently, however, there appears to have been some significant improvement in the latter, but only a slight change in what citizens think about the responsiveness of elected officials.

Figure 3.4 (on pages 84–5) looks more closely at the determinants of system responsiveness. Not surprisingly, certain factors turn out to be more influential than others. Based on these results, it appears as though perceptions of system responsiveness are most heavily contingent upon citizens' feelings toward the federal government, and to a lesser extent on the integrity of politicians and feelings toward the bureaucracy. Overall, however, the less confident citizens are in the federal government and the civil service, and the more they perceive politicians as being crooked/dishonest, the less likely they are to conceive of their political system as being responsive to their needs and demands.

Part II: The Changing Nature of Human Capital

It is important not to overlook the possibility that changing levels of human capital (i.e., the gamut of knowledge and skills that citizens acquire over the course of their daily lives)[82] might also play a significant role in this process by affecting both perceptions of personal efficacy as well as the process of electoral choice. According to the cognitive-mobilization argument, today's voters are said to possess the types of resources and skills required to participate more independently in

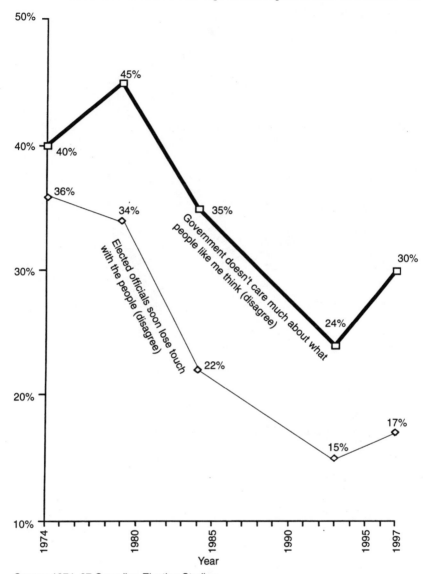

Source: 1974–97 Canadian Election Studies.

Government doesn't care much: Beta = –.26** (based on mid-60s and 70s versus 80s and 90s); *n* = 12,920

Elected officials soon lose touch: Beta = –.20** (based on mid-60s and 70s versus 80s and 90s); *n* = 3,053

** significant at p < .01

Figure 3.3 Perceptions toward government responsiveness (or external efficacy)

Confidence in governmental institutions

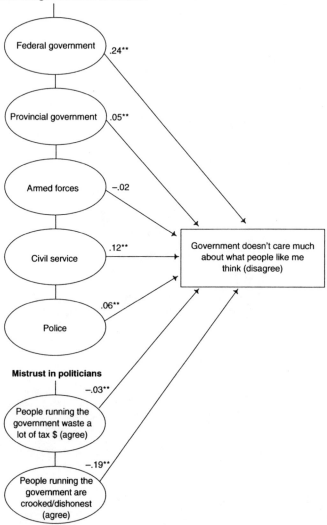

Source: 1965–97 Canadian Election Studies.

Note: The effects of confidence in the federal and provincial governments are considered independently from the effects of confidence in institutions such as the armed forces, the civil service, and the police.

** Beta coefficients significant at p < .01

Figure 3.4 Predictors of perceptions toward government responsiveness (or external efficacy)

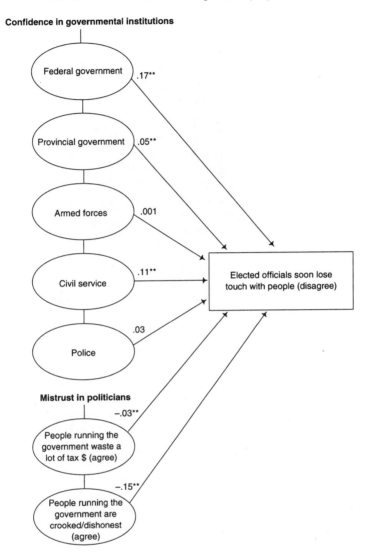

Confidence in governmental institutions

Federal government .17**

Provincial government .05**

Armed forces .001

Civil service .11**

Police .03

Elected officials soon lose touch with people (disagree)

Mistrust in politicians

−.03**

People running the government waste a lot of tax $ (agree)

−.15**

People running the government are crooked/dishonest (agree)

politics.[83] In particular, improvements in information technology and mass communications have been implicated as greatly improving citizens' access to political information.[84] Figure 3.5 helps to validate this argument by demonstrating that over the last three or four decades a growing number of Canadian households have become better equipped, with two or more radios and cable TV. Newspaper sales have also exploded by more than fifty times. As well, the sale of

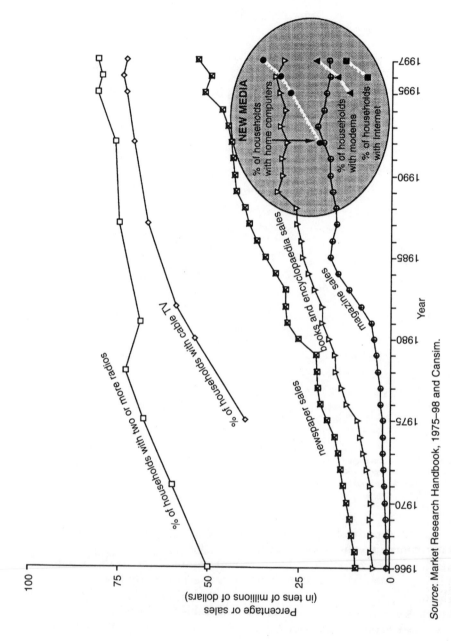

NEW MEDIA

% of households with home computers

% of households with modems

% of households with Internet

% of households with two or more radios

% of households with cable TV

newspaper sales

books and encyclopaedia sales

magazine sales

Year

Percentage or sales (in tens of millions of dollars)

100

75

50

25

0

1966 1970 1975 1980 1985 1990 1995 1997

Source: Market Research Handbook, 1975–98 and Cansim.

Figure 3.5 Access to information

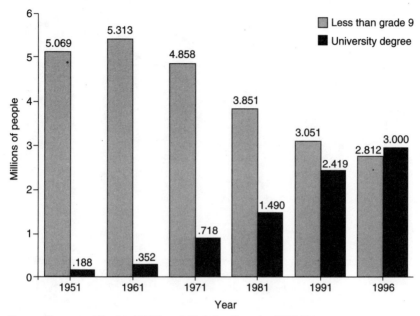

Source: Guppy and Davies (1998) and Statistics Canada, 1996 Census.

Figure 3.6 Levels of education

books and encyclopedias has grown by more than seventy times, while magazine sales have increased nearly twenty-fold. And let's not forget the so-called new media: over the last decade alone, the number of Canadian households with home computers, modems, and access to the Internet has all but doubled.[85] Admittedly, Internet use is still highly correlated with household income.[86] However, the latest evidence shows that, even within low-income households, as many as 7% of occupants admit to using the Internet at home, 6% at school, 4% at work, and 3% at a library.[87]

In addition, absolute levels of education have also improved.[88] Figure 3.6 shows that the number of Canadians aged fifteen and over with a university degree now outnumbers the number of citizens with less than a grade 9 education. Indeed, since the early 1950s, the number of Canadians graduating from universities has skyrocketed by more than 1500 per cent. Such profound structural shifts help to fuel the proposition that today's Canadian electorate may be more informed and better able to participate in politics.[89]

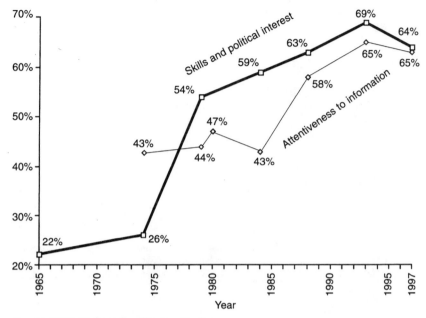

Source: 1965–97 Canadian Election Studies.

Attentiveness to information (high levels) = frequency of TV viewing + newspaper
   reading + radio listening
Cronbach's alpha = .9; Beta = .10**; *n* = 17,508

Skills and political interest (high levels) = interest in politics + interest in election
   campaigns + frequency of political discussion + level of education
Cronbach's alpha = .5; Beta = .30**; *n* = 17,861

** significant at p < .01

Figure 3.7 Levels of cognitive mobilization

Of course, there still remains the possibility that Canadians may not
be very interested in politics, nor very attentive to political news.
Nevitte's analysis,[90] for example, shows that for Canadians, politics
ranks as being less important than other relevant priorities such as
work, family, friends, leisure, and religion. However, this finding should
not be interpreted as suggesting that Canadians are totally oblivious to
what goes on in their political world. On the contrary, figure 3.7 shows
that compared to three decades ago, citizens today are significantly
more inclined to watch television news, to read about the news in
newspapers, and to listen to the news on the radio. Furthermore, in
addition to being better educated, Canadians are also more interested

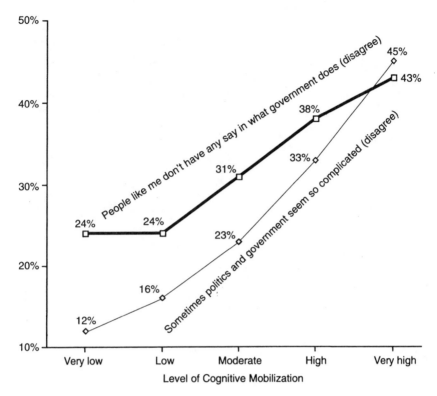

Source: 1965–97 Canadian Election Studies.

Cognitive mobilization = attentiveness to information (index) + cognitive mobilization (index)

Cronbach's Alpha = .6

People like me don't have any say in what government does (disagree): Beta = .13**; n = 10,208

Sometimes politics and government seem so complicated (disagree): Beta = .22**; n = 10,246

** significant at $p < .01$

Figure 3.8 Internal efficacy by cognitive mobilization

in politics and more involved in political debate. More than three in every five Canadians now qualify as being highly cognitively mobile.

The empowering effects of these shifts are clearly visible in the electorate's sense of internal efficacy. To put it simply, improvements in cognitive mobilization work to elevate citizens' understanding of politics and makes them more inclined to feel as though they can significantly influence the political system.[91] Figure 3.8, for example, indicates that

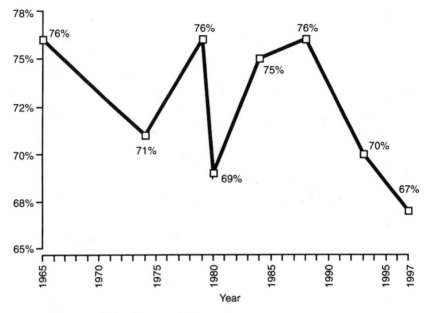

Source: Canadian Global Almanac, 1997.

Note: The Beta for voter turnout using the CES data is −.16**.

Figure 3.9 Voter turnout in Canada

Canadians who are highly cognitively mobile are twice as likely to disagree with the statement 'People like me don't have any say in what the government does,' and almost four times as likely to disagree with the claim 'Sometimes politics and government seems so complicated that a person like me can't really understand what's going on.' It remains to be seen, however, how improvements in human capital and internal efficacy might affect the vote. What impact, if any, do these changes have on the process of electoral choice?

Part III: Voter Turnout, Partisan Loyalties, and the Changing Coherency of Voter Rationale

Based solely on statistics of voter turnout, it is difficult to predict whether or not Canadians will continue going to the polls; the trend reported in figure 3.9 is relatively unstable and consequently hard to gauge. Looking back over the last decade or so, the data appear very much in line with those from other advanced industrial states;[92] Cana-

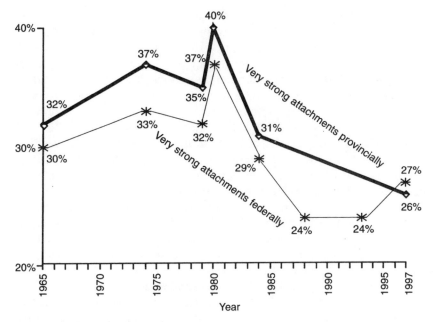

Source: 1965–97 Canadian Election Studies.

Federal attachments: Beta = −.06**; *n* = 14,637
Provincial attachments: Beta = −.04**; *n* = 10,138

** significant at p < .01

Figure 3.10 The intensity of federal and provincial partisan loyalties

dians too, it seems, are voting in fewer numbers. If, however, we
compare the low points of the 1990s to participation rates in 1980, or
1974 for that matter, the recent drop in voter turnout seems not all that
different from what we have seen in the past.

Not everyone, however, would agree. Inglehart, for example, sees the
more recent decay in voter turnout as being symptomatic of a broader
decline in 'long-term' partisan ties.[93] Younger, postmodern voters, he
argues, are not likely to continue supporting old-line political parties –
particularly if they are hierarchical and oligarchical. Consequently, to
the extent that parties continue to have difficulty mobilizing voters,
electoral participation is more than likely to decline.

At first blush, it would seem as though the Canadian evidence on
partisan intensity is very much consistent with what Inglehart suggests: figure 3.10 indicates that over the last two decades or so, the

number of strong partisans, both federally and provincially, has declined by an average of 12 per cent. Keep in mind, however, that Canadians are known for being notoriously flexible in their partisanship: 'rather than having a strong stable commitment to a political party, for both provincial and federal elections, [the average Canadian voter] is much more likely to be weakly committed, to swing from one party to another, and to prefer different parties in different elections.'[94] A weakening of partisan loyalties, therefore, might not be the best indication of voting habits, at least not in the case of Canada. Besides, higher levels of cognitive mobility would suggest that today's voters might be less likely to rely on party cues, and more likely to be independent and calculating when it comes to electoral choice.

Figure 3.11 attempts to test this proposition by probing the coherency of voter rationale. To what extent do Canadians' voting decisions coincide with their overall evaluations of party leaders? And how much do electoral choices correspond with voters' perceptions of which parties are best suited to deal with their most salient concerns?[95]

The results in this case point to a striking improvement in the coherency of voter rationale. To the extent that consistency serves as an approximate indication of reasoned decision-making, contemporary voters appear to be more calculating in their electoral choice. Whereas during the mid-1970s only one in every three Canadians voted for a party whose leader they preferred, and a party that they felt was most capable of dealing with their most critical issue concerns, today nearly half of all electoral decisions are consistent in this way.

The analysis presented in table 3.1 suggests that several different factors are at least partially to blame, some more than others, however. Perhaps the most surprising finding overall is that feelings of efficacy, both internal and external, have only a weak effect. Perceptions of government responsiveness, for example, have no discernible impact on electoral decision-making, while the perceived responsiveness of elected officials has only a weak effect. Contrary to earlier suggestions,[96] the evidence shows that Canadians who agree that 'elected officials soon lose touch with the people' are in fact more compelled than others to employ a highly coherent approach to electoral choice. Similarly, internally efficacious voters are also more inclined to make coherent electoral decisions, a finding that complements the argument made by Roese (this volume), namely, that 'self-efficacy predicts action.'

The most powerful influence overall comes as a direct result of differences in human capital. The most coherent voting decisions tend to be

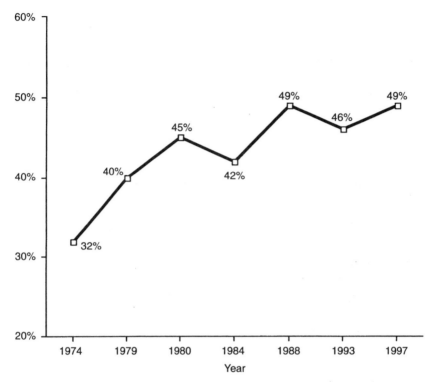

Source: 1974–97 Canadian Election Studies.

Note: This index of voter rationale measures the coherency between voting decisions, preferred political leaders, important election issues, and voters' perceptions of which parties are best suited to deal with important election issues. For example, if a voter supports a party whose leader they rate as being positive, and a party that they believe is most capable of dealing with their two most important issue concerns, they receive a score of '3,' meaning 'highly coherent.' If, on the other hand, a voter supports a party but feels negatively toward the party's leader, and knows very little about where the party stands on key issues, they receive a score of '1,' meaning 'not very coherent.'
Cronbach's alpha = .8; Beta = .14**; n = 14,047

** significant at $p < .01$

Figure 3.11 The coherency of electoral decision-making

made by those Canadians who are highly cognitively mobile, meaning that they pay fairly close attention to the news, they are highly educated, and they express a relatively keen interest in politics. Indeed, the impact of human capital turns out to be even more important than both the intensity of partisan attachments and the effects of various signifi-

TABLE 3.1
The predictors of coherent electoral decision-making (regression analysis: beta coefficients)

Predicators	Coherent electoral decision-making (highly coherent)
Feelings of efficacy	
– External efficacy:	
• Government doesn't care much about what people like me think (disagree)	–
• Elected officials soon lose touch with the people (disagree)	–.05**
– Internal efficacy:	
• Sometimes politics and government seem so complicated (disagree)	.05**
• People like me don't have any say in what government does (disagree)	.05**
Human capital	
– Cognitive mobilization (high levels)	.33**
Partisan attachments	
– Federally (very strong)	.11**
– Provincially (very strong)	–
Socio-demographics	
– sex (male)	.07**
– age (seniors)	–
– income ($50,000 or more)	.04
– English (vs. French)	.09**
– Protestant (vs. Catholic)	.02
– Ontario (vs. Atlantic)	.07**
– Quebec (vs. Atlantic)	.10**
– West (vs. Atlantic)	.08**
Constant	–.01
r-squared	.18

Source: 1965–97 Canadian Election Studies.

**significant at p < .01

cant social-group influences, such as sex, language, and region.[97] In accordance with earlier expectations, coherent voters, it seems, are more independent when making their electoral choices, basing their voting decisions more on the information they acquire and on their political know-how, as opposed to conventional social-group and/or partisan cues.

Conclusion

What, then, do the results of this analysis suggest about the future of representative governance? Does disenchantment with governmental institutions and political authorities pose a serious threat to the current system of representative government? The data in this case suggest the need for guarded optimism: while the majority of Canadians seem satisfied with the workings of their current democracy (see Nadeau, this volume), when compared to other Europeans Canadians appear much less content. Furthermore, support for the current political system is alarmingly fragile; any further decline in institutional confidence or increase in the public's mistrust of politicians could trigger an erosion of systemic support. Likewise, any further deterioration of confidence in the federal government or the civil service, or any more damage to the integrity of politicians, could detract significantly from perceptions of system responsiveness. Much more detailed research in this area is necessary in order to determine the optimal levels of institutional confidence and trust in political authorities required in order to maintain a high level of satisfaction with representative democracy and positive perceptions of system responsiveness, even though the latter appears to have only a weak impact on electoral choice.

As for whether or not Canadians will continue to vote, the answer is difficult to predict. The intensity of partisan loyalties, both provincially and federally seems to be in decline; however, Canadians are also known for their flexible partisan ties[98] and it would therefore be highly risky to forecast any further reduction in voter turnout based solely on declining levels of partisanship. Furthermore, evidence from the past suggests that certain elections entice greater participation than others, even after periods where it appears that voter turnout may be in decline. It could be, then, that given the 'right' election, possibly even the next election, we might once again see a sharp increase in turnout at the polls.

What is for certain, however, is that compared to three decades ago, Canadian voters are much more cognitively mobile today, meaning that they are more informed, better educated, and more involved in the political process. Such improvements in human capital contribute to making voters more understanding of politics and more inclined to feel as though they can significantly influence the political process. Furthermore, higher levels of internal efficacy are at least partially to blame for the improving coherency of voter rationale. And higher levels of cognitive mobilization mean that voters today are better able to make independent and calculated choices, such as basing their voting decisions on the information they acquire and on their political wherewithal, as opposed to conventional social-group and/or partisan cues. Surprisingly, rather than detracting from this process, negative perceptions of system responsiveness actually work to motivate voters to adopt a more coherent approach.

The results of these shifts are likely to have many profound consequences, especially for elected officials, parties, and electoral competition in general. Electorates with higher levels of cognitive mobilization are likely to be smarter, more demanding, and harder to please. Parties and politicians would be well advised to take as little as possible for granted, and they should be leery of being too reliant on voters' past allegiances. To acquire electoral support, parties and politicians might have to do more to convince voters that their policies are the most relevant and far superior to others. Sharper, more informed voters are not as likely to support a politician or party merely because they have done so in the past. This means, then, that parties and party officials will have to work harder to stay in touch with the needs and demands of the citizens that they represent, and they will have to find innovative ways to accommodate those concerns, while remaining within the confines of yesterday's institutional constraints. Elected officials, in particular, will have to do better at communicating with their constituents and be more representative of their needs, or they are likely to be held accountable for their actions.[99] Also, it is increasingly important for politicians to maintain the highest level of integrity; the legitimacy of the political system may depend on it.

In addition, the nature of electoral competition as we have come to know it is also likely to change. Electorates with higher levels of cognitive mobilization are probably likely to be more critical and deliberative when deciding how they are going to vote. Where there are credible alternatives to incumbents, voters may take more time to contemplate their electoral decisions, and the chances are greater that they may be more familiar with the necessary background information. Voters are likely to make their political decisions based on the news they receive through various media outlets, and on their personal experiences with both elected officials and the broader political system.[100] Increasingly, the main focus for voters is likely to be on which candidates and parties are best suited to deal with their most salient issue concerns.[101] Therefore, strategic use of the media (both print and electronic) is likely to become even more important for the purposes of attracting voter support. Intense competition between candidates might necessitate experienc-ing with the use of 'negative advertising' and/or more targeted communication.[102] The most effective communicators, in other words, stand to gain the most voter support. More research in this area is required not only to develop effective communication strategies, but also to explore more carefully the prospects of new media, such as the Internet.

Notes

I extend my sincere gratitude to my team members for their valuable feedback and suggestions. As well, I thank the various outside commentators who participated in our meetings for their useful insights; their constructive criticisms were especially enlightening. And, lastly, I extend my humble appreciation to Ms Judi Powell for her magnificent secretarial skills. Funding for this project was provided by the Social Sciences and Humanities Research Council of Canada.

1 S.M. Lipset and W.C. Schneider, *The Confidence Gap: Business, Labor, and Government in the Public Mind* (New York: Free Press, 1983); J. Nye, Jr, P.D. Zelikow, and D.C. King, *Why People Don't Trust Government* (Cambridge, MA: Harvard University Press, 1997); N. Nevitte, *The Decline of Deference* (Peterborough, ON: Broadview Press, 1996).

2 R.J. Dalton, 'Political Support in Advanced Industrial Democracies,' in P. Norris, ed., *Critical Citizens: Global Support for Democratic Governance* (Oxford: Oxford University Press, 1999); see also Neal Roese, this volume.

3 P. Norris, *Critical Citizens*; R. Inglehart, *Modernization and Post-modernization: Cultural, Economic, and Political Change in 43 Societies* (Princeton: Princeton University Press, 1997).

4 P. Norris, 'Introduction: The Growth of Critical Citizens?' in Norris, *Critical Citizens*; J. Nye, Jr, 'Introduction: The Decline of Confidence in Government,' in Nye, Zelikow, and King, *Why People Don't Trust the Government*.
   I am referring here to the Eastonian (D. Easton, *A Systems Analysis of Political Life* [New York: Wiley, 1965]) notion of 'diffuse' support for the broader political system, as opposed to 'specific' support for particular government policies. For a brief discussion of this difference, see A. Kornberg and H.D. Clarke, *Citizens and Community: Political Support in a Representative Democracy* (New York: Cambridge University Press, 1992).

5 Norris, *Critical Citizens*; Kornberg and Clarke, *Citizens and Community*; see also Richard Nadeau, this volume.
6 G. Almond and S. Verba, *The Civic Culture: Political Attitudes and Democracy in Five Nations* (Princeton: Princeton University Press, 1963); B.G. Farah, S.H. Barnes, and F. Heunks, 'Political Dissatisfaction,' in S.H. Barnes and M. Kaase, eds, *Political Action: Mass Participation in Five Western Democracies* (Beverly Hills, CA: Sage Publications, 1979).
7 R. Inglehart, 'Postmodernization Erodes Respect for Authority, but Increases Support for Democracy,' in Norris, *Critical Citizens.*

   Conventional wisdom holds that efficacious citizens are more inclined to participate in politics (see C. Pateman, *Participation and Democratic Theory* [Cambridge: Cambridge University Press, 1970]; see also Roese, this volume) and that perceptions of system responsiveness (or feelings of external efficacy) are significantly linked to conventional types of political participation (see Farah, Barnes, and Heunks, 'Political Dissatisfaction,' 435). Therefore, the more responsive a government, the greater the chances that citizens will vote.
8 Norris, *Critical Citizens*; R.J. Dalton, *Citizen Politics: Public Opinion and Political Parties in Advanced Democracies*, 2nd ed. (Irvine: University of California, 1996); R.J. Dalton and M.P. Wattenberg, 'The Not So Simple Act of Voting,' in A. Finifter, ed., *Political Science: The State of the Discipline II* (Washington: American Political Science Association, 1993); H. Klingemann and D. Fuchs, eds, *Citizens and the State* (New York: Oxford University Press, 1995); M. Kaase and K. Newton, *Beliefs in Government* (Oxford: Oxford University Press, 1995).
9 Inglehart, 'Postmodernization Erodes Respect for Authority, but Increases Support for Democracy'; D. Fuchs, G. Guidorossi, and P. Svensson, 'Support for the Democratic System,' in Klingemann and Fuchs, *Citizens and the State*; see also Nadeau, this volume.

   According to The Freedom House Index (see P. Norris, 'Conclusions: Electoral Reform and Electoral Change,' in Norris, *Critical Citizens*), the proportion of democracies worldwide has increased from 34% in 1983 to 41% 1997: 'Out of 194 states around the world (excluding independent territories), 81 countries could be classified as democratic ... 60 countries as incomplete or semi-democracies, and another 53 [as] undemocratic ...' (Ibid., 265). Representative democracy is now preferred in more countries than any other system of government.
10 In its most generic form, the term 'human capital' refers to the level of knowledge and skills acquired by individuals; it was developed originally through the work of economists such as Gary Becker ('Investment in

Human Capital: A Theoretical Analysis,' *Journal of Political Economy* 70(5) [1962]: part 2, supplement: 9–49; *Human Capital: A Theoretical and Empirical Analysis, with Special Reference to Education*, 1st and 2nd ed. [New York: National Bureau of Economic Research, 1964 and 1975]) and Theodore W. Shultz ('Investment in Human Capital,' *American Economic Review* 51(1) [1961]: 1–17; 'Reflections on Investment in Man,' *Journal of Political Economy* 70(5) [1962] part 2, supplement 1–8).

11 R. Inglehart, 'Cognitive Mobilization and European Identity,' *Comparative Politics* 3, October 1970: 45–70; R. Inglehart, *Culture Shift in Advanced Industrial Society* (Princeton: Princeton University Press, 1990); Inglehart, *Modernization and Postmodernization*; R.J. Dalton, 'Cognitive Mobilization and Partisan Dealignment in Advanced Industrial Democracies,' *Journal of Politics* 46 (1984): 264–84; R.J. Dalton, *Citizen Politics: Public Opinion and Political Parties in Advanced Democracies*, 1st ed. (Irvine: University of California Press, 1988); Dalton, *Citizen Politics*, 2nd ed.; T.N. Clark and M. Rempel, *Citizens Politics in Post-Industrial Societies* (Boulder, CO: Westview Press, 1997); Barnes and Kaase, *Political Action*; M.K. Jennings and J.W. van Deth, *Continuities in Political Action* (New York: Walter de Gruyter, 1989); R.J. Dalton and M. Kuechler, *Challenging the Political Order: New Social and Political Movements in Western Democracies* (New York: Oxford University Press, 1990).

12 H. Semetko and P. Valkenberg, 'The Impact of Attentiveness on Political Efficacy: Evidence from a Three-Year German Panel Study,' *International Journal of Public Opinion Research* 10(3) (1998): 195–210.

13 Norris, *Critical Citizens*.

14 For instance, at the state level, R. Rogowski ('Eckstein and the Study of Private Governments: An Appreciation, Critique, and Proposal,' *Comparative Political Studies* 31(4) [1998]: 444–63; 'Democracy, Capital, Skill, and Country Size: Effects of Asset Mobility and Regime Monopoly on the Odds of Democratic Rule,' in P. Drake and M. McCubbins, eds, *The Origins of Liberty* [Princeton: Princeton University Press, 1998]) reports that there is a strong link between higher levels of human capital and a greater demand for democracy. This relationship, it turns out, is even more powerful than the association between wealth and democracy.

15 R.J. Dalton, S.C. Flanagan, and P.A. Beck, *Electoral Change in Advanced Industrial Democracies: Realignment or Dealignment?* (Princeton: Princeton University Press, 1984); I. Crewe and D. Denver, *Electoral Change in Western Democracies: Patterns and Sources of Electoral Volatility* (London: Croom Helm, 1985); M. Wattenberg, *The Decline of American Political Parties: 1952–1988* (Cambridge, MA: Harvard University Press, 1990); H.D. Clarke and

M. Stewart, 'The Decline of Political Parties in the Minds of Citizens,' *Annual Review of Political Science* 1 (1998): 357–78; M. Franklin, T. Mackie, and H. Valen, *Electoral Change: Responses to Evolving Social and Attitudinal Structures in Western Countries* (New York: Cambridge University Press, 1992); Norris, *Electoral Change Since 1945* (Cambridge, MA: Blackwell Publishers Ltd., 1997).

16 Dalton and Wattenberg, 'The Not So Simple Act of Voting.'

17 Almond and Verba, *The Civic Culture.*

18 Norris, *Critical Citizens*; Kornberg and Clarke, *Citizens and Community.*

19 Lipset and Schneider, *The Confidence Gap*; Nye, Zelikow, and King, *Why People Don't Trust Government*; see also Roese, chapter 5, this volume.

20 Dalton, 'Political Support in Advanced Industrial Democracies.'

21 Nevitte, *Decline of Deference.*

22 Dalton, 'Political Support in Advanced Industrial Democracies,' 63.

23 H.D. Clarke et al., *Absent Mandate: Canadian Electoral Politics in an Era of Restructuring*, 3rd ed. (Toronto: McGraw-Hill Ryerson, 1996). For a more detailed analysis of what Canadians think about their politicans, see M. Mancuso et al., *A Question of Ethics: Canadians Speak Out* (Don Mills, ON: Oxford University Press, 1998).

24 Inglehart, 'Postmodernization Erodes Respect for Authority,' 250; *Modernization and Postmodernization.*

25 J. Nye, Jr, and P.D. Zelikow, 'Conclusion: Reflections, Conjectures, and Puzzles,' in Nye, Zelikow, and King, *Why People Don't Trust Government*; 'Introduction: The Growth of Critical Citizens?'; Kornberg and Clarke, *Citizens and Community.*

26 R. Inglehart, *The Silent Revolution: Changing Values and Political Styles among Western Publics* (Princeton: Princeton University Press, 1977); *Culture Shift; Modernization and Postmodernization.*

27 Inglehart, *Modernization and Postmodernization*, 29–30.

28 Inglehart, 'Postmodernization Erodes Respect for Authority,' 250.

29 Nevitte, *Decline of Deference.*

30 Inglehart, 'Postmodernization Erodes Respect for Authority,' 250. Citizens today are more inclined to sign petitions, join boycotts, attend unlawful demonstrations, join unofficial strikes, occupy buildings, and join new social movements. For a more thorough analysis of the rise in unconventional political participation, see Barnes and Kaase, *Political Action*; Jennings and van Deth, *Continuities*; Dalton and Kuechler, *Challenging the Political Order*; and Nevitte, *Decline of Deference.*

31 Kornberg and Clarke, *Citizens and Community.*

32 Ibid., 136.

33 Farah, Barnes, and Heunks, 'Political Dissatisfaction.'
34 Inglehart, *Modernization and Postmodernization*. See also Dalton, *Citizen Politics*, 2nd ed.; M. Dickerson and T. Flanagan, *An Introduction to Government and Politics: A Conceptual Approach* (Scarborough, ON: ITP Nelson, 1998), chap. 28; and M. Stewart and H. Clarke, 'The Dynamics of Party Identification in Federal Systems: The Canadian Case,' *American Journal of Political Science* 42 (1998): 197–216.
35 Inglehart, *Modernization and Postmodernization*, 311.
36 Klingemann and Fuchs, *Citizens and the State*.
37 Kaase and Newton, *Beliefs in Government*. O. Listhaug and M. Wiberg, 'Confidence in Political and Private Institutions'; O. Listhaug, 'The Dynamics of Trust in Politicians'; and R. Topf, 'Electoral Participation,' in Klingemann and Fuchs, *Citizens and the State*.
38 H. Schmitt and S. Holmberg, 'Political Parties in Decline,' in Klingemann and Fuchs, *Citizens and the State*, 122
39 Fuchs and Klingemann, *Citizens and the State*.
40 Fuchs, Guidorossi, and Svensson, 'Support for the Democratic System,' 350–1.
41 Fuchs and Klingemann, eds, *Citizens and the State*, 437.
42 Ibid., 436.
43 Dalton, *Citizen Politics*, 2nd ed.; A. Downs, 'An Economic Theory of Political Action in a Democracy,' *Journal of Political Economy* 65 (1957): 135–50; S. Rosenstone and J. Hansen, *Mobilization, Participation, and Democracy in America* (New York: Macmillan Publishing Co., 1993); S. Verba, K.L. Schlozman, and H. Brady, *Voice and Equality: Civic Voluntarism in American Politics* (Cambridge, MA: Harvard University Press, 1995).
44 See, e.g., B.R. Berelson, P.F. Lazarsfeld, and W.N. McPhee, *Voting: A Study of Opinion Formation in a Presidential Campaign* (Chicago: University of Chicago Press, 1954), chap. 14.
45 P. Sniderman, 'The New Look in Public Opinion Research,' in Finifter, *State of the Discipline II*, 219.
46 P.E. Converse, 'The Nature of Belief Systems in Mass Publics,' in Apter, ed., *Ideology and Discontent* (New York: Free Press, 1964); H. McClosky, 'Consensus and Ideology in American Politics,' *American Political Science Review* 58(2) (1964): 361–82.
47 Dalton, *Citizen Politics*, 2nd ed., 17.
48 Clark and Rempel, *Citizens Politics in Post-Industrial Societies*, 16.
49 N. Nevitte and M. Kanji, 'Orientations towards Authority and Congruency Theory: The Cross-National, Cross-time Evidence,' *International Journal of Comparative Sociology* 40 (1) (February 1998): 161–90.

50 Inglehart, *Modernization and Postmodernization*, 170.
51 Ibid., 21; Dalton, 'Cognitive Mobilization and Partisan Dealignment'; *Citizen Politics*, 1st ed.
52 Inglehart, *The Silent Revolution; Culture Shift; Modernization and Postmodernization*.
53 Dalton, *Citizen Politics*, 1st ed., 18.
54 Dalton, *Citizen Politics*, 2nd ed.
55 Rosenstone and Hansen, *Mobilization, Participation and Democracy*; Verba, Schlozman, and Brady, *Voice and Equality*.
56 Dalton, *Citizen Politics*, 2nd ed., 7; C.S. White, 'Citizen Participation and the Internet: Prospects for Civic Deliberation in the Information Age,' *The Social Studies* 88, Jan./Feb. 1997: 23–8; David L. Paletz, 'Advanced Information Technology and Political Communication,' *Social Science Computer Review* 14(1) (1996): 75–7; William G. Mayer, 'The Polls-Poll Trends: The Rise of the New Media,' *Public Opinion Quarterly* 58 (1994): 124–46.
57 Dalton, *Citizen Politics*, 2nd ed., 24.
58 Semetko and Valkenberg, 'The Impact of Attentiveness on Political Efficacy.'
59 X. Zhao and S.H. Chaffee, 'Campaign Advertisements versus Television News as Sources of Political Issue Information,' *Public Opinion Quarterly* 59 (1995): 41–65.
60 D.R. Shaw and B.H. Sparrow, 'From the Inner Ring Out: News Congruence, Cue-Taking, and Campaign Coverage,' *Political Research Quarterly* 52(2) (1999): 323–51; R.J. Dalton, P.A. Beck, and R. Huckfeldt, 'Partisan Cues and the Media: Information Flows in the 1992 Presidential Election,' *American Political Science Review* 92(1) (1998): 111–26.
61 C.R. Hofstetter et al., 'Information, Misinformation, and Political Talk Radio,' *Political Research Quarterly* 52(2) (1999): 353–69.
62 Clark and Rempel, *Citizens Politics*.
63 N.H. Nie, J. Junn, and K. Stehlik-Barry, *Education and Democratic Citizenship in America* (Chicago: University of Chicago Press, 1996).
64 Inglehart, *Culture Shift*, 5.
65 Dalton, *Citizen Politics*, 2nd ed.
66 See, e.g., Dalton, *Citizen Politics*, 2nd ed.; Sniderman, R. Brody, and Tetlock, *Reasoning and Choice: Explorations in Political Psychology* (New York: Cambridge University Press, 1991); S. Popkin, *The Reasoning Voter: Communication and Persuasion in Presidential Campaigns* (Chicago: University of Chicago Press, 1991); J. Zaller, *The Nature and Origins of Mass Opinion* (New York: Cambridge University Press, 1992).
67 See R. Johnston et al., *The Challenge of Direct Democracy* (Montreal and

Kingston: McGill-Queen's University Press, 1996); and E. Gidengil and N. Nevitte, 'Know More: Information, Interest and the Constitutional Proposals,' CPSA Meetings, Ottawa, 1993.

68 M.K. Jennings, 'Political Knowledge over Time and across Generations,' *Public Opinion Quarterly* 60 (1996): 228–52. Jennings also finds that as younger generations age, they become increasingly aware of current events, while the extent of their factual knowledge tends to stabilize by midlife.

69 Dalton and Waltenberg, 'The Not So Simple Act of Voting.'

70 Included within this analysis are data from the 1965, 1974, 1979, 1980, 1984, 1988, 1993, and 1997 CES.

71 For exact differences in question wording, please refer to the actual CES survey instruments, available at both the Institute for Social Research (ISR) at York University, Toronto, Ontario, and the Inter-University Consortium for Political and Social Research (ICPSR) at Michigan University, Ann Arbor, Michigan.

72 See Norris, ed., *Critical Citizens*; Kornberg and Clarke, *Citizens and Community*.

73 Norris, 'Introduction: The Growth of Critical Citizens?' 9; H. Klingemann, 'Party Positions and Voter Orientations,' in Norris, ed., *Critical Citizens*; Dalton, 'Political Support in Advanced Industrial Democracies.'

74 See Nevitte, *Decline of Deference*.

75 Similarly, Roese's analysis (chapter 5, this volume) shows that Canadians have also become less inclined to 'trust the government in Ottawa to do what is right.'

76 See N. Nevitte et al., 'The Populist Right in Canada: The Rise of the Reform Party of Canada,' in H.G. Betz and Stefan Immerfall, eds, *The New Politics of the Right: Neo-Populist Parties and Movements in Established Democracies* (New York: St Martin's Press, 1998).

77 For other prospective interpretations of why Canadians have become less trusting of elected officials, see Roese and Docherty (chap. 5) (chap. 6) in this volume.

78 S. Edwards, 'Canada's No. 1, United Nations says anew,' *National Post*, 29 June 2000.

79 These are not the only determinants, of course, but they are some of the most important.

80 Norris, 'Conclusions: Electoral Reform and Electoral Change.'

81 See Kornberg and Clarke, *Citizens and Community*; Farah, Barnes, and Heunks, 'Political Dissatisfaction'; Almond and Verba, *The Civic Culture*.

82 See M. Laroche, M. Merette, and G.C. Ruggeri, 'On the Concept and Dimensions of Human Capital in a Knowledge-Based Economy Context,' *Canadian Public Policy* 25(1) (1999).

83 See Inglehart, 'Cognitive Mobilization and European Identity' and Dalton, 'Cognitive Mobilization and Partisan Dealignment.'

84 Dalton, *Citizen Politics*, 2nd ed.; Clarke and Rempel, *Citizens Politics*.

85 Some of these changes, of course, may be directly attributable to increases in population. Nonetheless these data clearly show that access to political information has expanded significantly.

86 See P. Dickinson and J. Ellison, 'Plugged into the Internet,' in *Canadian Social Trends* (Statistics Canada Catalogue no. 11-008) Winter 1999; P. Dickinson and G. Sciadas, 'Canadians Connected,' *Canadian Economic Observer*, February 1999.

87 Dickinson and Ellison, 'Plugged into the Internet,' 8.

88 For a more detailed analysis, see N. Guppy and S. Davies, *Education in Canada: Recent Trends and Future Challenges* (Government of Canada: Minister of Industry, 1998).

89 Sniderman, 'The New Look in Public Opinion Research'; Sniderman, Brody, and Tetlock, *Reasoning and Choice*.

90 Nevitte, *Decline of Deference*.

91 This finding is consistent with those reported by Semetko and Valkenberg, 'The Impact of Attentiveness on Political Efficacy.'

92 See Inglehart, *Culture Shift* and *Modernization and Postmodernization*; Dalton, *Citizen Politics*, 2nd ed.; Dalton, Flanagan, and Beck, *Electoral Change*.

93 Inglehart, *Modernization and Postmodernizaiton*.

94 Clarke et al., *Absent Mandate*, 50; H.D. Clarke et al., *Political Choice in Canada* (Toronto: McGraw-Hill Ryerson, 1980).

95 Bear in mind, of course, that this analysis does not account for the possibility of strategic voting (see A. Blais and R. Nadeau, 'Measuring Strategic Voting: A Two-Step Procedure,' *Electoral Studies* 15 [1996]: 39–52; A. Blais et al., 'Voting Strategically against the Winner: The 1997 Canadian Election,' prepared for 1998 annual meeting of Midwest Political Science Association, Chicago, 23–6 April 1998; N. Nevitte et al., *Unsteady State: The 1997 Canadian Federal Election* [Toronto: Oxford University Press, 2000]), which may also be construed as independent and calculating, but not necessarily coherent.

96 See Almond and Verba, *The Civic Culture*; Kornberg and Clarke, *Citizens and Community*; Farah, Barnes, and Heunks, 'Political Dissatisfaction.'

97 According to socio-demographics, the most coherent voters tend to be males, English Canadians, and those who reside west of Atlantic Canada.

98 See Clarke et al., *Political Choice in Canada*; Clarke et al., *Absent Mandate*.

99 See D.C. Docherty, chapter 6, this volume.

100 Ibid.
101 See J.H. Pammett, 'The 1988 Vote,' in A. Frizzell, J.H. Pammett, and
     A. Westell, eds, *The Canadian General Election of 1988* (Ottawa: Carleton
     University Press, 1989); J.H. Pammett, 'Tracking the Votes,' in A. Frizzell,
     J.H. Pammett, and A. Westell, eds, *The Canadian General Election of 1993*
     (Ottawa: Carleton University Press, 1994); J.H. Pammett, 'Analyzing
     Voting Behaviour in Canada: The Case of the 1993 Election,' in H.G.
     Thorburn, ed., *Party Politics in Canada* (Scarborough, ON: Prentice-Hall
     Canada, 1996); J.H. Pammett, 'The Voters Decide,' in A. Frizzell and J.H.
     Pammett, eds, *The Canadian General Election of 1997* (Toronto: Dundurn
     Press, 1997).
102 R.K. Carty, W. Cross, and L. Young, *Rebuilding Canadian Party Politics*
     (Vancouver: UBC Press, 2000).

4. Civic Engagement, Trust, and Democracy: Evidence from Alberta

Lisa Young

There is considerable attitudinal and anecdotal evidence suggesting that Canadians have grown increasingly disenchanted with the quality of democratic life in the country over the past three decades. Public-opinion surveys report dissatisfaction with the quality of democracy, discontent with the quality of political representation, and growing support for direct democracy.[1] Certainly the behaviour of the Canadian electorate through the 1990s suggests little support for politics as usual: the Charlottetown Accord was defeated in a national referendum, and the national party system was shattered by the emergence of what appeared at the time to be two regional protest parties in the 1993 election. This growing dissatisfaction and discontent is a complex phenomenon that has eluded simple explanation. Some observers have suggested that poor institutional design or performance are to blame, while other studies have focused on changes in Canadian society, and most particularly changes in social structure and values held by individuals in that society.[2]

The purpose of this chapter is to test an alternative explanation for growing disenchantment with democratic life in Canada: the civil society / social capital explanation. This argument holds that declining involvement in the associations that constitute civil society contributes to a decline in 'social capital' – norms of reciprocity and trust – that in turn erodes the basis on which democratic governance flourishes. This argument has been brought to public attention by Robert Putnam, whose work has rapidly found its way into the media and reintroduced concern with civil society in policy-making in both Canada and the United States.

The civil society / social capital explanation will be tested using the 1999 Alberta Civil Society Survey. This study surveyed 1272 Albertans during a period from December 1998 to January 1999.[3] It should be acknowledged at the outset that there are certain limitations to basing this study on a survey conducted only in Alberta. Alberta is a relatively affluent province with low rates of trade-union membership and a political culture that favours minimal government. Public-opinion studies have demonstrated that levels of support for direct democracy and disenchantment with the federal government are higher in Alberta than elsewhere in the country. Thus, considerable caution should be used in generalizing findings from Alberta to the rest of the country. That said, the Alberta Civil Society Survey is the only Canadian data set available that includes items allowing this hypothesis to be tested. It should be noted at the outset that this is only a preliminary study. Because the civil society / social capital argument relates, at least in part, to societies in the aggregate, there are limits to the conclusions that can be drawn using individual-level survey data. In light of these limitations, the findings reported in this chapter should be treated as preliminary.

Civic Engagement, Trust, and Democracy

The civil society / social capital literature offers a potential explanation for civic disengagement that warrants careful consideration and empirical investigation. The basic argument is as follows: advanced industrialized nations, particularly the United States, have in recent years experienced a decline in the quality of civil society. This decline is manifested in decreasing levels of associational membership and a tendency away from recreational activities in groups. With this decline of civic engagement comes a decline in interpersonal trust. The existence of a relationship between civic engagement and interpersonal trust is predicated on the assumption that involvement in the life of the community instils in individuals the habits and practices of cooperation. Those who are engaged in the community, according to this theory, are more likely to be predisposed to trust others, and assume that others will behave according to a sort of unwritten code enshrining norms of reciprocity. Trust, in turn, is necessary to a functioning democracy. Numerous empirical studies conducted over the past forty years have shown a correlation between interpersonal trust and the persistence of democratic institutions.[4] According to Brehm and Rahn, '[t]hese norms [of reciprocity] become part of a community's social capital, allowing people to make inferences about the intentions of others even when direct knowledge about them is unavailable. Generalized trust allows people to move out of familiar relationships in which trust is based on knowledge accumulated from long experience with particular people. If outcomes in a democracy are inherently uncertain ... such global trust may be necessary in order for people to support democratic arrangements.'[5] From this notion, it is clear that declining trust could potentially affect confidence in and willingness to engage with democratic governance.

The past decade has witnessed a resurgence of interest among social scientists studying industrialized democracies in the idea of 'civil society' and 'social capital.'[6] There are several reasons for this resurgence of interest; they include influence from scholars studying the importance of civil society in democratization processes in Eastern Europe and developing nations, and the publication of Robert Putnam's provocative works *Making Democracy Work* and 'Bowling Alone.' As William Galston observed, 'seldom has a thesis moved so quickly from scholarly obscurity to conventional wisdom ... Putnam's argument has touched a nerve. Most Americans believe that during the past forty years, important aspects of their society may have changed for the worse.'[7]

One might speculate that this resurgence of interest is at least in part a reaction to the conditions of postmodern or postindustrial social organization. In a heterogenous society where there are ever fewer shared beliefs, cultural references, and practices, where the population is increasingly mobile and thus unrooted, where familial ties are strained by distances, where family structure has been transformed, and where we often seem to lack common purpose and common identity, the communitarian impulse of the civil-society and social-capital argument is without doubt highly attractive to many. That said, this literature frequently comes under attack for its nostalgic portrait of a bygone era as the golden age of civil society. Critics point out – entirely correctly – that such nostalgia can contain an unrealistic and possibly undesirable longing to return to an era that predates women's entry into the paid workforce, greater freedoms for women, increased legal and social tolerance of ethnic and sexual diversity, and a relaxation of punishing social norms dressed up as conventional morality.

The term 'civil society' refers to the associations that form in the space between the state and the purely private realm. More precisely, we can think of civil society as referring to the realm of private volun-

tary association, ranging from neighbourhood committees to philan-
thropic enterprises.[8] There is no consensus regarding the precise definition of civil society. In some accounts, civil society is understood to
encompass the market; in others, it is seen as an intermediary realm
that excludes the market.[9] The notion of civil society is particularly
important to American political thought, in large part because of the
emphasis Tocqueville placed on it, arguing essentially that Americans'
propensity for banding together in voluntary associations (everything
from town councils to charitable organizations) was their greatest de-
fence from state tyranny.

Closely related to the idea of civil society is the concept of social
capital. Putnam defines social capital as the 'features of social life –
networks, norms and trust – that enable participants to act together
more effectively to pursue shared objectives.'[10] Following the work of
sociologist James Coleman, Putnam argues that social capital is a public
good, a property of a community rather than an individual. Societies
rich in social capital, he argues, are characterized by 'virtuous circles' in
which interpersonal trust encourages cooperation among citizens; cooperation, in turn, breeds trust.[11] Treated in this way, social capital
'focuses on those cultural values and attitudes that predispose citizens
to cooperate, trust, understand and empathize with each other – to treat
each other as fellow citizens rather than as strangers, competitors or
potential enemies.'[12]

According to Putnam, social trust can arise from two related sources:
norms of reciprocity and networks of civic engagement. Norms of
reciprocity are the unwritten rules of social obligation (like raking
leaves from our lawns in the fall) enforced through social approbation
and disapproval. This can be thought of as generalized reciprocity – a
continuing relationship of exchange that is at any given time unre-
quited or imbalanced, but that involves mutual expectations that a
benefit granted now should be repaid in the future.[13] Effective norms of
reciprocity, Putnam argues, are likely to be associated with dense networks of social exchange. Networks of civic engagement – neighbourhood associations, choral societies, cooperative sports clubs, and the
like – encourage cooperation and reciprocity in a community. Such
networks provide a means of punishing those who flout norms of
reciprocity; they reinforce norms by facilitating communication and
improving the flow of information about the trustworthiness of individuals.[14] Putnam's emphasis on participation in formal associations
(bowling in an organized league versus bowling regularly with a group

of friends) echoes the claim of Tocqueville and others that participation in formally organized voluntary associations is essential for generating democratic norms among citizens as they teach the civic virtues of trust, moderation, compromise, and reciprocity and the skills of democratic discussion and organization.[15]

This conclusion is not universally accepted, however. As Newton observes, 'it seems, on the face of it, implausible to ascribe a crucial role to voluntary organizations when they account for only a few hours a week of life, and even then for only a small minority of activists.'[16] The influences of education, socialization within the family, and experiences in the workplace all potentially have a greater effect than does participation in voluntary organizations. If face-to-face interaction in non-hierarchical groups is, in fact, important to instilling Putnam's 'habits of the heart,' it is possible that the most important type of interaction occurs not in formal associations, but in informal groups that 'come together casually and irregularly to play darts, discuss a novel, study religion, raise consciousness, organize a street party or a neighbourhood watch scheme, run a baby-sitting circle or a car pool, organize a support group, or simply drink in a bar.'[17]

The civil society / social capital approach has drawn criticism from a number of quarters. One point of contention is the distinction made between civic and political engagement. Critics argue that civic engagement may well yield the hypothesized social and economic benefits, but cannot yield political benefits. For example, Benjamin Barber argues that only political activity that encourages deliberation and exchange of ideas can engender the understanding of the public good that is needed to develop public policy.[18] In a similar vein, intriguing research by American sociologist Nina Eliasoph suggests that the hypothesized relationship between civic engagement and confidence in government may be illusory.[19] Eliasoph became an active participant-observer in three sets of social networks in a suburban area of California. These groups were civic volunteers (who raised money for a local high school and worked on anti-drug campaigns), country-and-western dance enthusiasts, and environmental activists opposed to nuclear plants in the area. In her study, she found that within the first two groups, which fit most closely into Putnam's notion of civil society – choral leagues and voluntarism – participants did everything they possibly could to avoid talking publicly about political matters. Eliasoph concluded that 'the people I met wanted to create a sense of community, but did not want to talk politics ... Civic etiquette made imaginative, open-minded, thoughtful conversation rare in public.'[20] The most interesting findings of this study were that the volunteers 'wanted to embody the republican ideal, but were loath to face the difficulty of living it out in communities that are more inextricably enlaced in national and global politics than in de Tocqueville's day ... [T]hey encouraged one another not to talk about issues that could not be solved simply by local citizens' banding together and looking out for one another. The belief called for political avoidance.'[21] This determined apoliticism and distaste for the political is deeply rooted in American society and may not be alien to Canada.

In a study based on public-opinion surveys in western Europe in the 1990s, Jan van Deth found evidence to support the hypothesis that higher levels of social capital *decrease* political salience (defined as the importance placed on politics). Individuals in these postindustrial democracies who had the greatest access to social capital – in the form of education, income, and associational involvement – place less emphasis on politics than do their less-capitalized counterparts. Van Deth concludes from this that politics becomes less salient as citizens become more autonomous and resourceful. In other words, social capital allows these citizens to rely on their own resources and ingenuity rather than looking for political solutions to problems.[22] The findings from the Eliasoph and van Deth studies raise serious questions about the hypothesized linkages in the civil society / social capital literature.

Research Design

To test the civil society / social capital argument, this paper uses data from the 1999 Alberta Civil Society Survey. More specifically, the paper will test the hypothesis that civic engagement, or involvement in the associations that make up civil society, contributes to interpersonal trust, which, in turn, contributes to confidence in political institutions and trust in government. To determine whether there is any relationship between these variables, simple bivariate analysis is used. To determine the strength of these relationships relative to other potential explanatory variables, linear regression analysis is employed.

It should be noted that this research design is looking for such relationships at the *individual*, rather than the aggregate, level. Although Putnam and others argue that social capital is a property of communities, not individuals, other scholars have argued convincingly that the concept can be measured at an individual level. According to Brehm and Rahn, 'social capital is an aggregate concept that has its basis in individual behaviour, attitudes and predispositions. Multiple institutions nurture the habits and values that give rise to social capital, including community and other voluntary organizations, families, church organizations, and cultural patterns.'[23] Brehm and Rahn specify that, at the individual level, social capital can be understood as 'the reciprocal relationship between civic participation and interpersonal trust.'[24] Further research would be required to determine whether these relationships exist at the aggregate level.

Civic Engagement

The term 'civic engagement' refers to individual involvement in the associational life that constitutes civil society. For Putnam, a decline in civic engagement in American society is closely related to declining interpersonal trust. In fact, much of his analysis is predicated on the observation that membership in all sorts of organizations, from the PTA to bowling leagues, is on the wane in the United States.[25] Directly comparable measures are not available for Canada. In fact, what little evidence is available suggests a reverse pattern. Statistics Canada's tracking of voluntarism rates shows an increase between 1987 and 1997. Over that period, voluntarism rates in the Canadian population increased slightly from 27 per cent to 31 per cent.[26] Voluntarism is not, however, synonymous with civic engagement. The latter encompasses other activities such as participation in organized religion, recreational sporting teams, and the like.

For the purpose of this study, three distinct measures of engagement have been developed. The first, *civic engagement*, relates to involvement in non-political, non-market civic organizations. As table 4.1 demonstrates, the majority of associational memberships included in the Alberta Civil Society Survey fall into this civic engagement category. They include service clubs, volunteer groups, neighbourhood associations, religious groups, ethnic organizations, recreational associations, and parents' groups. The category of 'other groups' was also included with civic groups on the assumption that most other organizational involvement would be neither market-related nor political in nature. Of the civic groups, religious groups (churches, temples, and mosques) claimed the greatest membership (38% of respondents), followed by recreational associations (28%), neighbourhood associations (18%), and volunteer groups (16%). Of the groups included in this category, volunteer-

TABLE 4.1
Membership and activity in groups

Group type	% belonging	Of those who belong:				
		% contribute/pay membership	% occasional participants	% regularly attend mtgs	% active volunteers	% leaders
I. Civic groups						
Religious	38	7	32	28	18	14
Recreational	28	9	20	27	26	18
Neighbourhood	18	19	30	9	29	14
Volunteer	16	6	12	5	52	26
Other	12	13	17	17	32	21
Parents'	10	6	20	8	49	17
Ethnic	5	15	43	14	22	6
Service club	5	17	10	13	31	29
II. Professional						
Business/Prof.	23	37	24	17	11	11
Union	15	59	23	12	3	4
III. Political						
Political party	11	52	23	4	19	2
Pol. action grp	4	33	17	5	25	20

Source: Calculated from Alberta Civil Society Survey.

group memberships were the most likely to involve significant engagement – 26% of respondents belonging to such groups were leaders and 52% active volunteers.[27]

The second measure is *professional engagement*, which includes only two classes of associational involvement: unions and professional or business organizations. It should be noted that membership in many unions and some professional associations (like the Bar association) are not voluntary, but rather a precondition for employment. More extensive involvement, such as regularly attending meetings or playing a leadership role is, however, voluntary. Among respondents to the survey, 23% reported membership in a business or professional organization, and 15% reported union membership. Of those, 37% and 59% respectively played no role other than contributing membership fees.

Along with these two measures of civic and professional engagement, we have also developed a third measure: *political engagement*. The two kinds of associational membership included in this measure are membership in a political party and membership in a political action group other than a political party. Among respondents, 11% reported membership in a political party, and 4% in a political action group.[28]

It should be noted that the boundaries between civic, market, and political organizations are not as clearly delimited as they might first appear. Unions and professional associations may involve themselves in the formal political process by supporting a political party; arguably, union activism is a political action. That said, union membership itself is more closely related to market involvement than to political activity. Similarly, neighbourhood associations might become highly politicized when lobbying for policy change of some sort, ethnic organizations may well enter the political fray, and religious groups could mobilize their followers for political activity. Nonetheless, the location of such groups is within civil society, and engagement with the formal political sphere is not their primary reason for being.

For all three measures of engagement, additive scales were constructed such that a respondent would receive one point on the scale for membership in a category of groups, an additional point if they were occasional participants, two additional points if they regularly attended meetings, three additional points if they were active volunteers, and four additional points if they acted as leaders in the group. This measure captures both breadth and intensity of associational involvement. For instance, an individual who was an inactive member of three categories of groups would receive a score of three, as would an individual who regularly attended meetings in one category of group.[29]

Determinants of Engagement

Before considering the presence of relationships between civic engagement, interpersonal trust, and confidence in government, it is useful to consider the factors that affect the degree of individuals' involvement in the associations that make up civil society. This is of particular importance when considering possible policy directions stemming from the research. Several studies regarding civic engagement suggest possible demographic and other determinants of this type of involvement. The most prominent of these is Putnam's 'Strange Disappearance of Civic America' in which he tests a series of potential explanations for declining civic involvement. Putnam finds that education is by far the strongest correlate of civic engagement. He concludes that 'well-educated people are more likely to be joiners and trusters, partly because they are better off economically, but mostly because of the skills, resources, and inclinations that were incorporated to them at home and at school.' Rising levels of education, he argues, have partially offset the general trend toward civic disengagement. Putnam also finds that residents of the largest metropolitan areas are slightly less trusting and slightly less likely to be group members. Putnam finds a strong generational effect, with members of postwar generations less likely to be engaged than their predecessors were. He identifies what he calls 'the long civic generation' – those born from the early 1930s to 1945 – as the last civic generation in America.[30]

The ultimate culprit in the decline of civil society in the United States, according to Putnam, is television. The rise of television as a major component of leisure time coincided with generational disengagement. Television, he argues, 'privatizes our leisure time,' resulting in a decline in civic engagement. This is to some degree supported by Brehm and Rahn, who find that, among Americans, each additional hour of television each night has a dampening effect on civic participation of equivalent magnitude to the positive effect of $1000 of additional income.[31]

Putnam also rules out several potential causes for civic disengagement: mobility, on the grounds that the overall rate of mobility of the American population has not increased in the period in question; and the changing role of women, as he finds that working women belong to slightly more voluntary associations than do housewives, although housewives on average spend more time on voluntary activities. Fi-

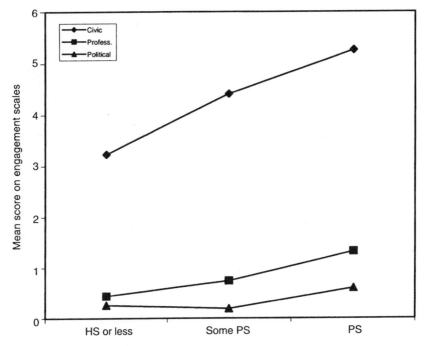

Figure 4.1 Engagement by education

nally, although he finds a correlation between marriage, especially if the family includes children, and civic engagement, he thinks higher divorce rates may be a consequence rather than a cause of declining social capital.[32]

Findings

Analysis of the 1999 Alberta Civil Society Survey data demonstrates that post-secondary education is a strong predictor of civic, professional, and political engagement. As figure 4.1 illustrates, people who have completed at least one post-secondary degree are more likely than others to be involved in community organizations, professional groups, and political groups. In fact, regression analysis shows that post-secondary education is the strongest determinant of the two latter forms of engagement, and the second strongest predictor of civic engagement (see table 4.2). This is essentially consistent with Putnam's findings.

The strongest predictor of civic engagement in Alberta, precisely as

TABLE 4.2
Determinants of civic, professional, and political engagement

	Civic		Professional		Political	
	Beta	Beta weight	Beta	Beta weight	Beta	Beta weight
Constant	1.976**		0.067		−0.068	
Post-secondary education	1.301*	0.135	0.576**	0.179	0.358**	0.169
Age (in years)	0.037**	0.116	0.010*	0.092	0.010**	0.138
Hours of TV/week	−0.066**	−0.138	−0.013*	−0.081	−0.006	−0.060
Hours of newspaper/week	−0.022	−0.020	0.026*	0.074	−0.001	−0.005
Hours of e-mail or Internet	−0.015	−0.029	−0.004	−0.020	0.004	0.031
Married	−0.903**	0.100	0.017	0.006	−0.077	−0.039
Children 6–12	1.114**	0.111	0.095	0.028	−0.025	−0.012
Full-time employment	−0.688*	−0.078	0.169	0.057	−0.148*	−0.076
Household income >$70K	0.759*	0.080	0.443*	0.141	−0.049	−0.024
Female	0.115	0.013	−0.044	−0.015	−0.064	−0.033
Rural	0.963**	0.092	0.014	0.004	0.064	0.028
Years living in current residence	0.035*	0.074	0.002	0.013	0.012**	0.115
R-squared	0.148		0.109		0.085	

*Significant at $p < .05$
**Significant at $p < .01$

Putnam suggests, is time spent watching television. The more hours of television watched each week, the less likely one is to be involved in civic organizations or professional organizations. Figure 4.2 shows that the more television one watches, the lower the mean score on all three categories of engagement. It should be noted that measuring the number of hours of television watched each week is a crude measure. There is, presumably, a qualitative distinction to be made between the individual who watches public-affairs programs regularly because of an interest in community or national affairs and the individual who devotes a similar number of hours of television each week to watching the Jerry Springer show (feeding an interest in affairs of another sort entirely). To a considerable extent, Putnam's assumption that newspaper reading is positively correlated with civic engagement is borne out in

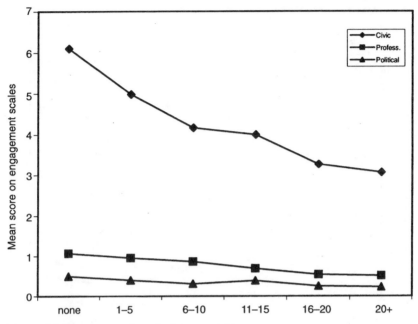

Figure 4.2 Engagement by television watching

these findings (see figure 4.3), although the relationship is less clear than the relationship with television watching, and did not have a significant effect in the regression analysis. Hours spent on the Internet or with e-mail at home has a mixed effect, again not statistically significant in the regression analysis.

Also in keeping with Putnam's conclusions, we find that age has a strong and significant positive effect on all three forms of engagement. People born before the Second World War are more likely than their younger counterparts to be involved in civic and political organizations. That said, once the intensity of involvement is taken into account, we find that people in their late thirties and early forties are slightly more engaged than those over fifty-five (see figure 4.4). When this analysis is broken down by gender, we find that the pattern Putnam hypothesizes holds true among men, but not among women (see figure 4.5). Among women, civic engagement peaks among 35 to 44 year olds and declines among subsequent cohorts, which suggests a life-cycle explanation related to child-rearing rather than the cohort effect Putnam suggests. Moreover, people aged 35 to 54, at the prime of their working

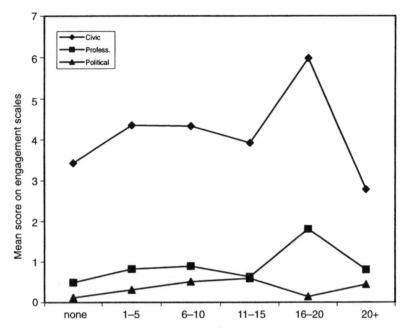

Figure 4.3 Engagement by newspaper readership

life, are more likely to be engaged in professional organizations than either their younger or older counterparts. Given the importance of professional life, and given that professional engagement may well instil Putnam's 'habits of the heart' just as effectively as civic engagement, this finding should not be overlooked.[33] In short, the data do not entirely support Putnam's argument about the existence of a civic generation born before the Second World War.[34]

Putnam's conclusion that increased mobility does not account for decreased engagement is thrown into question by the findings presented in figure 4.6. The figure shows that the longer one has lived at one's current residence, the greater the degree of civic and political engagement. This pattern holds even when controlling for age. This finding suggests that patterns of social organization that require people to move frequently for educational and job-related reasons do, in fact, have a dampening effect that on civic engagement in the years subsequent to each move.

Traditional family forms are also correlated with engagement. Re-

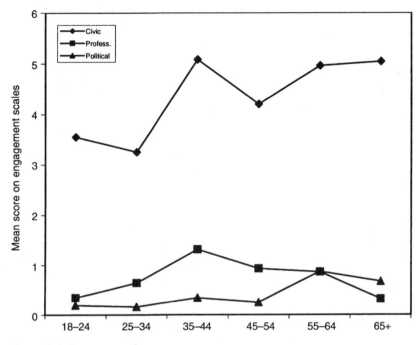

Figure 4.4 Engagement by age

spondents who are married or widowed are more heavily engaged, at least in the civic and political categories, than those in common-law relationships or who are divorced or separated. Some of this variation may, however, be explained by the effect that having children in the home has on civic engagement. Among women, those with children five and under are substantially more heavily engaged than those without. There is no similar effect among men. For both men and women, the presence of children aged six to twelve in the home substantially increases the degree of civic engagement. The substantial effect that having children has on civic engagement, especially among women, suggests that age differences in civic engagement may, in fact, be as much a lifestyle effect as a cohort effect. Figure 4.7 shows levels of civic engagement broken down by marital status and gender. This suggests that the dampening effect of divorce on civic engagement is far more pronounced among men than among women, which may at least in part reflect the tendency for women to have primary custody of children in the event of marital breakdown.

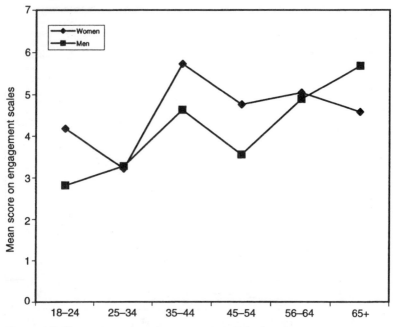

Figure 4.5 Civic engagement by age and gender

There is also some evidence suggesting that very traditional family form – male breadwinners and female homemakers – encourages civic engagement (see figure 4.8). Women who identify their primary occupation as homemaker score higher, on average, on civic engagement than women who work outside the home. Having a wife who is a homemaker does not have any effect on men's civic engagement, however.

Overall, Putnam's findings regarding the determinants of civic engagement in the United States are borne out by the findings from the ACCS. Engagement in civic organizations is greatest among those with post-secondary education and among older Albertans. Just as Putnam suggests, these two effects to some degree cancel one another out: civic engagement would be declining greatly in Alberta were it not for the positive effect of more access to post-secondary education. Television watching and frequent moves appear to dampen civic engagement. Finally, individuals living in traditional family forms appear to be more likely to be involved in their communities.

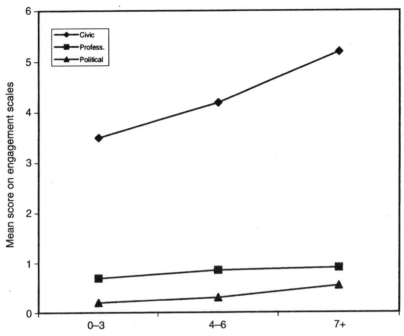

Figure 4.6 Engagement by years at current residence

Civic Engagement and Interpersonal Trust

The civil society / social capital argument is predicated on the assumption that civic engagement fosters interpersonal trust. According to the argument, it is in this relationship that social capital emerges. In their individual-level study of social capital in the United States, Brehm and Rahn found civic engagement and interpersonal trust to exist in a 'tight reciprocal relationship, with the effect of participation on trust substantially greater than the reverse.' They also found that general life satisfaction was strongly related to interpersonal trust, that wealth and education facilitate trust, and that victimization (measured by fear at night and experience of burglary) were negatively associated with trust.[35] Analysing World Values Survey data, John Helliwell found positive correlations between levels of trust and civic engagement in Canada. His findings suggest that types of membership do not significantly affect levels of trust; rather, it is the extent of involvement that matters.[36]

To test for the effect of civic engagement on interpersonal trust among

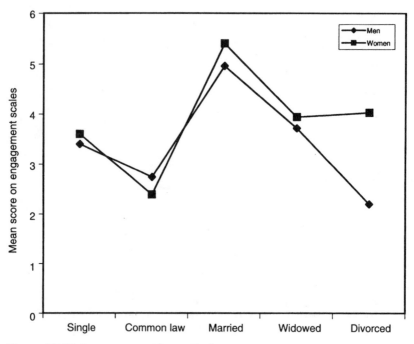

Figure 4.7 Civic engagement by marital status

respondents to the ACCS, a three-item index of interpersonal trust was developed, incorporating the following three items:

- Most people are basically good.
- Most people can be trusted.
- Most people try to take advantage of you (coding reversed).[37]

Findings

All three measures of engagement are positively correlated with interpersonal trust, but civic engagement is the most strongly correlated[38] (see figure 4.9). Regression analysis (see table 4.3) determined that civic engagement was the third strongest predictor of interpersonal trust, lending support to the civil society / social capital argument. The more extensively involved a respondent is in the community, the greater the level of interpersonal trust he or she is likely to express.

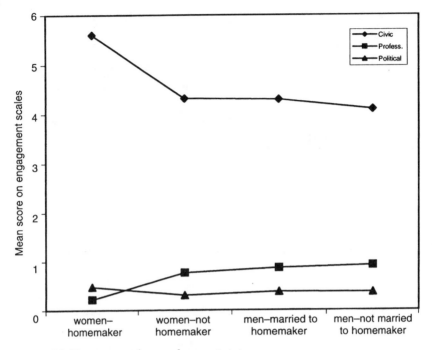

Figure 4.8 Engagement by employment status

The strongest predictor of interpersonal trust in the regression model was fear of walking in one's neighbourhood at night. Although one might argue that such fear is, in fact, an element of interpersonal distrust, it is possible to conceive of otherwise trusting individuals who correctly assess risks entailed in walking in their neighbourhood at night. The results of the regression analysis also confirm Brehm and Rahn's finding that general life satisfaction (in this case measured as the response 'very happy' to the question 'Taken all together, how would you say things are these days: very happy, pretty happy, not too happy?') has a relatively strong and statistically significant effect.

Age and post-secondary education are predictors of both civic engagement and interpersonal trust. Age has a strong positive effect on interpersonal trust: figure 4.10 shows that individuals under the age of 35 are substantially less trusting than their older counterparts, and that those aged 55 to 64 are the most trusting overall. To a lesser degree, post-secondary education had a positive effect on interpersonal trust.

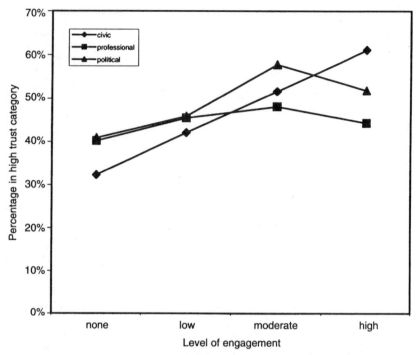

Figure 4.9 High levels of interpersonal trust

Other predictors of civic engagement – television watching, newspaper reading, and residential mobility – had no statistically significant effect in the regression analysis.

Although fear of crime and general life satisfaction have the strongest effect on interpersonal trust, civic engagement is nonetheless an important predictor of trust. This finding confirms the general argument set out in the civil society / social capital literature, as well as Brehm and Rahn's empirical findings regarding the American case. That said, it should be noted that age and post-secondary education are relatively strong predictors of interpersonal trust. Members of Putnam's civic generation are, in fact, more trusting than younger Albertans, and post-secondary education has a strong positive effect on interpersonal trust.

Foley and Edwards suggest that 'civil society' is far too vague a concept, and advocate empirical inquiry that focuses on the particular form of civic engagement that has the positive effects Putnam and

TABLE 4.3
Determinants of interpersonal trust

	Beta	Beta weight
Constant	**8.224**	
Post-secondary education	**0.566**	**0.091**
Age (in years)	**0.027**	**0.142**
Married	0.266	0.047
Full-time employment	0.169	0.029
Household income >$70K	0.329	0.051
Female	0.293	0.051
Rural	0.124	0.018
Years in current residence	0.020	0.043
Hours TV/week	0.015	0.05
Hours newspaper/week	0.003	0.004
Civic engagement	**0.091**	**0.137**
Professional engagement	−0.038	−0.019
Political engagement	0.035	0.012
Very happy overall	**0.796**	**0.109**
Fear	**−1.139**	**−0.178**
R-squared	0.135	

Note: Variables in bold statistically significant at 0.05; Ordinary
least squares regression

others hypothesize. They suspect that social-movement organizations, grassroots interest groups, and grassroots political associations are far more likely to generate these effects than the apolitical choral societies and bowling leagues Putnam favours.[39] Bivariate analysis broken down by category of group supports Putnam's claim, however. This analysis shows statistically significant relationships between interpersonal trust and activity in volunteer groups, neighbourhood associations, church groups, recreational groups, professional and business groups, and political parties. Activity in service clubs, ethnic groups, unions, and political action groups were *not* related to interpersonal trust. The strongest relationships with interpersonal trust were found with neighbourhood groups, recreational groups, and volunteer activity. These are all essentially apolitical groups, although neighbourhood associations can on occasion be involved in political activity, while recreational and voluntary groups are less likely to be. In terms of instilling interpersonal trust, then, Putnam's arguments are supported by the ACSS data.

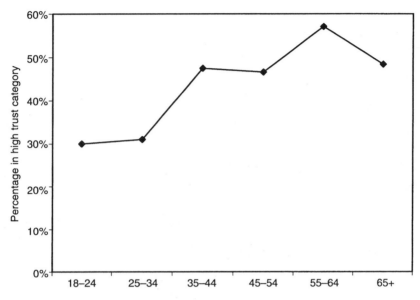

Figure 4.10 Interpersonal trust by age

Determinants of Trust and Confidence in Government

The final, and arguably most crucial, component of the civil society /
social capital argument holds that civic engagement and interpersonal
trust are the necessary preconditions for democratic government. Once
again, this argument was originally put forth at the aggregate level: in
communities with engaged populations and high levels of interpersonal trust, democratic government could to some degree extend to
trust in government. If this were translated to the individual level of
analysis, it would suggest that interpersonal trust would be positively
correlated with trust in government and confidence in public institutions. The hypothesized relationship between interpersonal trust and
trust or confidence in political institutions is, arguably, the most contentious element of the civil society / social capital thesis. As Newton
observes, 'to place a high level of trust in ordinary people (horizontal
trust) is one thing, to place the same level of trust in politicians (vertical
trust) may be another.'[40] Moreover, distrust of government might be
understood equally as a rational assessment by an informed citizen.
This is the argument put forward by the cognitive-mobilization school.[41]

The empirical findings of other studies suggest support for both the civil-society and the cognitive-mobilization approaches. Brehm and Rahn, analysing American survey data, found that greater civic engagement accompanies less confidence in government, directly refuting their hypothesized relationship.[42] In other words, involvement in community organizations *reduced* confidence in government. Interpersonal trust, however, had a positive effect on confidence in government institutions. This effect was substantial, but smaller than the effect of three other variables: a belief that public officials are not interested (negative effect), general life satisfaction (positive effect), and positive economic expectations (positive effect). These findings lend some support to the hypothesis that civic engagement contributes to interpersonal trust, which in turn contributes to confidence in government.

Other analyses have, however, drawn different conclusions. In his analysis of World Value Survey data in this volume, Roese concludes that declining trust in government is not related to declining interpersonal trust, but rather is part of an increasing distrust of large institutions. He also concludes that economic shifts do not explain declining trust in government. Rather, he argues that a sense of efficacy and political activism were the two strongest predictors of trust in government. More specifically, he found a negative relationship such that individuals who had a strong sense of efficacy and were politically active were less trusting of government overall. Roese's conclusions are consistent with the findings of Nevitte, who concludes that declining confidence in political institutions among Canadians can be attributed to age, education, interest in politics, and post-materialist value orientations.[43] More specifically, Nevitte found that those individuals who were younger, better educated, and more interested in politics and postmaterialist in orientation tended to be *less* confident of political institutions than their counterparts.

Findings

Several measures of trust in government and confidence in institutions were employed to probe the linkages between civic engagement, interpersonal trust, and confidence in governmental institutions. Respondents were asked the degree to which they trusted the federal and the provincial government, and how much confidence they had in a number of institutions, including the federal and provincial governments, the Supreme Court, the police, and political parties. They were also asked

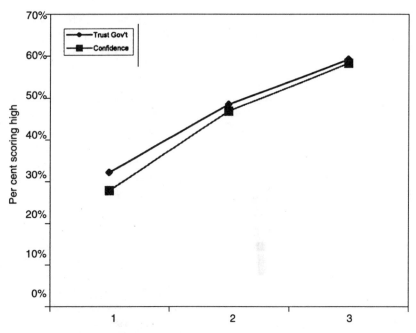

Figure 4.11 Effect of interpersonal trust

about confidence in a number of non-governmental institutions, including the United Way.

Statistical analysis showed interpersonal trust to be a strong predictor of trust in government and confidence in political institutions (see figure 4.11). In regression analysis, interpersonal trust was a statistically significant predictor of every measure of trust in government and confidence in political institutions (see table 4.4). Interpersonal trust was the strongest predictor of trust in the federal government, confidence in the police, and confidence in political parties. This finding lends some support to the civil society / social capital argument, as it confirms – at least at the individual level – the presence of a relationship between interpersonal trust and confidence in government and political institutions. It should be noted, however, that these analyses show only that interpersonal trust and confidence in government are correlated; the possibility remains that causation runs in the opposite direction, with confidence in public institutions inspiring trust in other individuals.[44]

Civic engagement has little direct effect on trust in government or

TABLE 4.4
Determinants of trust in government and confidence in political institutions (Beta coefficients)

	Confidence Fed. gov't	Trust Fed. gov't	Confidence Police	Confidence Parties	Confidence Sup. court	Confidence Prov. gov't	Trust Prov. gov't
Post-secondary ed'n.	**0.072**	**0.063**	0.043	-0.003	**0.101**	-0.029	-0.059
Age in years	**-0.096**	**-0.142**	0.001	-0.043	**-0.082**	**-0.098**	**-0.175**
Married	0.051	0.032	**0.140**	0.052	0.030	**0.061**	0.057
Full-time employmt	0.013	-0.004	0.054	0.021	0.018	0.051	-0.013
Hhld income > $70K	**-0.128**	-0.048	-0.041	-0.064	-0.004	**-0.075**	**-0.067**
Hhld income < $30 K	-0.011	0.043	**0.075**	0.046	-0.029	-0.037	-0.018
Female	**0.070**	0.039	**0.068**	0.022	-0.005	-0.046	-0.035
Rural	**-0.076**	**-0.071**	-0.039	**-0.076**	**-0.113**	-0.044	**-0.058**
Civic engagemt	0.045	0.033	0.058	**0.067**	0.092	0.029	0.025
Professional engagemt	0.003	0.033	-0.052	-0.038	0.019	**-0.119**	-0.058
Political engagemt	-0.043	**-0.075**	**-0.068**	0.003	**-0.075**	**-0.082**	**-0.094**
Trusting	**0.119**	**0.213**	**0.248**	**0.146**	**0.137**	**0.081**	**0.112**
Very happy	0.003	0.044	0.050	**0.076**	0.035	**0.063**	0.030
Efficacious	**0.080**	0.052	-0.001	**0.097**	0.055	**0.076**	0.052
Federal Reform supp.	**-0.097**	**-0.132**	0.009	0.043	**-0.162**	**0.335**	**0.303**
Federal Liberal supp.	**0.159**	**0.119**	**0.064**	0.046	0.035	0.017	-0.028
R-square	0.119	0.146	0.124	0.069	0.117	0.18	0.168

Variables in bold statistically significant at 0.05

confidence in public institutions. The bivariate relationship between civic engagement and the measures of trust and confidence was statistically significant only for confidence in the Supreme Court, political parties, the police, and the federal government. In the regression analysis, civic engagement was a statistically significant predictor only of confidence in political parties. Breaking civic engagement down into its constituent parts, we find that only church involvement, membership in an ethnic group, and membership in a recreational association have a consistent positive relationship with the measures of trust and confidence (data not shown). Overall, these findings suggest that if civic engagement has any meaningful effect on confidence in government, it is mainly indirect. That is, it occurs through the effect of civic engagement on interpersonal trust, and of interpersonal trust on trust and confidence in political institutions.

Measures of trust and confidence in government cannot be separated from evaluations of government performance and respondents' partisan attachments and ideological predispositions. It is not surprising that political affiliation had a strong effect on trust and confidence in both levels of government. Regression analysis showed that the strongest predictor of confidence in the federal (Liberal) government and the fourth strongest predictor of trust in the federal government was identification as a federal Liberal. Identification as a federal Reform supporter had a strong and statistically significant negative effect on both measures. Even more striking was the very strong effect of provincial Progressive Conservative affiliation on trust and confidence in the PC provincial government of Alberta (see table 4.4).

Political efficacy (measured as those who agree or strongly agree with the statement 'The average person can influence political decisions') was a statistically significant predictor of confidence in the federal government, the provincial government, and political parties (see table 4.4). At first glance, this appears to contradict Roese's finding that a sense of efficacy contributed to *less* confidence in government, not more. It should be noted, however, that Roese is employing a measure of general efficacy, while this study employs a measure of political efficacy. No measure comparable to that employed by Roese was available in this data set. It is a rather different thing to conclude that those who believe they can influence political outcomes have the greatest confidence in the political system than to conclude that those who believe they can control their surroundings have greater confidence. Nonetheless, the finding does suggest the need to probe the efficacy–trust in government relationship more thoroughly in future studies.

The regression analysis found support for Roese's conclusion that political activism contributes to distrust in government. Political engagement has a statistically significant negative effect on all the measures of trust and confidence in government, with the exception of confidence in the federal government and in political parties. When political engagement is broken down into its component parts, we find that membership in a political party has a weak negative effect on all measures of trust and confidence except confidence in political parties. Membership in a political action group has a stronger and consistently negative effect. This lends some support to the cognitive-mobilization approach, as it suggests that individuals who are more closely involved with the political system are dissatisfied with what they see. That said, it is also possible that much of the political activism reported is of a uniquely Albertan variety – membership in the anti-statist Reform party or membership in a group hostile to government like the Canadian Taxpayers' Federation or the National Citizens' Coalition.

The effect of age on measures of trust and confidence in government is intriguing. Both the civil-society and the cognitive-mobilization approaches suggest that age should be positively correlated with trust in government and confidence in political institutions. According to Putnam, generations born after the Second World War are less civic and should, consequently, be less trusting of others and less trusting in government and public institutions. Similarly, the cognitive-mobilization approach holds that younger, better-educated, and more cognitively mobile generations will prefer newer, non-traditional modes of political participation, while older generations will remain more supportive of traditional political institutions.[45]

Contrary to these expectations, we find that among respondents to the ACSS, respondents under the age of thirty-five are the least trusting of others, but the *most* trusting of governments, and have the greatest confidence in political institutions (see figures 4.12 and 4.13). As table 4.4 shows, age has a statistically significant negative effect on all but two of the measures of trust and confidence. Younger baby boomers (age 35–44) express the least confidence in political institutions. These findings are not entirely inconsistent with Nevitte's findings. In his analysis of 1990 survey data, he finds that the cohort the least confident in government institutions are those aged 25 to 34.[46] This is essentially the same cohort that is aged 35 to 44 in the 1999 ACSS. The relationship

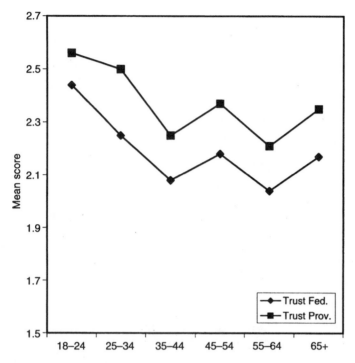

Figure 4.12 Trust in government by age

between interpersonal trust exists among all age cohorts, demonstrating that age and interpersonal trust have independent effects on confidence in government.

The generational effect shown in these findings is intriguing. If, in fact, it demonstrates a cohort effect and not a life-cycle effect, then it suggests that confidence in government will increase over time as new generations replace the cynical baby boomers in the population. Figure 4.14 shows the relationship between age and confidence in government institutions among Canadians (using 1997 Canadian Election Study data). Although the pattern is slightly less stark than in the ACCS data, the same pattern holds: respondents aged 33 to 52 in 1997 (the same cohort as those aged 35 to 54 in the 1999 ACCS) were the least confident in political institutions.[47] If these same patterns hold over time, we can expect the current crisis of confidence in government to wane somewhat as baby boomers become a smaller proportion of the population.

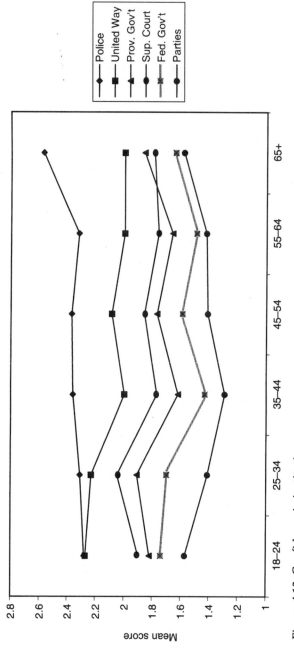

Figure 4.13 Confidence in institutions

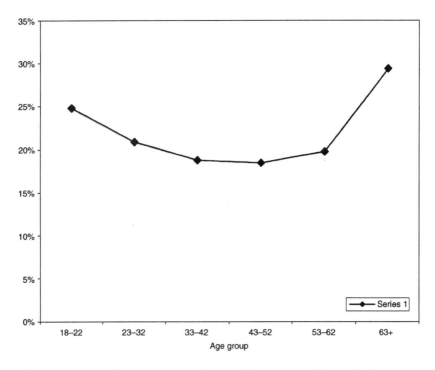

Figure 4.14 Canadians expressing high confidence in public institutions

This analysis of survey data from Alberta suggests that there is some evidence supporting the basic civil society/social capital argument. Civic engagement does, to some degree, predict interpersonal trust. In part, the relationship between the two concepts can be attributed to their common determinants: age, post-secondary education, being married, and relative affluence. Beyond this, however, there is some evidence that involvement in the associations that make up civil society does foster trust of one's fellow citizens. Although civic engagement is not directly correlated with trust and confidence in political institutions, interpersonal trust is a strong predictor of both trust and confidence in political institutions. This finding lends some credence to the argument made by Putnam and others that declining civic engagement and interpersonal trust may, in turn, contribute to declining confidence in political institutions.

Policy Implications

At the outset of this paper, it was noted that the findings presented were only preliminary. They are based on survey results from one somewhat atypical province (Alberta) and the results themselves are not entirely conclusive. More extensive research should be undertaken before policy initiatives based on these findings are launched. That said, it is useful to consider at least in a preliminary way the kinds of policy initiatives that might respond to the findings of this study. Developing such policy is a difficult task. The civil-society argument is at its heart communitarian: it envisions extensive voluntary, collective undertakings in the realm of civil society as the basis on which democratic governance rests. If civil society in Canada or the United States has declined in recent decades, it is due in part to an atomistic, individualist ethic in those societies. Moreover, civil society is by definition outside the realm of the state. There are limits, then, to the capacity for public policy to reinvigorate civil society. In a society that values individual autonomy and diversity, there is little room for state intervention in certain areas. For example, regular attendance at religious services is portrayed in much of this literature as an important predictor or element of civic engagement. Requiring, or even directly encouraging, such attendance would, however, be a highly contentious and inappropriate role for government in a modern liberal state.

Furthermore, it is worth noting that the notion of civil society is highly flexible, and can be used to further existing agendas at either end of the political spectrum. As William Galston observes, 'this new emphasis on civil society can be hijacked: on the right, as a battering ram against government; on the left, as a vehicle for reopening the battles of the 1960s against liberalism in the name of participatory democracy.'[48] The flexibility of the notion of civil society and the potential for specific, pre-existing agendas to be played out in the name of fostering civil society reinforce the imperative to develop policy closely related to research findings when attempting to address changes in the character of civil society.

In light of these cautions, the emphasis in the following discussion will be on barriers to interpersonal trust and civic engagement, and consideration of potential remedies to these barriers. The discussion will follow the logic of the research findings, looking first at the relationship between interpersonal trust and confidence in government, and then at the relationship between civic engagement and interpersonal trust. Finally, some broader issues regarding size of government, the role of the state in managing relationships with the voluntary sector, and the importance of institutional performance will be considered.

Bolstering Interpersonal Trust

The analysis of ACSS data found that interpersonal trust was a strong predictor of trust in government and confidence in political institutions. This relationship existed independently of the effect of age. Analyses of the determinants of interpersonal trust, in turn, found that older and better-educated Albertans tended to be more trusting. While there is little that can be done about the effect of age, it is noteworthy that higher education has positive effects beyond its economic benefits. As Newton observes, '[E]ducation provides us with a common knowledge of a set of dates, places, names, events, concepts, references and quotations that help the social interaction of otherwise disparate individuals. Schools ... develop an understanding of abstract ideas such as citizenship, trust, fairness, equality, universalism, the common good, and the golden rule.'[49] The tendency toward treating secondary and post-secondary education primarily as a site for practical job training to some degree takes away from this socialization function of education. Moreover, to the degree that post-secondary education becomes financially unviable for substantial numbers of Canadians, existing differentials in both income and generalized trust will be reinforced rather than alleviated. Ensuring the accessibility of post-secondary education, then, is one means by which reserves of interpersonal trust may be maintained, if not bolstered.

The finding that fear of walking in one's neighbourhood at night was a strong predictor of low interpersonal trust raises the question of crime rates and perceptions of crime rates. It is impossible to determine whether the respondents who indicated a fear of walking in their neighbourhoods at night were responding to exaggerated perceptions of crime rates or actual risk of crime. Given evidence that Canadians' general perception is that crime rates are increasing when in fact they tend to be decreasing, there may be some role for public information campaigns to alleviate fears.

Civic Engagement and Interpersonal Trust

One of the strongest determinants of interpersonal trust among respondents to the ACSS was civic engagement, or involvement in a range of voluntary community organizations. To encourage interpersonal trust, governments can encourage civic engagement. It must, however, be acknowledged at the outset that most of the determinants of civic engagement identified in this study are beyond the reach of public policy. There is, for example, little that government can do directly to discourage television watching.

The findings that traditional family form is correlated with civic engagement might suggest the potential for policies encouraging such formations. Such policies would, however, be entirely inappropriate responses to these findings. First, the conclusion that divorce correlates with disengagement, particularly among men, does not necessarily tell us that divorce *causes* disengagement. It is entirely possible that the personal traits that contribute to disengagement also contribute to a propensity to divorce. A more useful way of thinking about the finding that traditional family form – and especially the single-income, two-parent family – is positively correlated with civic engagement would be to think in terms of time made available for community involvement. In its national survey on giving, volunteering, and participating, Statistics Canada found that the most common reason given for not volunteering was a lack of time.[50] Certainly, the advent of the two-income family has created time pressures on both women and men. This is compounded by economic pressures to work long hours or substantial overtime and, in some cases, to work at more than one job. To the extent that time pressures limit community involvement, more flexible working hours might facilitate engagement in non-work activities as well as alleviating other time pressures experienced by families. Some corporations make time available to individuals involved in the company's community events, again facilitating such engagement.[51]

Although government can legislate issues surrounding work hours and can create incentives for corporations to encourage voluntarism, it must be acknowledged that the onus for changing such practices is primarily on corporations (or on governments as employers). This raises the issue of the relationship between the market and civil society. William Galston notes that if civil society in the United States is to be bolstered, 'free market conservatives would have to acknowledge that the operation of the contemporary economy isn't always compatible with a strong civil society. While social capital is largely place-specific, our corporations give less and less weight to historic community ties.'[52] Citizens working long hours in jobs they perceive to be insecure are less available for community involvement than are individuals with secure employment and expectations of reciprocity from their employers.

Governments can facilitate civic engagement by creating legislative and regulatory frameworks that encourage the formation of voluntary associations and reduce barriers to their activities. The Canadian Panel on Accountability and Governance in the Voluntary Sector (appointed by a group of national voluntary associations) recommended that governments, along with the private sector, support capacity-building in the voluntary sector through financial contributions and by lending expertise. The panel also recommended following recent British practice, with the creation of compacts between government and the voluntary sector outlining the essentials of good practice on both sides, and allowing for consultation with the voluntary sector in policy-making. In addition, the panel recommended changes to the process for gaining tax status as a charity, creation of a Voluntary Sector Commission to increase financial accountability in the sector, and reform of the regulations for financial management of voluntary organizations.

The compact on relations between government and the voluntary sector adopted by the British government[53] is predicated on the assumption that 'voluntary and community activity is fundamental to the development of a democratic, socially inclusive, society.' In the compact, the British government undertakes to recognize the independence of the voluntary sector, to provide multi-year strategic funding to it, to evaluate new policies in terms of their potential effect on the voluntary sector, and to promote effective working relationships between government and the sector.

Although it may be difficult for government to take measures that directly encourage civic engagement, it is useful to think of civic engagement as a collateral benefit of programs designed to achieve other objectives. For example, a day-care centre run by a parents' collective draws those parents into a community organization, while a for-profit day-care centre run by a corporation treats parents simply as consumers of a service. To the extent that the civil-society argument holds true, the former organization creates a social benefit related to social capital that the latter does not. Programs delivered in such a way as to invite citizen participation add to the stock of social capital in a community. Addressing the question of how to strengthen bonds of community and citizenship in the contemporary United States, Janoski calls for increased participation in decision-making at work and in the community. Participation rights, he argues, 'are a way to carry societies toward connection.'[54] In a similar vein, Jonathan Lomas and Gerry Veenstra suggest that organizing government structures such as regional health boards in such a way as to optimize connection and collaboration would enhance social capital, in addition to serving the primary purpose of effective health delivery.[55] Such participation in the community and in the delivery of government programs would be consistent with public calls for greater citizen participation in decision-making and greater government responsiveness to citizens' demands.

Although greater citizen involvement in decision-making regarding service delivery is a desirable objective, it should be noted that there is a qualitative distinction between such measures and the offloading of responsibilities by government. There is little evidence that the retreat of the state in fact encourages the creation of social capital.

Does Government 'Crowd Out' Civic Engagement?

Some proponents of civil society argue that government has 'crowded out' civil society by assuming many of the functions formerly performed by private voluntary groups. The growth of the welfare state, according to this argument, reduced the need for private charitable organizations. As the state retreats in the contemporary era, then, civic organizations should spring up to replace it. Making essentially this argument, Galston notes that as the City of New York retrenches, 'newly revitalized neighbourhood organizations are springing up, in part to form new partnerships with the public sector, but also to fill the gap through their own voluntary efforts.'[56]

The argument that the state displaces voluntary efforts, thereby discouraging the formation of social capital, is not supported by the empirical findings of Thomas Janoski's cross-national study. This study compared rates of voluntarism in social democratic and liberal societies. Liberal societies were those that had smaller welfare states and less emphasis on social citizenship, including both the United States and Canada. The study found that once religious activity and union membership were taken out of the equation, rates of voluntary association membership were not substantially different in the two sets of countries, although the rates were slightly higher in the liberal countries. The United States, with its minimalist welfare state, actually has almost identical rates of voluntary-association membership (excluding unions and churches) to social democratic nations like Sweden, Norway, and the Netherlands, and differs little from Canada.[57] This suggests that in comprehensive welfare states, government is not crowding out voluntary effort.

Arguably, the notion that the state crowds out civil society assumes far too simple an understanding of the relationship between society and the state. In the Canadian model in particular, voluntary associations often rely heavily on government funding for their very existence. For example, a study of seventy-two non-profit social welfare agencies in the four western provinces and Ontario found that, on average, 81 per cent of the groups' annual revenues were from government.[58] Volunteers were nevertheless an integral component of service delivery by these agencies, which had sixty volunteers on average. This suggests that state support and voluntarism are complementary, rather than competitive. Again, a distinction can be drawn between partnerships between community associations and government for service delivery (which encourages civic engagement) and privatization of services (which turns social services into a commodity to be delivered by the lowest bidder).

Political Arrangements and Institutional Performance

If we accept that civic engagement and interpersonal trust contribute to confidence in political institutions, it does not necessarily follow that concerns about political arrangements and institutional performance are irrelevant. The preliminary findings in this paper suggest that the society-centred civil society / social capital hypothesis offers only a *partial* explanation for disenchantment with government and political institutions. Moreover, the statistical findings point to a *correlation* between interpersonal trust and confidence in government, but do not specify the direction of causation.

In their critique of Putnam's argument, Foley and Edwards argue that Putnam fails to take into account a political variable.[59] This variable includes both political organizations (social movements, interest groups, political parties) that play an important role in society and the prevailing political settlement that governs who plays, the rules of the game, and acceptable outcomes. Political settlements, they argue, are often the work of the best-financed or most influential elements of civil society. In this sense, political arrangements can represent a betrayal of the trust civil society placed in politicians and political parties. In short, their argument is that distrust in the political class may be a result of betrayal of trust rather than of a decline in civil society.

In a similar vein, Margaret Levi suggests that institutions, including government institutions, can influence trust, possibly by providing reassurance that defectors from societal norms will not go unpunished. Levi argues that states with a capacity to monitor laws, bring sanctions against lawbreakers, and provide information and guarantees about those seeking to be trusted are states capable of producing interpersonal trust.[60] Beyond performing these basic functions, states can further engender trust by appearing to be fair. An important means to this end is involving citizens in the policy-making process 'so that they become aware of what is at issue and are included in the give and take that leads to compromise.'[61] Finally, Levi argues that states are most likely to engender interpersonal trust when they reciprocate citizens' trust in government. Governments that deliver on their promises and treat citizens with respect, she argues, make citizens more trusting and more trustworthy.

Brehm and Rahn find empirical evidence supporting Levi's argument that the state can engender interpersonal trust. In their model, the strongest determinant of interpersonal trust is confidence in government institutions. This finding 'implies that poor performance by government can initiate downward spirals in social capital by first undermining trust, and then feeding into the reciprocal cycle.'[62] Similarly, cross-national research undertaken by Muller and Seligson concludes that low levels of interpersonal trust are not an impediment to democratization, but that long-term experience of democracy engenders interpersonal trust. Interpersonal trust, in their findings, is a product of democracy rather than a cause of it.[63] Given these findings, it is apparent that a policy approach that treated citizen disengagement and disenchantment solely as a function of social arrangements would risk exacerbating the problem by ignoring the important issue of governmental and institutional performance. In practical terms, this means that recommendations for institutional change such as those made by Docherty and Nadeau in this volume should be taken seriously. Such reforms should focus on increasing responsiveness to citizens and also on encouraging 'trustworthy' behaviour on the part of political actors.

Conclusion

The analysis presented in this chapter offers a tentative and partial explanation for citizen discontent. It finds some evidence supporting the civil society / social capital argument. Involvement in community organizations appears to contribute to interpersonal trust, which, in turn, is correlated with trust in government and confidence in political institutions. Although there are significant constraints on the capacity of government to encourage civic engagement, development of mechanisms for citizen consultation and community-based administration of services may be effective. There is little evidence that government retrenchment will encourage the development of social capital, but there is evidence suggesting that government performance can affect generalized trust.

Further research into the relationships between civic engagement, interpersonal trust, and confidence in government is required. Such research should be national in scope and sensitive to the regional and interprovincial variations that are likely to appear. It is also important that future research probe the relationships between these variables at the societal, or aggregate, level in addition to the individual. That will allow for a more thorough evaluation of the argument at the level of social organization and societal norms.

Notes

1 See Mebs Kanji (chap. 3) and Richard Nadeau (chap. 2), this volume.
2 For a review of possible explanations for this phenomenon, see Joseph Nye, 'In Government We Don't Trust,' *Foreign Policy* 108 (1997): 99–111.
3 The Alberta Civil Society Survey was undertaken by the Research Unit for the Study of Civil Society at the University of Calgary. Funding for the survey was provided by the Donner Foundation. Neither RUSCS nor the Donner Foundation bears any responsibility for the analysis presented here.
4 See Gabriel Almond and Sidney Verba, *The Civic Culture: Political Attitudes and Democracy in Five Nations* (Princeton, NJ: Princeton University Press, 1963) and Ronald Inglehart, *Culture Shift in Advanced Industrial Society* (Princeton: Princeton University Press, 1990). This is, however, contested by other findings: see Edward Muller and Mitchell A. Seligson, 'Civic Culture and Democracy: The Question of Causal Relationships,' *American Political Science Review* 88(3) (1994): 635–52.
5 John Brehm and Wendy Rahn, 'Individual Level Evidence for the Causes and Consequences of Social Capital,' *American Journal of Political Science* 41(3) (1997): 999–1023.
6 For an excellent review of this literature, see Pauleen O'Connor, *Mapping Social Cohesion*, CPRN Discussion Paper no. F.01, 1998; available at http://www.cprn.ca.

7 William A. Galston, 'Won't You Be My Neighbor?' *The American Prospect*, no. 26 (1996): 16.

8 Bob Edwards and Michael W. Foley, 'The Paradox of Civil Society,' *Journal of Democracy* 7 (3) (1996).

9 Thomas Janoski, *Citizenship and Civil Society: A Framework of Rights and Obligations in Liberal, Traditional and Social Democratic Regimes* (Cambridge: Cambridge University Press, 1998), 12–13.

10 Robert Putnam, 'Tuning in, Tuning Out: The Strange Disappearance of Social Capital in America,' *PS: Political Science and Politics* 28 (December 1995): 664.

11 Robert Putnam, *Making Democracy Work: Civic Traditions in Modern Italy* (Princeton: Princeton University Press, 1993), 171.

12 Kenneth Newton, 'Social Capital and Democracy,' *American Behavioral Scientist* 40(5) (1997): 575–86.

13 Putnam, *Making Democracy Work*, 171–2.

14 Ibid., 173–4.

15 Newton, 'Social Capital and Democracy,' 579.

16 Ibid., 579.

17 Ibid., 581.

18 O'Connor, *Mapping Social Cohesion*, 13.

19 Nina Eliasoph, *Avoiding Politics: How Americans Produce Apathy in Everyday Life* (Cambridge: Cambridge University Press, 1998).

20 Ibid., 230.

21 Ibid.

22 Jan van Deth, 'Interesting but Irrelevant: Social Capital and the Saliency of Politics in Western Europe,' *European Journal of Political Research* 37 (2000): 115–47.

23 Brehm and Rahn, 'Individual Level Evidence,' 1000.

24 Ibid.

25 Robert Putnam, 'Bowling Alone: America's Declining Social Capital,' *Journal of Democracy* 28 (1995): 666.

26 Statistics Canada, *Caring Canadians, Involved Canadians: Highlights from the 1997 National Survey of Giving, Volunteering and Participating* (Ottawa: Minister Responsible for Statistics Canada, 1998), 27.

27 A Statistics Canada survey of civic participation found slightly different patterns of associational involvement. Respondents to the survey most frequently reported activity in work-related organizations, followed by sports or recreation, religious, community or school-related, cultural/educational/hobby-related, service club, and finally political organizations. See Statistics Canada, *Caring Canadians*, 43.

28 Reported membership in political parties is surprisingly high.

29 Reliability analysis produced alpha scores of 0.4124 for the civic engagement index, 0.1674 for the market engagement index, and 0.2460 for the
political engagement index. This suggests that the civic engagement index
captures most closely the concept it is trying to measure. The alpha scores
for the professional and political engagement indexes are poor; this reflects
a low degree of correlation among items included in them. They were
nonetheless retained because they reflect the definitions of market-related
and political engagement. Where appropriate, all three indices are
disaggregated to demonstrate the effect of particular kinds of engagement
on other variables.

30 Putnam, 'Tuning In, Tuning Out.'

31 Brehm and Rahn, 'Individual Level Evidence,' 1015.

32 Putnam, 'Tuning In, Tuning Out.'

33 A 1997 Statistics Canada survey, which included work-related groups in
its definition of organizations, found that the age cohort the most likely to
participate was aged 45–54, followed by the cohort aged 35–44, and then
by the cohort aged 55–64. Looking at participation rates for voluntarism,
the same survey found that the cohort aged 35–44 was the most active,
followed by the cohort aged 45–54, and then by the cohort aged 15–24.
This directly contradicts Putnam's 'long civic generation' argument. See
Statistics Canada, *Caring Canadians*, 44, 29.

34 The measure of civic engagement being employed in this analysis is highly
sensitive to variations in the level of involvement; respondents score the
highest if they hold a leadership position in one of the categories of organizations. This could produce an age effect, as younger individuals might
not be considered eligible to hold a leadership position in an organization.
To test for this, an alternative measure was created that coded holding a
leadership position the same as being an active member of a group. The
age breakdown on the measures of engagement did not change at all with
this alternative measure.

35 Brehm and Rahn, 'Individual Level Evidence,' 1015–16.

36 See O'Connor, *Mapping Social Cohesion*.

37 The alpha score measuring the reliability of this scale was 0.4476.

38 Pearson's correlation coefficient of 0.203 for civic engagement, as compared to 0.06 for professional and 0.09 for political.

39 Edwards and Foley, 'The Paradox of Civil Society,' 49.

40 Newton, 'Social Capital and Democracy,' 579.

41 See Russell J. Dalton, *Citizen Politics in Western Democracies: Public Opinion
and Political Parties in the United States, Great Britain, West Germany and*

France, 1st ed. (Chatham, NJ: Chatham House, 1988); and Neil Nevitte, *The Decline of Deference* (Peterborough, ON: Broadview Press, 1996).

42 Brehm and Rahn, 'Individual Level Evidence,' 1015.

43 See Nevitte, *Decline of Deference*.

44 It should be noted that interpersonal trust is also positively correlated with confidence in non-governmental organizations, including small business, the United Way, and organized religion.

45 Nevitte, *Decline of Deference*, 55.

46 Ibid., 57; see figures 3–4.

47 This index was compiled from four measures of confidence: in the federal government, the provincial government, the courts, and the civil service. The alpha measure of reliability for the index was 0.6645.

48 Galston, 'Won't You Be My Neighbor?' 16.

49 Newton, 'Social Capital and Democracy,' 580.

50 Statistics Canada, *Caring Canadians*, 38.

51 It must be recognized that corporations pursue their own public-relations objectives in their charitable activity; in this sense, these are not entirely voluntary undertakings.

52 Galston, 'Won't You Be My Neighbor?' 17.

53 United Kingdom, *Compact on Relations between Government and the Voluntary and Community Sector in England* (London: Queen's Printer, 1998).

54 Janoski, *Citizenship and Civil Society*, 233.

55 O'Connor, *Mapping Social Cohesion*, 4.

56 Galston, 'Won't You Be My Neighbor?' 17.

57 Janoski, *Citizenship and Civil Society*, 134–5.

58 Canada West Foundation, *Alternative Service Delivery Project: Research Bulletin* (Calgary: Canada West Foundation, 1999).

59 Edwards and Foley, 'Paradox of Civil Society.'

60 Margaret Levi, 'A State of Trust,' in V.A. Braithwaite and M. Levi, eds, *Trust and Governance* (New York: Sage, 1998), 85; see also M. Levi, 'Social and Unsocial Capital: A Review Essay of Robert Putnam's *Making Democracy Work*,' *Politics and Society* 24 (1996): 45–55.

61 Levi, 'A State of Trust,' 92.

62 Brehm and Rahn, 'Individual Level Evidence,' 1014.

63 See Muller and Seligson, 'Civic Culture and Democracy.'

5. Canadians' Shrinking Trust in Government: Causes and Consequences

Neal J. Roese

This chapter confirms that Canadians are increasingly less trusting of the Canadian government, but also that this trend is common to other Western industrial nations. If trust is indeed decreasing among Canadians, an important issue for the next century is the means by which the government might regain the public's trust. The evidence suggest that declining trust is not a product of general isolation or disenfranchisement, but on the contrary is related to increasing feelings of empowerment and also increasing political activism among Canadians. Attempts to regain the public's trust should be cognizant of, but possibly also capitalize on, the fact that Canadians are on average becoming more sophisticated and active in their political participation.

Are Canadians Becoming Less Trusting of Government?

This chapter centres on the implications of declining trust by Canadians in their government. Trust refers to an individual's confidence that other people, objects, or institutions will behave as expected or as promised. On a more basic level, every society is held together by trust. If one cannot trust other individuals to do as they say, then an intrinsic bond connecting individuals is broken. Interpersonal trust – the trust existing among individuals in their daily interactions – has been taken by many to be a cornerstone of mental health, with declines in interpersonal trust associated with depression, anxiety disorders, and even schizophrenic disorders. This chapter focuses on a more general form of trust – the trust individuals have for the institution of government.

Traditionally, observers have assumed that reduced trust in government constitutes, at worst, a symptom of the decline of democracy. If trust is indeed decreasing among Canadians, an important question is raised: what will be the means by which governments might regain the public's trust?

This chapter explores the issue of trust in government in five parts. First, the consequences of declining trust in government are considered. These consequences speak to the issue of 'why' it is important to consider trust at all. Second, evidence for a decline in trust in government in Canada is reviewed. Third, several patterns are examined that help to clarify the nature of trust, particularly in terms of how general or wide-ranging the effect might be. Fourth, possible causes of reduced trust in government are examined from a psychological standpoint. And fifth, possible causes of reduced trust in government are examined with regard to political attitudes and activist behaviours. The conclusions examine the public policy implications of the findings from the analysis.

1. Consequences of a Decline in Interpersonal Trust

Why is it important to understand trust? Consequences that emerge from a decline in trust have been studied in a variety of contexts, and span several academic disciplines. For example, at the purely interpersonal level, a low level of trust is considered to be a symptom of emotional and social maladjustment, and extreme lack of trust is associated with mental disorders ranging from depression to schizophrenia.[1] Trust has also been conceptualized at the institutional level as a property of large organizations: government and corporations, for example, can be interpreted by citizens as relatively more or less trustworthy.[2]

Generally speaking, two overarching interpretations of reduced trust in government present themselves, one negative and one positive. The negative interpretation, which is relatively more common in academic discourse, centres on individual political disengagement.[3] The positive interpretation, by contrast, centres on the value of healthy scepticism born of increasing individual cognitive sophistication.[4] Summarized first are several arguments and evidence regarding the negative interpretation.

1. Reduction in trust can contribute to excessive self-interest and behaviours that are deleterious at the group level. For example, the depletion of deteriorating, non-renewable resources is exacerbated by the behaviour of individuals who are low in trust, but slowed by

individuals demonstrating relatively greater levels of trust.[5] In essence, belief that government is untrustworthy increases 'looking out for number one.'

2. Reduced trust may cause reduced political involvement. The electorate as a whole may withdraw from the political process, effectively dismantling the democracy and leaving power and governance to elites. Reduced trust generally breeds an environment of cynicism and self-interest, while participation in voluntary pro-social activities wanes.[6] The findings in this report contradict this notion, showing that increased political involvement may unleash narrowly specific forms of distrust.

3. Decreased trust may exacerbate the disenfranchisement of already marginalized members of society. One specific form that this may take is the encouragement of unsubstantiated conspiracy theories involving secret government plots.[7]

4. Reduced trust affects politicians themselves, in that it may encourage an 'obsessive concern with their public image.'[8] This may then result in heightened attention to public poll information at the expense of more informative, directly data-driven sources of information. Clearly, politicians expect to preserve a balance between attention to popular concerns (a hallmark of democracy) and attention to internally derived agendas. If politicians fear that they have lost public confidence, the delicate balance between these forces may be severely disrupted.

By contrast, the positive interpretation notes that blind trust in any person or institution is detrimental to one's own interests, and that a healthy scepticism is closely intertwined with heightened attention to, vigilance toward, and knowledge about an institution. In short, scepticism might be associated with a greater rather than lesser political engagement. Turning to the evidence examined here, we find that it tends to support this latter, positive interpretation.

2. Evidence for a Decline in Trust

Trust refers to the confidence one has that people, objects, or institutions will behave as expected or as promised. Trust is a straightforward psychological state that can be directed toward numerous objects, from close others to corporate entities to nation states. The focus of this report is on trust in the Canadian federal government. Evidence from a variety of sources indicates that Canadians have over several decades become less trusting of the federal government to 'do what is right.'[9]

TABLE 5.1
Decline in trust in government

Question	Year			
	1965	1968	1988	1993
Trust	58%	58%	48%	33%
Crooked	24	–	46	45
Waste	36	–	65	79

Source: Canadian National Election Survey.

Note: For the 'Trust' question, the percentage refers to the proportion of people selecting 'just about always' or 'most of the time' in response to the question 'How much of the time can you trust the government in Ottawa to do what is right?' For the 'Crooked' question, the percentage refers to the proportion of people indicating that 'quite a few of the people running the government are a little crooked.' For the 'Waste' question, the percentage refers to the proportion of people indicating that 'people in the government waste a lot of the money we pay in taxes.'

Canadian National Election Survey. This survey provides information on trust from the mid-1960s through to the 1990s. The survey contains several questions regarding trust, the most of important of which concerns the extent to which respondents feel they can 'trust the government to do what is right.' From 1965 to 1993, responses to this question show a decrease in trust (see table 5.1). The drops from 1984 to 1988, and from 1988 to 1993 are statistically significant. Questions focusing on perceptions of politicians' crookedness and politicians' wasting of tax dollars show similar patterns (in these cases, perceptions of crookedness and waste increased; see table 5.1.

World Values Survey. This survey was conducted in 1981 and 1990 in several dozen nations around the world, providing insight into changes in trust over time not only for Canada but other industrial democracies. A 'trust score' was created by averaging responses to three questions regarding confidence in parliament, the civil service, and the legal system. On a scale of 1 to 4 (where 1 = no confidence at all and 4 = a great deal of confidence), trust declined between 1981 ($M = 2.54$) and 1990 ($M = 2.46$), $F(1, 2866) = 13.97, p < .0001$.[10]

Trust Relative to Other Western Nations. It is easy to generate explanations for a decline in trust that centre on particular political events in Canada, but these types of explanations cannot account for the fact that the same pattern appears in other Western nations.

Trust in government has declined in the United States in a manner that closely parallels the Canadian trend. A particularly useful index for gauging shifts in trust in the United States has been a 'trust in government index,' composed of responses to four questions included in the biennial National Election Survey run by the Center for Political Studies at the University of Michigan. Generally speaking, trust in government remained unchanged between 1958 and 1964, but declined steadily over the next twenty years,[11] with the most rapid declines occurring in the late 1960s and 1970s. Levels of trust rose briefly in the mid-1980s, then continued to decline into the 1990s.[12]

The World Values Surveys provide data on trust in government in many nations. Unless otherwise noted, findings in the remainder of this report derive from this source. For present purposes, the most instructive comparison is between Canada, the United States, and an aggregate of European industrial nations (Britain, France, Germany, Italy, and the Netherlands). Across all three, confidence in government declined between 1981 and 1990. Using the same 'trust score' mentioned previously (i.e., averaged responses to questions regarding confidence in parliament, the civil service, and the legal system), trust declined in the United States between 1981 ($M = 2.66$) and 1990 ($M = 2.57$), $F(1, 3850) = 17.73, p < .0001$. It also decreased among European nations between 1981 ($M = 2.45$) and 1990 ($M = 2.39$), $F(1, 12483) = 26.38$, $p < .0001$.

Thus, a decline in trust in government is not unique to Canada: it is clearly a feature common to other industrial democracies. This would suggest that we should refrain from looking for causes that are unique to Canada, such as specific domestic political scandals. Rather, the search might more profitably be directed to causes that have impinged upon many western nations over the same period of time.

3. Clarifying the Nature of Trust

The World Values Surveys provide information regarding a variety of personal beliefs and values that may or may not be related to trust in government. By looking at Canadians' responses to various questions related to trust, we can more clearly articulate the context for shifts in trust in government.

A decline in trust in government might be due to a general anomie or malaise that would contribute to distrust in both other persons and large institutions. Indeed, some have argued that modern industrial economies coupled with the rise of television produce a general social isolation or lack of connectedness between individuals.[13] This line of thinking was not supported, however. General interpersonal trust has in fact been *on the rise* in Canada. In response to the question 'Generally speaking, would you say that most people can be trusted or that you can't be too careful in dealing with people?', the proportion of Canadians selecting 'most people can be trusted' increased from 48.5 per cent in 1981 to 53.1 per cent in 1990, an increase that was statistically significant, $F(1, 2888) = 5.97$, $p = .015$. In other words, decreasing trust in government is not associated with a more general decline in interpersonal trust.

Another suggestion made by recent theorists[14] is that people have become more cynical about large institutions in general, and that this includes not only government but also large corporations. This argument holds some merit, as confidence in large corporations has also declined among Canadians. On a scale of 1 to 4 (where 1 = no confidence at all and 4 = a great deal of confidence), trust in 'major companies' declined from 1981 ($M = 2.58$) and 1990 ($M = 2.51$), $F(1, 2877) = 6.69$, $p = .01$. This trend, however, is somewhat weaker than the decline in trust in government. Interestingly, there is no such decline among Americans, who voiced exactly the same level of confidence toward major companies in 1981 ($M = 2.53$) as they did in 1990 ($M = 2.53$), $F(1, 4072) = .035$, $p = .85$.

To summarize, the decline in trust in government is not related to declines in interpersonal trust, but it does seem to be part of an increasing distrust of large institutions. These findings help to bracket and define the effect of interest. Distrust of government is focused and specific.

4. Psychological Factors

Although we have seen that there is not a general, pervasive lack of trust of fellow citizens, it might still be possible that specific psychological factors centring on feelings of reduced empowerment, reduced satisfaction, or reduced happiness might be at the heart of declining trust in government. For example, unemployment unleashes a host of negative psychological consequences, such as feelings of lack of control, anxiety, and depression.[15] Thus, any shifts in the economic status of Canadians would be expected to produce negative emotional consequences that might subsequently produce distrust in government institutions.

The above line of thinking was not supported, however, as there have been no shifts in Canadians' levels of satisfaction. In the following items, questions about satisfaction were answered using scales ranging from 1 to 10 (where 1 = dissatisfied and 10 = satisfied). In terms of general life satisfaction, Canadians in 1981 were just as satisfied with their 'life as a whole' ($M = 7.82$) as they were in 1990 ($M = 7.89$), $F(1, 2975) = 1.22$, $p = .27$. Canadians in 1981 were just as satisfied with the financial situation of their household ($M = 7.27$) as they were in 1990 ($M = 7.13$), $F(1, 2955) = 2.79$, $p = .10$; were just as satisfied with their jobs ($M = 7.97$) as they were in 1990 ($M = 7.88$), $F(1, 1773) = .86$, $p = .36$; and were just as satisfied with their home life ($M = 8.36$) as they were in 1990 ($M = 8.41$), $F(1, 2976) = .54$, $p = .46$. To conclude, there were no statistically reliable shifts in Canadians' satisfaction with their lives, finances, jobs, or domestic situations over the same period that saw a reliable decrease in trust in government. This finding seems to parallel a similar one in the United States, namely, that economic shifts cannot account for the entirety of declining trust in government.[16]

One psychological variable contains an important clue as to the nature of declining trust: self-efficacy, or perceived control. In psychological research, the extent to which an individual feels 'in control' of his or her life has numerous benefits, including improved health, more active social engagement, and greater resistance to the stressors of daily life.[17] More important, self-efficacy predicts action. People are more likely to engage in protest behaviour, volunteer for community service, and in general participate in civic life to the extent that they believe that they personally have the power to change outcomes. And Canadians increasingly do believe that they have this power. Canadians indicated 'how much freedom of choice and control' they felt they had over the way their 'life turns out' along a scale ranging from 1 to 10 (where 1 = none at all and 10 = a great deal). In 1981, Canadians gave an average rating of 7.25, but in 1990 this had jumped to 7.55, an increase that was statistically significant, $F(1, 2959) = 18.36$, $p < .0001$. This increase in self-efficacy – the belief that one has the ability and power to change the course of events – is an essential ingredient in a broader set of changes that correspond to declines in trust in government, as described in the next section.

5. Declining Trust Is Related to Increasing Political Activism and Awareness

The picture that emerges from the World Values Survey is that the decline in trust corresponds to an increasingly sophisticated and involved Canadian electorate (see Kanji's discussion of cognitive mobilization in chapter 3 of this volume). As Canadians become better educated, more aware, and more politically active, their sharper gaze has uncovered more that displeases them. This general pattern is revealed by variables that speak to this issue of citizen involvement.

The most important predictor of the decline in trust is political activism. The extent to which Canadians were engaged in political activities such as signing petitions, joining boycotts, attending demonstrations, joining strikes, and occupying buildings increased between 1981 and 1990. Canadians rated each of these five behaviours according to a 3-point scale, where 1 = would never do, 2 = might do, and 3 = have done. Thus, greater numbers indicate greater behavioural engagement in political activism. These five responses were averaged to produce an index. Canadians reported greater activism in 1990 ($M = 1.77$) than they had in 1981 ($M = 1.63$), an increase that was significant, $F(1, 2977) = 58.41, p < .0001$. Precisely the same pattern occurred in the Unites States and in Western Europe.

In addition, it seems that this rise in activism does directly explain at least some of the decline in trust in government. In other words, those individuals who indicated relatively greater distrust of government also tended to show greater activism. This type of mediation was supported by the finding that activism was a reliable covariate in the difference between 1981 and 1990 in trust in government, $F(1, 2862) = 33.12, p < .0001$. The magnitude of that difference in trust was reduced from $F = 13.97$ to $F = 9.27$, indicating that activism mediated (i.e., explained) some but not all of that decline in trust.

The activism index of Canadians' political behaviour is supplemented by measures of particular political attitudes (see table 5.2). There has been an increase both in proselytization (i.e., how often an individual attempts to persuade friends, relatives, or fellow workers to share his or her view) and in self-reported interest in politics. In the first case, respondents used a scale to indicate frequency of proselytization (where 1 = never and 4 = often). Canadians reported greater frequency in 1990 ($M = 2.60$) than in 1980 ($M = 2.46$), $F(1, 2982) = 16.88, p < .0001$. Interest in politics was reported using a scale where 1 = not at all interested and 4 = very interested. Canadians reported greater political interest in 1990 ($M = 2.63$) than in 1980 ($M = 2.39$), $F(1, 2977) = 44.94, p < .0001$. Although these variables shifted reliably over time, they were not reliable mediators of the decline in trust. That is, they appear to have shifted coinci-

TABLE 5.2
Comparison of key variables, 1981–1990

	1981	1990
Trust in government	2.54	2.46
Trust in major companies	2.58	2.51
Activism	1.63	1.77
Self-efficacy	7.25	7.55
Persuade friends	2.46	2.60
Interested in politics	2.39	2.63
Left vs right	5.85	5.64

Source: World Values Survey.

dentally, rather than in a manner that is more deeply related to trust in government.

General political leanings, on the other hand, did appear to underlie at least part of the decline in trust in government. Canadians described their own political orientation on a scale where 1 = left and 10 = right. The statistically reliable shift over time would best be described as a movement toward the centre of the political spectrum, $F(1, 2372) = 8.73$, $p = .003$. The theoretical mid-point of a 10-point scale is 5.5. In 1981, Canadians described their political orientation with a mean value of 5.85, whereas in 1990 they placed themselves at 5.64, which is closer to the mid-point of the scale (it is also a shift to the left, but note that the mean in 1990 still sits within the 'right' half of the scale). This shift toward the political centre mediated the decline in trust in government, as it was a marginally significant covariate in the difference between 1981 and 1990 in trust in government, $F(1, 2317) = 5.37$, $p = .021$. The magnitude of that difference in trust was reduced from $F = 13.97$ to $F = 6.34$, suggesting that political orientation underpinned some (but certainly not all) of that decline in trust.[18]

Summary. The above variables that shifted between 1981 and 1990 were entered as predictors into a regression analysis in which the trust index was the dependent variable. Only 1990 Canadian data were used. This analysis revealed only two reliable, independent predictors of trust: self-efficacy and political activism (see table 5.3). For comparative purposes, the same regression was run for the United States and also western Europe. Roughly the same pattern was obtained in the U.S. as in Canada, but in Europe there was a tendency for more of these variables to be independently predictive of declining trust. In Canada,

TABLE 5.3
Predictors of trust in government, 1990 Canada sample

Predictor	Canada	U.S.	Europe
Activism	−.12*	−.16*	−.11*
Self-efficacy	−.08*	−.07*	−.05*
Persuade friends	.00	−.01	−.04*
Interest in politics	−.01	.09*	.17*
Left vs right	−.02	−.06	−.12*

Source: World Values Survey.

*significant at p < .01

however, the extent to which individuals believed that their own actions could change external events, coupled with the extent to which they actually engaged in politically oriented actions, reliably predicted trust. In other words, the more empowered Canadians felt, the less they trusted their government.

It should be noted that this finding is somewhat different than one found by Young (chapter 4, this volume). In her analysis of data from Alberta, Young found that self-efficacy was related to greater rather than less confidence in government. The two measures of efficacy were not entirely the same, however: general perceptions of control in the present analysis; specific political efficacy in Young's analysis. Thus, Young concluded that 'it is a rather different thing to conclude that those who believe they can influence political outcomes have the greatest confidence in the political system than to conclude that those who believe they can control their surroundings have greater confidence.'

6. Analysis and Recommendations

This analysis of the decline in trust in government among Canadian citizens paints an overall picture that is encouraging. Declining trust has not, as some have warned, coincided with greater citizen disengagement and thus a weakening of the essence of democracy. To the contrary, declining trust is closely related to increases in personal feelings of empowerment, political activism, and political awareness. As well, interpersonal trust, defined in terms of the individual's perceptions of other individuals encountered on a daily basis, is increasing rather than decreasing, and hence is not a component of the observation that trust in government is shrinking. Canadians are becoming more interested in the way their government does business, and they are thus directing a keener gaze toward specific government actions. Moreover, this pattern is not unique to Canada, but characterizes the United States and western European nations as well.[19]

To be sure, however, this is hardly a complete picture of trust in Canada. Numerous other factors likely play a role, but were not available for direct analysis, or are of relatively lesser utility because they are impossible to alter in the service of improving trust. Several examples of additional factors influencing trust in government are listed below:

(1) Changes in the media. Over the last thirty years, popular news coverage has evolved from being a relatively passive conveyor of information into a more active investigator of scandal.[20] For example, politicians' adulterous liaisons were largely ignored by the press of the early 1960s, but were headline news in the late 1990s. Content analyses of news coverage have revealed that stories about politicians and government have become more evaluative and more negative over the last two decades. Campaign advertising has also, of course, become more negative in tone,[21] but in addition, news media replay and analyse these negative ads, such that the 'combination of negative ads plus negative coverage demarkets government and contributes to a popular view of bad government.'[22]

(2) Changes in prosperity. The focus of this explanation has been on the increases in prosperity enjoyed by Western nations over the last forty years.[23] According to this postmaterialist argument, greater prosperity shifts one's focus of attention generally away from basic needs such as food and shelter to issues of luxury, leisure, and acquisition. Heightened expectations (particularly as a consequence of the 1950s economic boom in North America) are difficult to meet, and the government is increasingly held accountable for problems whose solutions were either previously seen to be unattainable or outside the purview of government.

Summary and recommendations. Overall, the results of the present investigation suggest that greater empowerment and action by individuals has been tightly related to declines in trust in government. Although the media and the relative prosperity of the West may also influence trust in government, these variables were not available for direct analysis. What follows are some brief suggestions for policy based directly on the findings of this report.

(1) Trust might be regained to the extent that the government recognizes and caters to its citizens' increasing political involvement. Nadeau (chapter 2, this volume) discusses some relatively ambitious changes

that would accommodate the changing citizenry, including parliamentary reform. The changes he discusses are certainly compatible with the present conclusions, but my recommendaitons here, in contrast, focus on more modest and immediately achievable goals. As we enter a new century, Canadians are extremely well positioned to take advantage of new information technologies that might contribute to greater 'transparency' in the process of government, thereby satisfying the increasing appetite for information about government. For example, the Internet could be used to make detailed information on government procedure available to the general public. At present, some information is available on Government of Canada web sites, but these continue to be extremely limited.

(2) Political advertising and publicly available information referred to avoid overly simplistic sloganeering and appeal to basic emotions. If part of the shift among Canadians centres on increased political awareness, then political messages should be compatible with this change. Among theorists who study persuasion, a rule of thumb is that slogans and emotional appeals are effective only to the extent that the audience is inattentive or disengaged. Persuasion among highly involved individuals occurs more effectively when messages are coherent and well supported with detailed information.[24]

It should be emphasized that the public information referred to here is not politicians' election campaign advertising, which many have noted is increasingly emotional rather than informative.[25] Such advertising is often under the direct control of individual politicians and is unlikely to change as long as such politicians believe in the effectiveness of emotional appeals. Rather, the argument here is that aspects of the operation of government per se, such as brochures, web documents, and television commentary by civil servants might focus more effectively on basic information, conveyed in larger quantities, in a clear yet sophisticated manner.

(3) A third suggestion is that the information made available to the public be as much about procedures as it is about outcomes and events. That is, information that emphasizes the fairness of a variety of government processes can contribute to greater trust. This conclusion derives from a wealth of research in social psychology indicating that satisfaction levels for outcomes (from small group decisions to local election outcomes) are influenced not only on the basis of pure self-interest (i.e., whether the outcome benefits the individual personally) but also and importantly on the extent to which the outcomes were presumed to follow from fair and just procedures.[26]

7. Conclusions

Limitations of This Research. This overview of survey findings is essentially a snapshot of the period in Canada between 1981 and 1990. The report itself was written in 1999. Mebs Kanji's report (chapter 3, this volume) report does suggest that the patterns have changed somewhat, in that confidence in government has rebounded and increased through the 1990s, but that confidence in politicians per se has continued to decline. The question then is whether patterns described in this report can tell us anything about the next century. Although it is impossible to predict the future, and rather difficult to collect reliable information on the present, there is at least some indication that the period focused upon here is representative of a broader trend. Specifically, data from the Canadian National Election Survey and its American counterpart show declines in trust in politicians beginning in the 1960s and extending into the mid-1990s. It is likely, then, that the pattern observed through the 1980s provides a snapshot that is representative of a trend extending over several decades.

    Coda. Trust reflects an individual's confidence that other people, objects, or institutions will behave as expected or as promised. This report confirms that Canadians are increasingly less trusting of the Canadian government, but also that this trend is common to other Western industrial nations. If trust is indeed decreasing among Canadians, an important issue for the future is the means by which the government might regain the public's trust. Evidence here suggests that declining trust is not a product of general isolation or disenfranchisement, but on the contrary is related to increasing feelings of empowerment and also increasing political activism among Canadians. Attempts to regain the public's trust should be cognizant of, but possibly also capitalize on, the fact that Canadians are on average becoming more sophisticated and active in their political participation.

Notes

This project was prepared for the Project on Trends, funded by the Social Sciences and Humanities Research Council of Canada.

  1 J. Steel, 'Interpersonal Correlates of Trust and Self-Disclosure,' *Psychological Reports* 68 (1991): 1319–20.

  2 E. Allen Lind and Tom R. Tyler, *The Social Psychology of Procedural Justice* (New York: Plenum, 1988) and T.R. Tyler and Roderick M. Kramer, eds,

Trust in Organizations: Frontiers of Theory and Research (Thousand Oaks, CA: Sage, 1996).

3 See, e.g., Robert Putnam, *Bowling Alone: The Collapse and Revival of American Community* (New York: Simon and Schuster, 2000) or Garry Wills, *A Necessary Evil: A History of American Distrust of Government* (New York: Simon and Schuster, 1999).

4 See Mebs Kanji (chap. 3) and Robert Nadeau (chap. 2), this volume, for a fuller examination of this trend, labelled 'cognitive mobilization.'

5 See P. Brann and M. Foddy, 'Trust and the Consumption of a Deteriorating Common Resource,' *Journal of Conflict Resolution* 31 (1987): 615–30.

6 See A.C. Cadenhead and C.L. Richmond, 'The Effects of Interpersonal Trust and Group Status on Prosocial and Aggressive Behaviors,' *Social Behavior and Personality* 24 (1996): 169–84; and P. Kumar and R. Ghadially, 'Organizational Politics and Its Effects on Members of Organizations,' *Human Relations* 42 (1989): 305–14.

7 See T. Goertzel, 'Belief in Conspiracy Theories,' *Political Psychology* 15 (1984): 731–42.

8 See Seymour Martin Lipset and William Schneider, *The Confidence Gap: Business, Labor, and Government in the Public Mind*, rev. ed. (Baltimore: Johns Hopkins University Press, 1987), 376.

9 Text in quotation marks represents the exact wording that appeared in the surveys discussed.

10 The statistical tests provided in the main text use the standard notation found in social-science publications. For readers unfamiliar with this notation, the key indicator is the p value. The smaller this value is, the more reliable and meaningful is the difference between two means. For present purposes, a cut-off $p = .01$ was used, meaning that p values less than .01 were treated as statistically reliable, whereas p values greater than .01 were taken to indicate that two means were essentially the same.

11 See also Lipset and Schneider, *The Confidence Gap*.

12 See also G. Orren, 'Fall from Grace: The Public's Loss of Faith in Government,' in Joseph S. Nye, Jr, Philip D. Zelikow, and David C. King, eds, *Why People Don't Trust Government* (Cambridge, MA: Harvard University Press, 1997), 77–107.

13 See Robert D. Putnam, 'Tuning In, Tuning Out: The Strange Disappearance of Social Capital in America,' *PS* 28 (1995): 664–83 and Putnam, *Bowling Alone*. See also Lisa Young, this volume.

14 See Lipset and Schneider, *The Confidence Gap* and Joseph Nye, Jr, 'In Government We Don't Trust,' *Foreign Policy* 108 (1997): 99–111.

15 See S.M. Montgomery et al., 'Unemployment Pre-Dates Symptoms of

Depression and Anxiety Resulting in Medical Consultation in Young Men,' *International Journal of Epidemiology* 28 (1999): 95–100.

16 See R.Z. Lawrence, 'Is It Really the Economy, Stupid?' in Nye, Zelikow, and King, *Why People Don't Trust Government*, 111–32.

17 See Albert Bandura, *Self-Efficacy: The Exercise of Control* (New York: W.H. Freeman and Co., 1997).

18 During this same time, American political orientation shifted to the centre (Ms = 5.92 vs. 5.74) in essentially the same way as in Canada, while western Europeans held steady just left of centre (Ms = 5.12 vs. 5.14).

19 See R. Inglehart, 'Postmaterialist Values and the Erosion of Institutional Authority,' in Nye, Zelikow, and King, *Why People Don't Trust Government*, 217–36; and Neil Nevitte, *The Decline of Deference: Canadian Value Change in Cross-National Perspective* (Peterborough, ON: Broadview Press, 1996).

20 See Thomas E. Patterson, *Out of Order* (New York: Vintage Books, 1994).

21 See Stephen Ansolabehere and Shanto Iyengar, *Going Negative: How Attack Ads Shrink and Polarize the Electorate* (New York: Free Press, 1995).

22 Nye, 'In Government We Don't Trust,' 110.

23 Ibid., 99–111.

24 See Alice H. Eagly and Shelley Chaiken, *The Psychology of Attitudes* (Orlando, FL: Harcourt Brace Jovanovich, 1993).

25 Especially the variety readily viewed on television; see Ansolabehere and Iyengar, *Going Negative*.

26 See Lind and Tyler, *The Social Psychology of Procedural Justice*.

6. Citizens and Legislators: Different Views on Representation

David C. Docherty

The image of the highly regarded politician, dutifully attending to local interests while at home, thinking and debating national interests while in Ottawa, is at best a vague memory in the minds of many Canadians, and more likely strange fiction in the minds of others. Elected officials – municipal, provincial, territorial, or federal – are not among the best respected members of Canadian society. Evidence of the plight of politicians in the public's mind is hard to escape. Polls in Canada have consistently shown that Canadians do not trust politicians or respect the institutions in which they serve. Other studies indicate that most Canadians see politicians as political chameleons, willing to say anything to get elected, only to lose touch with Canadians soon after they win office.[1] Gallup polls show that fewer than one in five Canadians have a great deal of trust in the House of Commons, compared to 43 per cent of Canadians who hold the big banks in respect.

This lack of trust in elected officials in hardly unique to Canada. Members of Congress and state representatives in the United States face a similar lack of public credibility, to the point where citizens are increasingly turning towards recall and term limits as a method of keeping these seemingly distant politicians in check. However, the high cost of electioneering in the United States, seen by most astute political observers as the reason for high re-election rates and a disenfranchised public, are unique to the U.S. experience.

Nor is a sense of detachment reserved only for public lawmakers. In his work in this volume, Neal Roese has argued that a lack of trust among citizens goes beyond politicians and parliament. Canadians are becoming less trusting in government in general. While Canadians are exhibiting a lack of trust that reaches beyond elected officials, this is perhaps small comfort to Canadian politicians, many of whom lose their jobs at election time.[2]

Despite Canada's high turnover rates, evidence of our ability as voters to punish unpopular politicians, Canadians seem just as unhappy with the type of role that provincial and national legislators are playing. Recall is alive in British Columbia, and while no member has lost his or her seat yet, there has been a concerted effort to recall the entire government. In Ontario, the Progressive Conservative government gathered strong support for a bill called 'The Fewer Politician's Act,' which cut the size of the Ontario Legislative Assembly by over 20 per cent, from 130 to 103. Federally, the Reform party (now the Canadian Alliance) has found some success in running for an office they openly criticize. Perhaps paradoxically, candidates from all parties run for federal political office claiming they are 'not a politician.' It may be that elected office is the only job in the world where everyone seeking it tries to be as underqualified as possible.

One can hardly blame would-be politicians for such an approach to job-hunting. It appears that Canadians have unreasonably high expectations of MPs, and then have little regard for them once they are elected. As Mancuso and colleagues found in their study of ethics, 43.3 per cent of Canadians believe that MPs should be held to a higher ethical standard than other Canadians.[3] Unfortunately, a substantial minority of voters, 34.1 per cent, feel that MPs actually have lower ethical standards than a typical Canadian.[4] It should not be surprising that the net result of unrealistic expectations is an increasing lack of trust, not just in politicians, but also in the institution in which they serve. How can Canadians have faith in their MPs to properly represent them if they lack faith in the ethical standards of members of parliament?

Part of the fallout of this increased cynicism is a call for changes to our institutions of representation. Among other possible changes, Canadians are beginning to embrace the notion of recall of members during their terms, are receptive to more referenda on important national questions, and seek Senate and House of Commons reform to provide representatives with more incentive to follow local demands. Yet it is far from clear what the net effect of any of these changes will be. Nor is it clear that our present members of parliament are not performing functions that are a necessary part of responsible government.

Finally, both scholars and citizens should be careful to recognize that just as the values of Canadians have changed in the past generation, so too have the representative responsibilities of members of parliament. Before moving ahead with any reforms that might mollify a cynical public, it is imperative that we understand exactly what Canadians seek in a representative and how far away our MPs are from that ideal.

The dissatisfaction of voters is undoubtedly rooted in a number of causes. Much of the blame can be placed at the feet of the parties themselves, who often govern in seeming direct contradiction to their campaign platforms. Certainly the most public example of this was the Liberal party's ill-fated pledge during the 1993 election campaign to eliminate the GST. Canadians are reminded of this broken promise with nearly every purchase they make. Inside the House of Commons, high levels of party discipline that effectively prevent members from voting according to constituency wishes spur the notion that politicians are out of sync with their voters. At the societal level, Neil Nevitte argues,[5] Canadians are less deferential as a whole, and this lack of deference in the political arena is partially a result of the post–Charter of Rights society and partially a reflection of postindustrial changes on a global scale.

In an interesting departure, Richard Nadeau (chapter 2, this volume) succinctly argues that Canadians are more satisfied with democracy than we might think, particularly in comparison to other industrial nations. This chapter does not dispute Nadeau's findings. It may be true that, as a nation, we reflect high levels of satisfaction with basic concepts of democracy (at least when we are contrasted with other nations). But the fact that we are sceptical about our politicians, hold them in low regard, and have little hesitation in voting them out of office with regularity is clear to most observers and practitioners of elected politics. In an attempt to complement Nadeau's more compara-tive examination of satisfaction with democratic practices, this chapter does not look at democracy as an approach to governance, but rather considers how Canadians view parliament and the men and women who are elected to serve in it. It is reasonable to assume that someone can distrust a politician but be more sanguine about the democratic system that allows that politician to be thrown out of office.

This chapter argues that the crisis of confidence in elected officials is at least partially a result of a gap in views on what constitutes effective representation in Canada. Drawing on a number of secondary data sources, the chapter seeks to identify the gap that exists between what the public sees as important representative duties and what members of parliament view as critical aspects of their job. Specifically, it traces the evolution of two parallel developments: the changing attitudes of Canadians towards their representatives and the changing view that members of parliament have towards their representative responsibilities.

This chapter argues that citizens and MPs differ in what they see as an elected legislator's primary duty. Members of parliament, it will be argued, are in fact deserving of more respect than the public seems willing to provide. They see their job as helping constituents in non-partisan ways, and take great pleasure in one-on-one constituency help. At the same, MPs are guilty of not keeping most voters informed about the workings of Ottawa, something the public sees as a priority. In addition, the public wants its members to pay more attention to partisan policy concerns. There are, of course, many other reasons for public cynicism towards political officials, but these lie beyond the scope and intent of this chapter, which begins with a brief discussion of the theoretical and historical aspects of representation in a Westminster-style parliamentary system. It then examines the increasing development of a cynical public. Canadians are more prone to see politicians as ambitious opportunists, and this view transcends sectors of the population. The chapter then looks at how politicians view their jobs, arguing that, for most members, the best type of service is one that removes them from the partisan battles of the legislature.

Methodology and Data Sources

A rich literature exists on levels of public support for representative institutions and respect for elected and other public figures. The chapter draws extensively on these secondary data in order to investigate trends in public views towards politicians and the role of the member of parliament as a representative. There are far fewer data available on how members see their role in terms of representation.

The section on public views on representation uses a combination of survey instruments, most of which were undertaken for academic purposes. The largest set of these are the Canadian National Election Surveys of 1984 through to 1997 (CNES). These surveys, headed by a group of political scientists during and after each national election, were funded through Social Science and Humanities Research Council grants. The 1984 survey was undertaken by Canadian Facts Inc., while the 1988,

1993, and 1997 studies were administered by the York University Institute for Social Research. In addition, this section also uses the Harold Clarke and Alan Kornberg Political Support in Canada (PSC) survey of 1993. All these surveys contain similar questions on political trust. In particular, each contains a question asking Canadians if they view members of parliament as losing touch with the electorate soon after their election to office. This question is a prominent feature of the analysis that follows. The 1993 PSC survey also asks a series of important 'contact' questions, and is therefore used instead of the 1993 CNES where applicable. Sample sizes from the survey are provided in each of the respective tables.

The section on public views on representation also makes some use of Gallup Canada data. Since the late 1980s Gallup Canada has asked a series of 'respect' questions, measuring public respect for various governmental and non-governmental organizations, institutions, and associations. Finally, a 1993 Gallup Canada poll asked Canadians to rank the importance of various responsibilities of members of parliament.[6]

There is far less quantitative data available on the self-identified representative roles of members of parliament. Behavioural studies of MPs from the 1960s and 1970s concentrated more on informal power and influence arrangements inside the House of Commons and less on the representational roles of members.[7] More recent work has begun to pay attention to the representational aspect of members' political careers.[8] As part of an earlier project, this author conducted mail surveys with members of the 34th Parliament of Canada, candidates for office for the 1993 general election, and rookie members of the 35th Parliament of Canada.[9] The section on members' views on representation makes extensive use of these now secondary data sources.

Representation in a System of Responsible Government

The Canadian political system, based on the Westminster model, is a system of responsible government. Of course, this begs the question, who is responsible to whom? As James Mitchell and Sharon Sutherland state, responsibility in our system 'ensures the democratic accountability of ministers to the elected legislature.'[10] In addition, it also guarantees that the appointed and meritocratic bureaucracy is also accountable and responsible to elected officials and, through them, the public. While such an arrangement serves to make a nice schematic drawing in introductory Canadian political-science texts, with the citizens holding the ultimate authority and bureaucrats and cabinet the least, the reality is more complex, and historically unique.

In his now classic study of representative and responsible government, Anthony Birch delineates three major forms of representation: the representative as agent, the representative as an elected official, and the representative as someone who characterizes a particular group or class of individual.[11] In Canada we have traditionally assumed the second form of representation to be of primary importance. Unless representatives are elected, their legitimacy is suspect. Among the many public-image problems facing the Senate, the greatest may be the fact that it is an appointed body, with no input from the public as to senatorial selections. And although our blend of single-member districts and a plurality electoral system means that most members are elected with far fewer than half the votes, the direct election of members of the House of Commons is a democratic strength of our system.

This is not to suggest that our system only provides for elected representatives. In fact, the House of Commons also allows for degrees of Birch's two other forms of representation. At the very least, we expect our elected members to act as agents of local concerns. The concept of agent lies at the heart of some public discontent about elected officials. Three problems exist for MPs with the 'agent' approach to representation.

First, members of parliament often find it difficult to act in a manner that pleases most of their constituents. Particularly in a multi-party system such as Canada's, often more people vote against a winning candidate than for that individual. Members of parliament are therefore left in the unenviable position of representing a political party *plus* a riding where more than half of voters would have preferred a different agent. Second, knowing the views of your constituents is a problematic, if not impossible, task. Riding-level polling data on all important issues of the day simply do not exist in Canada. Nor do members have the resources to gather such information. In the absence of quantitative information on constituency desires, members instead must rely on phone calls, letters, and visits to the constituency office, letters to the editor of local papers, and mail-back portions of riding newsletters, which tend to exaggerate extreme views.

Finally, MPs are often privy to information on issues that voters do not have. Issues that may seem black and white to the electorate are often seen in various shades of grey by lawmakers. Former members of parliament have commented that it is difficult to argue with constituents who, without access to complete knowledge of policy choices, take issue with members who make difficult decisions, cognizant of the domino effect that a riding-desired decision might have.[12]

Birch's third type of representation is the representation of groups or segments of society. More contemporary views of representation see this as a move towards mirror representation, where a deliberative body should mirror, or at least reflect, the society it represents.[13] Women can only be properly represented, it is argued, when a critical mass of women are sitting and voting in a legislature. Likewise, members of ethnic or racial minorities should expect to have their communities represented in the legislative arena. Mirror representation as a goal is one logical extreme of Birch's theory. For Birch, the notion that a representative speaks for a group of society is sufficient.

Naturally, the representation of segments of society is not restricted to classifications of race, ethnicity, or gender. Economic interests, be they business, union, agricultural, or resource based, expect a certain level of representation in the House of Commons. Prime ministers of Canada, for example, typically choose a rural MP to serve as Minister of Agriculture, a lawyer to serve as Minister of Justice, and a member from one of the coasts to serve as the Minister of Fisheries and Oceans. This representative function is one of a number of important criteria for selection to cabinet.[14]

In addition, members of the opposition parties are institutionally encouraged to represent specific interests, be they economic, social, biological, or linguistic. The role of the shadow cabinet is seen as critical for the proper accountability function of parliament. Specific members represent the same group interests that cabinet does, often with similar connections to the portfolio they are tagging.

The problem of representing segments of society for members of parliament is often one of workload. As elected representatives, members are expected to represent and serve their constituents first. A cabinet post or a critic's portfolio adds a second, societal role. Finally, members often speak for groups they associate with or have connections to outside of their parliamentary role. Women MPs are seen to represent the collective interests of women. As one of only two openly gay MPs in Canada, BC's Svend Robinson is seen as a voice for the concerns of gay men and lesbian women across the country, be they from Burnaby, British Columbia, or Cornerbrook, Newfoundland.

All of this suggests that Birch's notions of representation were never deemed to be mutually exclusive. While we naturally assume all representatives to be elected, even within a democratic society, this is not always the case. We expect representatives to act in our interest, but cannot always define what our interest is. Finally, we elect representatives based on territorially defined units, but are accustomed to hearing our local member of parliament speak on behalf of interests outside our riding.

Myriad other studies exist on styles and forms of representation. It was nearly a generation ago when Heinz Eulau discussed three types of representational styles in trying to understand what, at the time, was considered a 'crisis in representation.'[15] For Eulau elected representatives followed one of three styles: trustee, delegate, or politico. This delineation still has some resonance in the Canadian legislative system today, albeit not in the form Eulau first envisioned.

Trustees are members who believe they are elected to use their own judgment and wisdom and not rely on that of their constituents. The theory behind this notion of independent member is that voters select the wisest in their community and agree to live by the decisions he or she makes in the community's (and indeed nation's) best interests. Hanna Pitkin describes this as the original Burkean view of representing 'unattached interests.'[16] As Burke in his infamous speech to the electors of Bristol stated, once chosen, an individual is no longer a 'member from Bristol, but he is a member of Parliament.'[17] A trustee would argue that members are privy to better and more information than are voters. But even beyond the Birch distinction, a trustee would rank interests. The local interest should, according to trustee representatives, be second to the national interest. If this means voting against riding desires to protect a greater good, then no sacrifice is even seen to be made.

Delegates, by contrast, hold no quarter with national interests. They see themselves as merely voices of local expression, elected to follow the wishes of a majority of their constituents. Such individuals are beholden neither to their party nor to some abstract notion of national interest. For delegates, the only national interest is the aggregated views of a majority of local interests. Such a view of representation finds a home in the American form of congressional government. Different offices hold different responsibilities, with members of the House of Representatives charged with staying close to local interests.[18] This notion of representation is one that sticks closest to the ideal of direct democracy. In the absence of a system that provides for votes on every issue, an elected representative should try and act as a spokesperson for the riding on every issue.

The culture of delegate status is not one that is easily arrived at in Westminster-based parliaments, where party discipline takes priority over local interests. Still, there has been more than one party try to infiltrate the Canadian parliament with a delegate-style status. The first strong movement of this type came from the Progressive party in the early 1920s. The party, like most populist-based political movements, reflected a combination of anger at the existing political system and a frustration at the policies the 'system,' and those working within it, were seen to produce. The Progressive party enjoyed moderate success with such delegate-style promises of grassroots democracy, opposition to party discipline, and support for recall and more referenda.[19] Unfortunately, the principles of the party served to undermine its survival. Electing fourteen more members than the third-place Conservative party in the 1921 election, the Progressives refused to assume their role as Official Opposition. The party soon split and never really recovered.

The Reform, and subsequently the Alliance, parties have emerged as the contemporary version (at least in terms of style) of the Progressive party.[20] Elected with many of the same promises, the Reform party became the most successful 'delegate style' party in Canadian history. Reform met with both problems and successes while attempting to stay true to its grassroots ideals. Some of these achievements and failures will be discussed in subsequent sections. Suffice it to argue at this point that they managed to maintain a cohesive party presence in the House of Commons through a combination of strong leadership and a willingness to embrace party solidarity, if not party discipline.

Finally, Eulau describes the third type of representative as a 'politico' who embraces elements of both the trustee and delegate in his or her approach to elected office. This type of legislator agrees that constituents should have their views represented in parliament, but appreciates that this goal is more easily accomplished in theory than in practice. Much like Birch's representative as agent, the politico finds it difficult to determine the views of a majority of constituents. A minority of vocal opposition might appear stronger than a majority of acquiescent support. And like the agent, the politico appreciates that individuals might not have access to additional information that might cast policy problems in a different light. Like the delegate, the politico takes the wishes of constituents seriously. And like the trustee, the politico is cognizant that many constituents might not have the larger interests of the community, or country, at heart.

Few would argue that Canadian MPs serve as delegates of their constituencies. But neither are they trustees, at least not solely trustees, for occasions when members of parliament decide on an issue independent of constituency or party views are rare. If asked in these terms, the Canadian public might suggest that members are delegates of party leaders. In the public mind, the role of caucus is minimal, and individual MPs all too quickly heed the word of their leader, with constituency concerns and the wishes of the voters a distant secondary factor.[21]

Yet such a characterization is unfair. Not only do newly elected members of parliament represent a challenge to this traditional understanding of representational styles, but many veteran MPs are also less beholden to their leaders today than previous parliamentarians have been. Just as members of the Reform/Alliance caucus have eschewed the role of professional politician, so also have they been committed to acting as constituency delegates, shunning the views of their leaders and advisers and instead following the lead of their voters. They have been joined in this view since 1993 by many new Liberals, who are looking to their ridings for direction as much as they are turning to caucus and their leader's office.

The evidence of this apparently growing 'delegate' style is noticeable in the survey responses of members of parliament.[22] When asked whose direction is more important to deciding how to vote on an issue in the House of Commons, their leader and party or their constituents, MPs from more recent parliaments tend to side with voters. A survey of MPs in the last Mulroney government found that only 30 per cent of members would place district ahead of party and leader, compared to 59 per cent of rookie MPs in the first Chretién government.[23] Yet as the next section will argue, this change in approach has gotten politicians nowhere. Members of the public are just as, if not more, cynical about the motives and abilities of members to represent them today as they were fifteen or twenty years ago. Members of parliament, at their most basic level, believe they are providing as close to delegate style of representation as the Westminster system allows. The public, however, is not buying. If there is a gap between the public and the men and women whom the public elect, it is likely to be found in this area.

The next two sections explore the gap that exists in the understanding of elected representation in Canada. The real problem, it will be argued, is two-fold. First, Canadians want a style of representation that is difficult to provide within the present confines of the Westminster parliamentary system. Second, members of parliament believe they are providing proper representative service. This view of service is buttressed by the support most members get from a critical group in every riding, those individuals who seek the advice and services of MPs. The problem for members is that this group does not include the majority of the voters in their districts. Understanding how representation should work is a good precursor to, but does not replace, the first-order question, what do the public and members believe constitutes good representation?

Public Attitudes towards Parliament and Its Members

It's a nasty crowd out there. If the 1960s were the decade of love, the 1990s could easily be called the decade of cynicism. And among those who feel the brunt of this cynicism are elected officials in Canada. Rising deficits and increasing levels of taxation have made the lot of politicians difficult, and the public has not hesitated to indicate their discontent. Clarke and colleagues have argued convincingly that the blame for public dissatisfaction can find a home with both politicians and the public alike.[24] Those seeking power have been content to offer relatively painless promises to try and solve long-term structural and economic problems. The public has been quick to believe these short-sighted promises. Once the next government finds that their proffered solutions do not work, the backlash is inevitable.

The macro-level indicators provide mixed evidence of the level of public distrust. Since 1980 Canada has been governed by five consecutive majority governments. Brian Mulroney and Jean Chrétien each managed back-to-back-to-back majorities, something few prime ministers have been able to do. And as argued elsewhere in this volume, levels of satisfaction with democracy are relatively stable in Canada, and high compared to most other nations, both developing and industrialized. Yet levels of electoral turnover are at record highs. The 1984 general election saw the biggest drop in Liberal seats in history. The 1993 election saw the same fate befall the Conservatives and produced the largest turnover in Canadian history. Even the re-election of the Tories in 1988 and Grits in 1997 produced high levels of turnover, with cabinet and backbench incumbents alike being rejected at the polls.

The micro-level indicators are less puzzling. Canadians did not trust

TABLE 6.1
Trust in government

	Canada	United States	Mexico
Always	2.9%	5.9%	7.8%
Most of the time	16.8	35.5	16.6
Some of the time	53.5	47.7	51.3
Never	26.4	10.9	24.3
Sample size (N)	1694	1789	1520

Source: World Values Survey 1990.

Note: Question wording, 'How much do you trust the government in [Ottawa] to do what is right? Do you trust it always, most of the time, some of the time, never?'

people seeking elected office. It may be small comfort that Canadians are not alone in this view. Despite high second-term approval ratings for U.S. President Bill Clinton, for instance, American voters were not about to embrace their politicians as morally upright individuals with impeccable integrity. Table 6.1 illustrates the levels of trust for politicians in North America at the beginning of the 1990s.

Surveys at single points in time are always difficult to interpret. However, the discrepancy between nations is startling. Compared to voters in the United States, Canadians are far less trusting of their government. While only one in ten Americans stated they would never trust their government to do what is right, over one-quarter of Canadians said this, slightly higher than Mexicans' views on their government. Asking trust-in-government questions can be problematic. The term 'government' means different things to different people, both within and across nations. In addition, cross-sectional survey data do not allow researchers to detect any trends or, the alternative, relative consistency across time.

Table 6.2 examines levels of respect for various political and private institutions in Canada, including the House of Commons, political parties, the federal government, banks, and organized religion. The findings send rather mixed signals to public officials. Compared to non-governmental organizations, respect for the public sector is low. However, a great deal of variation exists within state or semi-state organizations.

Non-governmental organizations and institutions regularly rank higher in public respect than do political or state institutions.[25] Churches

TABLE 6.2
Respect for institutions in Canada over time

	1999	1997	1995	1993*	1989**
Organized religion					
Great deal	43.5%	44%	46%	41%	55%
Some	31.6	31	28	34	29
Very little	23.2	21	22	23	15
Large corporations					
Great deal	30.4	30	32	22	33
Some	46.5	44	39	49	43
Very little	19.5	22	23	27	20
Federal government					
Great deal	29.6	28	27	15	17
Some	47.7	43	44	38	39
Very little	20	25	25	46	41
Political parties					
Great deal	11.2	10	12	9	18
Some	49.1	49	44	39	46
Very little	36.8	37	40	49	33
House of Commons					
Great deal	21.8	23	19	16	30
Some	48	41	43	45	43
Very little	23.1	28	28	33	21
Total *N*	1005	1006	1005	1004	1021

Source: Gallup Canada Inc. Omitted from survey are combined 'Don't Know' and 'Refused' responses.

*1992 for 'Federal government' percentages
**1990 for 'Federal government' percentages

fare quite well, especially when contrasted to other large organizations. However, the level of trust among Canadians generally is quite low, and political and governmental bodies are not alone in struggling for better approval ratings. In fact, as the table illustrates, Canadians are almost as cynical about large corporations as they are about various branches of the federal state. In terms of public respect and confidence, large corporations do only about 5 per cent better than the federal government.

Canadians feel most of their cynicism towards political parties. While never leading the pack in public support, parties have not always been the pariah they now appear to most. In 1979, after the election of Joe Clark as prime minister, nearly one-third of all Canadians (30%) felt this way.[26] Political parties hit a low point in 1991 (not shown in the table), when only 7 per cent of Canadians admitted to having a great deal or quite a lot of respect for parties. The failure of the Meech Lake Accord and public anger at the lack of consultation on matters of constitutional reform certainly cast most political actors and parties in a bad light during this period.[27] Politicians and parties were seen at perhaps their most unresponsive during this period. Parties have been slow to recover their public credibility since the failure of Meech Lake. While nearly half of Canadians had some respect for parties in the past two years, this must be little solace to those running for office under a party banner.

By contrast, respect for the institution of the House of Commons has fared slightly better over time. Generally, about one-fifth of Canadians have a great deal or quite a lot of respect for the House of Commons and another 40 per cent have some respect for the elected assembly of Canada. If one combines the 'Great Deal' and 'Some' responses in this latter category, over 70 per cent of Canadians in April 1999 felt that the federal legislature is worthy of some respect. This is the highest combined percentage since 1989.

There is little direct evidence to explain this increased support for parliament. Part of the explanation is regional. There is greater respect for the Commons in the Atlantic provinces, Quebec, and Ontario than there is in the West. In the latter region, respect runs well below the national average, while it is higher than average in the other three regions. Middle-age Canadians (aged 40–64) are more likely to hold the elected half of parliament in high regard, while younger Canadians and seniors are slightly less enthusiastic. Those with university degrees are more inclined to view parliament positively, compared to every other educational ranking (such as college degree or high school diploma). Finally, there is a slight gender gap in respect for parliament, with 23.5 per cent of males having a great deal of respect for parliament, compared to just over 20 per cent of women.[28]

The discrepancy between political parties and the House of Commons suggests that voters distinguish between the role of parliament and the partisan nature of parties. This ability to separate parties and parliamentarians is consistent across sectors of society. There are no real differences in views of parties across region, gender, income, or education level, which suggests that the views of Canadians with regard to how parties conduct themselves are robust and, more important, negative. Within the Canadian electoral system, political parties are key actors, the primary mobilizers of public support outside of parliament.[29] There is more support among the public for the internal mustering of political action than there is for the external struggle for backing among the voting population.

Such a differentiation suggests that Canadians have more faith in the instruments of governance than they do in the men and women who run for elected office under a party banner. This is not inconsistent with the finding of Nadeau (chapter 2, this volume) that the public is not disenchanted with our democratic framework. Nor is it inconsistent with the findings of Roese (chapter 5) on public trust and Mancuso and colleagues on the ethical standards of politicians and parties.[30] Further, public cynicism towards politicians is readily apparent in every recent election survey in Canada. The public believes that members of parliament place election well ahead of representation as a goal. As a result, once elected, the perception is that members are non-caring, have already achieved their objective of election, and turn their minds away from the constituency. Table 6.3 illustrates the increasing evidence of a cynical population. The number of Canadians who believe that politicians will say anything to get elected has risen steadily since the first election of Brian Mulroney. Politicians, as candidates, are increasingly seen as self-interested. Many Canadians are voting for individuals they assume will soon ignore them. Who are these Canadians and have the group dynamics of this cohort changed in the past fifteen years?

The simple answer is that they are most Canadians and that these views have risen only slightly since 1984. There is not a single defining demographic characteristic among the group that views politicians as short-sighted. This is at least partially due to the overwhelming majority of those who share this perspective. With anywhere between 70 and

TABLE 6.3
Attention paid to politics and how voters see MPs staying in touch

MPs soon lose touch	Interest in politics generally		
	Not much interest	Fairly/somewhat	Very interested
1984			
Strongly agree	34.3	25.1	27.7
Agree	48.1	49.9	45.2
Disagree	13.9	20.2	18
Strongly disagree	3.7	4.8	9
N	1122	1392	588
1993			
Agree	82	80.5	77.2
Disagree	18	19.5	22.8
N	339	865	224
1997			
Strongly agree	40	36.3	40.4
Agree	43.9	46.8	41.5
Disagree	11.7	13.3	12.1
Strongly disagree	4.4	3.6	6
N	1142	1657	977

Source: 1984 and 1997 Canadian National Election Studies; 1993 Political Support in Canada Study.

80 per cent of Canadians holding this view, it should be difficult to find any distinguishing features. In the four election periods studied, residents of Atlantic Canada were more inclined to see politicians as staying in touch rather than losing touch. Western Canadians are more likely to agree with the statement that politicians soon lose touch. Yet the differences are not dramatic, nor statistically significant. With each election, the size of the cohort not trusting politicians to stay in touch grows, but only by 1 or 2 per cent. The net result of this incremental increase has been a steady move from about three-quarters of Canadians to about 85 per cent. For example, in the Atlantic provinces in 1984, 76.7% of respondents expected MPs to lose touch; in 1997, the number so responding was 83.3%. The largest gain has been in the West, where the size increased from 77.4% to 86.1%.

On average, females are more trusting of politicians, but again the difference is minor. A little over four-fifths of all males are cynical of politicians' ability to stay in touch compared to just under four-fifths of all females. Standard socio-economic indicators fare little better than region and gender as predictors. It is true that the higher the level of education obtained, the more inclined the respondent will be to trust politicians to keep their word. However, the differences between individual-level education groups is not overwhelming. Likewise, higher-income Canadians have higher levels of trust for politicians, but again all levels are high.[31]

If there is one indicator of trust of politicians that does consistently produce significant differences, it is the simple measure of how much attention Canadians pay to politics. In 1988 and 1993, a clear pattern emerged. The more attention people paid to politics, the more likely they were to see politicians as keeping their word and staying close to the electorate after the election. As table 6.3 demonstrates, the differences within years were significant. In 1984 the difference between the two bookends was just under 10 per cent. In 1988 the difference was half of that, but ran in the expected direction. By 1997, the relationship was altered. Those who paid the least attention to politics were still more inclined to view politicians as losing touch. However, Canadians who followed politics closely were now just as dubious about the willingness of politicians to stay in touch as those not generally interested in the political process. This finding complements Lisa Young's study in this volume on civic and political engagement in Alberta. While the measures are admittedly different, it is not too much of a stretch to equate Young's findings, that followers of politics (via the news) are more inclined towards civic and political participation, with the view that members of the public who follow politics are more likely to trust politicians to keep their word. In both cases there is a measure of trust, either in individuals to hold to their word, or in the system to provide opportunities for change.

The fact that there are few demographic or socio-economic differences among Canadians on the question of members' motives or approaches to elected office suggests the problem of confidence in representation is real. It is deeply rooted throughout Canadian society, and shows little sign of abating. If anything, the problem is increasing. In addition, it suggests that effectively addressing this problem is not simply a matter of targeting one segment of society. Young well-educated Westerners seeking office (Reform's Jason Kenney, for example) may appeal to a particular cohort in society, but that group is unlikely to trust him more simply because he 'is one of them.' The same holds true for veteran politicians who represent different cross-sections of society (Charles Caccia in urban Toronto, George Baker in rural Newfoundland, for example). Their approach to representing constituents may resonate with their own voters, but across the country this style of representation is no more trusted – nor are politicians who assume this approach – than any other. Distrust of office seekers runs throughout Canadian society.

With such overwhelming doubt about the motives of politicians, perhaps the better question is who in the population thinks politicians are doing a good job? While little direct evidence exists, the data that are available suggests it is that segment of the population that has the most contact with members of parliament. An interesting comparison can be made between two national surveys taken five years apart that ask two related, but very different questions. The 1988 national election survey asked individuals about actual contact with their member of parliament. By contrast, the 1993 survey on political support in Canada asked respondents how likely they thought MPs would be to help them in various tasks. The differences, as delineated in table 6.4 below, are informative. The expectations of receiving help and the experience of receiving help are two very different things.

Compared to the public at large, the segment of society that has contact with members of parliament tends to be very satisfied with the assistance they receive. Whether it is simply to voice an opinion, obtain some information, or actually seek assistance from the member (or his/ her staff) on an issue, a plurality of contacters are very satisfied with the response of the member. When combined with those who indicated some satisfaction, these pluralities all become majorities. This distinction between expectations and actual experience with members supports the earlier findings of Ferejohn and Gaines, who found that contact with members was likely to increase support for their district activities.[32] Knowledge of a member's activities is almost a precondition to approval of their day-to-day tasks. Individuals who have not contacted members or who do not have knowledge of their day-to-day tasks in the riding are less prone to give their member the benefit of the doubt and more inclined to greet their member's job functions with scepticism.

Interestingly, the type of contact has a positive influence on the level of satisfaction voters find with members of parliament. The more demands one places on a member or his or her office, the more satisfied the constituent is likely to find himself/herself. A strong majority of those who seek help with a personal problem leave the member's office very satisfied. Nearly 85 per cent of constituents seeking this type of

TABLE 6.4
Expectations and realities of MP's district service*

	1988	1993
MP listens to your opinion		
Very satisfied / Likely	44.4%	5.0%
Somewhat satisfied / Likely	32.4	41.1
Not very satisfied / Likely	7.5	27.8
Not at all satisfied	15	
N	176	1085
Contact MP for information		
Very satisfied	49.6	
Somewhat satisfied	29.6	
Not very satisfied	6.4	
Not at all satisfied	8.8	
N	236	
MP helps riding		
Very likely		14.6
Somewhat likely		43.3
Not very likely		15.7
N		1085
MP helps with personal problem		
Very satisfied / Likely	55.3	9.9
Somewhat satisfied / Likely	26.7	24.4
Not very satisfied / Likely	6.8	39.4
Not at all satisfied / Likely	8.7	
N	157	1082

Source: 1988 Canadian National Election Study; 1993 Political Support in Canada.

*The possible responses varied according to the question asked. In 1988 respondents were asked if they had contacted their member or his/her office and what level of satisfaction they received. Possible responses were 'Very Satisfied, Somewhat Satisfied, Not Very Satisfied and Not At All Satisfied.' In 1993 individuals were asked how likely they thought their member of parliament would be to properly respond to various interactions. The possible responses in this instance were 'Very Likely, Somewhat Likely and Not Very Likely.' In addition, because the 1988 survey is based on respondents who have actually had contact with their member of parliament or his/her office, the sample size is greatly reduced.

assistance leave the MP's office at least somewhat satisfied. Arguably, many businesses would be extraordinarily happy with this type of client response. For those who have not yet contacted their member but expect to at some point in the future, the figures are almost completely reversed. A clear majority felt that should they seek the assistance of a member for a personal matter, they would be very unlikely to come away satisfied.

Members can therefore take some solace in the fact that, when approached, their job approval rating is likely to increase. The fact that only a small proportion of the riding seek a member out in this manner leaves MPs with a problem. The gap in what is important in terms of representative responsibilities is becoming more clear. Assistance with personal problems can be associated with Anthony Birch's or Hanna Pitkin's understanding of the representative as agent. Individuals entrust their elected officials to act on their behalf. The end goal is stated (resolution of a pension dispute, for example), but the constituent does not direct the legislator on how to achieve this goal, knowing the member has far more expertise in this field.

Listening to constituents' opinions is a indirect example of the member-as-delegate role. It is presumed that when a member hears from constituents on certain matters (tax increases or gun-control legislation, for example), the member will repeat those concerns to various officials (elected and others) in Ottawa. This is an indirect measure of delegate representation for two reasons. First, the survey question does not ask whether voters expect members to act on their concerns. Citizens could be simply venting anger. Similarly, voters could be expressing thanks or appreciation for the actions of a member in a House vote, without having first asked their MP to take such a position. Second, timing is important. Citizen contact might concern an issue yet to be decided (an upcoming vote) or a matter that has already been dealt with (a previous vote or government action). If it is the latter, then the member did not act as a delegate.

What exactly do Canadians want of their representatives? As it turns out, they are not particularly interested in the one function on which members seem to get the highest approval ratings, namely, helping individuals with problems. Table 6.5 ranks five different types of responsibilities for elected members. The representative roles are based on an earlier cross-national study between the United States and the United Kingdom.[33]

The so-called 'agent' role ranks lower than any other responsibility. Canadians share this view with U.S. voters, who do not place great weight in the 'helping people' function.[34] By contrast, voters in Great Britain are more inclined to see merit in the agent responsibility, ranking it third of five. This difference is worth noting, since both the Canadian and U.S. systems have gone to greater lengths to institutionalize this function. In both nations, the legislature covers the cost of

TABLE 6.5
Most important representative roles: a 3-country comparison

Role	United States*	Great Britain*	Canada**
Helping people	5(11%)	3(19%)	5
Protecting district	3(15)	1(26)	2
Oversight	3(15)	6(4)	4
Keeping in touch	1(30)	2(24)	1
Policy	2(19)	5(11)	3
Don't know, all, none	6(10)	4(16)	

*Table 1.6 in B. Cain, J. Ferejohn, and M. Fiorina, *The Personal Vote* (London: Harvard University Press, 1987).
** The Gallup Poll, 1993.
Figures for the United States and Great Britain available in percentages only. The author has converted them to rankings for comparative purposes. In addition, the wording of the actual questions was changed to reflect internal national understandings of representation. Wording for the questions by nation can be found in appendix B.

constituency offices and staff, in some cases providing more than one office per riding.[35] While these constituency offices have been slower to develop in Canada than in the United States, their existence has been part of the development of the modern professional parliament that began during the Pearson era and was well ensconced in the early Trudeau years.[36] Great Britain was slower to provide members with these services, and the 'local surgeries' held on the weekends when the part-time member was in the district continued into the early Thatcher years.[37]

Canadians and Americans also share similar views on the importance of other representative duties. Both emphasize the 'keeping in touch' function, seeing it as the most important duty of an elected representative. It is difficult to understand exactly why this duty receives such strong support in both nations, and receives a strong second place ranking among British respondents. Voters may feel that members of parliament lose touch, but they still see them as the link between the bureaucratic and executive world of their nation's capital and the 'real world' of their ridings. The 'keeping in touch' responsibility straddles the agent and delegate role for members. In letting constituents know exactly what is going on in Ottawa (or Washington, or Westminster), members are being called on to take an active part not in representation, but rather in making sure that people in the district are not left out of the so-called loop.

Protecting the interests of the riding is a concern for citizens in all three nations, but particularly in Canada and Great Britain. This function is closely tied to the delegate function of members, and seems to indicate the public's concern that members will forget about the riding once they are in parliament. The focus of this duty is not in helping individuals with problems, or in letting the riding know what Ottawa is thinking, but rather in ensuring that Ottawa knows what the riding is thinking, and more importantly, that the riding not be ignored by federal policy makers. Perhaps surprisingly, there is no discernable difference on the issue of protecting local interests among the regions of the country. Voters in the Atlantic provinces were no more inclined to rate this activity as important than residents of Ontario and Alberta and British Columbia. There was also strong support for this task among respondents in Quebec.

Citizens in the United States place more emphasis on the importance of policy work than do Canadians and the British. However, as Cain and colleagues argue in their cross-national comparison, this is largely do to structural differences in the two systems. Members of Congress enjoy huge latitude in developing policy and legislation, while in Westminster the 'backbench MP is virtually irrelevant to the policy making process.'[38] As Searing points out in his exhaustive study of British MPs, even the members who see themselves as 'policy advocates' are really more like watchdogs, checking the executive more than producing innovative legislation and policy alternatives.[39] The limited role of MPs is not unknown to constituents who look to their representatives to play a different role, presumably one where members hold more influence.

In sum, there is evidence that the public in Canada is not far removed from citizens in other states in its expectations about public service. What Canadians seek from their representatives is someone who will protect local interests while at the same time ensuring that they are kept informed of the intentions and actions of the nation's decision makers. What citizens place little importance on is the problems of their neighbours, or at least those problems that require the assistance of their local member of parliament.

These expectations of representation cannot easily be defined in terms of either the delegate, trustee, or agent styles. As a result, public expectations do not easily fit within one style of representation, which makes it more difficult for elected officials to respond with a consistent approach to their elected duties.

Member's Attitudes toward Their Elected Responsibilities

If the public does not produce a consistent style of representation, how do members of parliament respond? When it comes to exploring the gap that exists between MPs and the public, understanding what the public seeks in elected officials reveals only half of the picture. Unfortunately, there is far more data available on questions of public confidence (or lack thereof) in members than there is on how members actually go about their job.

It is safe to argue that while members of the public have been increasingly sceptical about politicians from the early 1980s on, members of parliament have not been reluctant to change their approach to representation. This change, perhaps highlighted most clearly in the election of 1993 and the conduct of members of the 35th Parliament, was in many ways a result of the public's dissatisfied mood. In the aftermath of failed Meech Lake Accord and the defeat of the Charlottetown referendum, political leaders understood the public mood. Canadians felt the old elite system did not allow for enough consultation with citizens. Canadians demanded a new say, and were tired of parties and party leaders that relied on traditional methods of governing.[40]

Party discipline became one of many targets of voters' wrath. And leading the fight against party discipline was the Reform Party of Canada. The Reform party's rapid rise on the Canadian political scene was first of all a creature of Western alienation, and of a strong sense that the Progressive Conservative party under Brian Mulroney was no different than the Liberal party in its understanding of Western needs. As David Laycock reminds us, the success of the Reform party 'cannot be understood in simple regionalist terms.' Instead, the party represented a dramatic departure from traditional styles of representation, and a style of membership in the Commons that 'existed independently of region.'[41] With its populist, grassroots background and calls for term limits, more referenda, and recall legislation, the Reform party entered the 1993 election challenging traditional notions of leader-centred party discipline. In simple terms, Reformers pledged to place constituency demands ahead of party loyalty, and in this way move the Canadian MP to a delegate style of representation.

Reform was not alone in playing up this approach to governing. The Conservatives, under Kim Campbell, promised a new style of consensual politics. The Liberals' campaign Red Book promised more free votes in the Commons to allow members to reflect better the views of

TABLE 6.6
Representational style of MPs and candidates in 1993

	MPs of 34th Parliament (1988–93)	Candidates 1993
Delegate of riding	30%	79%
Delegate of party/trustee	70	21
N	113	241

Source: Table adapted from D.C. Docherty, Mr. Smith Goes to Ottawa, 145–9.

Canadians, not party leaders. Private members were also to be allowed a greater role in the development and initiation of public policy, in part to allow members to participate in the policy functions previously denied them.

Most non-incumbent candidates for office in 1993 saw themselves as delegate-style representatives. This approach stood in direct contrast to the veteran office holders of the Mulroney era, who were more inclined to favour the trustee, or at least leader-dominated, traditional method of parliamentary representation. Table 6.6 compares the representational perspectives of members of the 34th Parliament (1988–93) with non-incumbent office seekers for the 1993 general election. Both cohorts were asked to choose between party solidarity, and possible promotion by their leader, and the role of the elected delegate who follows the wishes of the constituency over all else. Individuals who stated they would always be beholden to their constituents for direction on legislative and policy matters fit the delegate profile. Those who stated they would follow party over constituency on non-crucial matters might best be described as delegates of the party leadership, or more kindly as trustees of the public interest.[42]

The difference between the two groups suggests that a huge gulf exists between those with experience in representation and those seeking experience. Members of the 34th Parliament, where 70 per cent said they would sacrifice constituency views for party unity, were more inclined to view themselves as party delegates. The numbers are nearly reversed among candidates in 1993, with nearly four-fifths of all office seekers claiming they would never place party above constituency.[43] Standard bearers for the Reform party were the most likely to claim the riding delegate mantle. Ninety-eight per cent of responding Reform party candidates stated there would never be an issue that would cause them to chose party over the men and women who sent them to

TABLE 6.7
Ranked importance of an MP's duties

Responsibility	MPs, 34th Parliament, 1988–93	Rookie MPs, 35th Parliament	Public
Protecting interests of constituency	3	1	2
Helping people who have personal problems with government	1	3	5
Ensuring bureaucracy is administrating government policy	5	5	3
Keeping in touch with constituents about what government is doing	4	2	1
Debating and voting in parliament	2	4	4

Source: D.C. Docherty, Mr. Smith Goes to Ottawa, 190.

Ottawa. But Liberal candidates also demonstrated strong ties to their ridings, with nearly two-thirds favouring a representational style of riding delegate. Of those candidates who were successful in their election bid, 75 per cent placed riding over party, and only one-quarter identified themselves as potential delegates of their party, or what Eulau called a trustee.

This admittedly secondary evidence suggests that there is variation not only in what citizens expect to see in a representative but also in what candidates and actual office holders see as their primary duties and responsibilities. More comparative evidence of this latter gap can be found in table 6.7. Members of the 34th Parliament and candidates were asked to rank the importance of five representative duties of members (the table only shows the responses of successful candidates, that is, those who won office for the first time in 1993; it is important to note, however, that these rookies were asked this question *as candidates, prior* to their election to national office). The responses of the public, as shown above in table 6.5, are shown in the final column of this table. A clearer picture of the 'gap,' or how members may actually lose touch soon after their election, begins to emerge. Rookie MPs reflect the views of citizens to a much greater degree than do more mature legislators. In this light, it does appear that MPs lose touch with the public they are elected to serve. Time spent in office makes MPs forget the desires of those individuals who originally sent them to the nation's capital.[44]

As indicated earlier, members of the public place great emphasis on the keeping-in-touch function and that of protecting the interests of the whole riding. Candidates see the former function as quite important, the second most of the five possible tasks. Members of parliament themselves see it as not critical at all, ranking it fourth of five. MPs might well be seen to be losing touch if they fail to place stock in keeping in touch. Likewise, while the public ranks the protection of local interests as the second most important duty, new office holders see this as their primary duty. The riding delegate style is thus paramount in the minds of both voters and new office holders.

Despite the limited opportunity for members to participate in the policy process, veteran MPs were inclined to rank their parliamentary work as a high-priority issue. This is perhaps natural given the amount of time members spend in Ottawa, but curious given the lack of opportunities available to members to have meaningful input into policy initiation. This aspect was not a high priority among members of the public – a response consistent with the weight citizens have given to the delegate style of representation.

While a lack of interest in communicating government policy or protecting the riding may signal 'losing touch' to voters, it does not translate into a lack of concern on members' parts with the plight of their constituents. Members of the 34th Parliament indicated that their most important duty was to help individuals who had problems with a government department. Interestingly, this is the duty that Canadians ranked last. This is where the true gap lies. Canadians do not see the job of MP as one of helping individuals, at least not compared to larger, riding-wide functions. Given that members think of this as their central task, it is little wonder that Canadians do not think MPs listen or respond as they should.

Recognizing where the deviation between public wishes and legislators' views on representation rests is much easier than identifying the cause of this discrepancy. From a legislator's perspective there are numerous possible reasons that they might view individual service as their primary responsibility. First, members see such work as an effective way of maintaining their reputations as problem solvers. People in the riding who encounter problems with government agencies or departments expect MPs to help resolve these difficulties.[45] There is little evidence that constituency work allows members to build the kind of personal vote support that members of Congress enjoy in the United States. So a reputation as an effective problem solver will not provide members with a buffer of support independent of voters' views on the member's party or leader.[46] However, in the minds of many MPs such a reputation is a prerequisite to a successful political career. As one member of the 34th Parliament stated, 'Helping people will not get me re-elected. But not doing it will sure get me defeated.'[47] This member recognized that while local service has few direct electoral benefits, it remains a requisite part of the job.

In addition, given the limited impact that members have in the public-policy field, it is not surprising that members turn their attention to a venue where success is more readily met. MPs are often successful in helping people in their ridings. An executive-centred parliamentary system makes tackling policy matters more frustrating. It is far easier to help a constituent wade through a maze of government programs and forms than it is to make sweeping policy changes. As a result, there may be a greater attachment to working on problems that can be resolved.

Further, whether individual MPs see themselves as delegates or trustees, they certainly share a common understanding of constituency work: it avoids conflict with one's own party. Given the primary role of party discipline within the Canadian legislative system, it is not surprising that many MPs would chose to attach greater importance to those activities that hold little, if any, overtly partisan content. Acting as a local troubleshooter means avoiding conflict with the party, its leader, and the government.

It should not be startling news then that the task most members rank as the most important is also one they enjoy performing. The reasons behind this enjoyment are similar to the reasons why members think it is important. Asked why they ran for office, most MPs indicate that it was to serve the community they live in. Helping individuals is a natural part of this community service. There is also a high degree of job satisfaction involved. Many members indicate that their parliamentary work can be frustrating. Committees meet and put a great deal of time and effort into studying policy, only to see the cabinet ignore well thought-out committee reports.[48] Committees and other aspects of parliamentary work may serve important legitimacy functions by allowing public access to the fringes of the policy process, but it is often difficult for members to see tangible results from these activities.[49] Alternatively, local work brings about concrete results, be they instantaneous – a constituent leaves the office satisfied with their problem now resolved – or part of a longer, harder process – the turning of sod at a community centre provided in part by federal funds.

Asked to rank these same five activities in terms of personal enjoyment, members in both the 34th and 35th Parliaments were consistent in their views. Protecting the interests of individuals and helping with their problems were the two most enjoyable tasks respectively. Tellingly, the least enjoyable task for both groups of members was the same – communicating government policy, or 'staying in touch.' Once again, the data point to the same conclusion: the gap between the public and parliamentarians is not a result of a lazy legislative body, but rather of members performing tasks the public writ large does not see as a priority, and not emphasizing those things the public thinks are more crucial to the representation process.

Finally, it is worthwhile exploring how the views of members of parliament alter even after a brief stint in parliament. After all, had the entry class of 1993 been consistent in their views, we should expect to see levels of trust increase. Yet as indicated earlier, in 1997 more Canadians than ever before thought politicians would lose touch with voters. Tables 6.6 and 6.7 indicate new members (when they first enter the parliamentary arena) hold views on representation that are closer to those of the public than to those of veteran politicians. What happened to them between the fall of 1993 and the national vote in 1997?

Simply put, the new members of the class of '93 drifted further away from the public and closer towards the men and women they replaced in the House of Commons. In this sense, they really did lose touch. For example, while nearly three-quarters of rookie politicians in 1993 said they would place constituency ahead of party (see table 6.6), asked the same question three years later, their support for this view drops to 59 per cent. Support for party discipline actually increased among rookie members over this same period.

The explanations for this change are many and a detailed examination of them lies beyond the scope of this paper.[50] However, a cursory analysis suggests that the pulls away from the riding and towards the legislature are difficult to resist. These tugs come from many sources. First, C.E.S. Franks and others have argued that the first term of members of parliament is the most difficult.[51] Rookie members are placed in a legislative organization that differs drastically from most of the working environments with which they are familiar. As a result, rookie members naturally turn to veteran members for guidance and direction, and begin to accept the views of veterans on issues such as representation style and the importance of constituency work. For rookie Reform MPs in 1993, there were no real veterans to turn to within their own caucus (Deborah Grey had been elected in a 1989 by-election and all other Reform MPs were rookies). As a result, these members turned to their leader and his office for advice, helping to solidify a traditional party hierarchy in a party that eschewed these very lines of authority.

This relationship with the leader acts as a further barrier to maintaining a delegate-style role. As long as party leaders control internal party and House positions, ambitious members of parliament have a vested interest in not openly criticizing or distancing themselves from their leader. This is particularly the case for rookie MPs on the government side, where many positions include an increase in pay, but it also applies to Opposition MPs, who hope to get key critic portfolios and wish a cabinet seat if and when their party takes hold of the reins of power. Despite John Nunziata's initial electoral success as an independent, winning candidates are overwhelmingly representatives of political parties. In fact, in the four general elections between 1984 and 1997, 1173 seats have been up for grabs (not including by-elections). Four of these have been won by independent candidates, for a success rate of a quarter of one per cent. Odds overwhelmingly favour candidates with a major party label. Incumbents are loath to break ties with their leader and party when their electoral careers are potentially at risk.

In addition, in the face of support for delegate-style representation, it must be remembered that within each party MPs share similar ideological outlooks. In most votes in the House of Commons, the similarity of views usually translates into party discipline, even when a 'whip' is not being used. The Reform party has defined itself as a party that does not believe in party discipline. At the same time, elected members of the party share similar conservative views on fiscal responsibility, social policy, and a limited state. An examination of votes on some third readings in the 35th Parliament suggests that these similar ideological views have the same impact as party discipline. An analysis of third-reading votes held in November 1994 and 1995, and April 1996 and 1997, showed Reform party MPs voted as a block on twenty-nine of thirty occasions.[52] The Reform party was just as likely to act in a unified manner as the traditional parties were.

At the same time, it must be acknowledged that the present and past parliaments have witnessed more high-profile breaches from party discipline than any of the modern parliamentary era (with the exception of issues in these and earlier parliaments designated as 'free' votes). From issues such as gun control and gay rights in the 35th Parliament to environmental issues in the 36th Parliament, members of all parties are less afraid to distinguish themselves from their party than were previous legislators. The most noticeable, and for voters heartening, change has been in the governing Liberal caucus. While Jean Chretién has been more aggressive than earlier prime ministers in punishing members who step out of line, this has not stopped Liberal backbenchers from publicly opposing their leader.[53] The net result has been a small challenge to accepted notions of party discipline. While this challenge may yet be too insignificant to register with a sceptical populace, it has gained notice from politicians and students of politics. And the fact that the challenge has been incremental places it in the company of most parliamentary reform in Canada. It is too soon to make any judgment about the long-term success or failure of this increase in independent-minded members.

The staggered challenges to a leader-dominated parliament and the resiliency of those factors that push members to their leader and party highlight the tendency of well-intentioned members to move from a riding-delegate to party-delegate style of representation. It should be noted, however, that this tendency does not necessarily indicate bad representation. While the public may think members are losing touch, and not acting in the best interests of the constituency, there is little evidence that this is actually the case. Members of parliament are providing important representational services – services that are in high demand from a cross-section of the constituency. The satisfaction levels of individuals who contact members' offices testify to the work that is performed by MPs and their staffs. There is a segment of the public that understands and appreciates the type of representation that members provide. For members, it is unfortunately a small segment of the population. The problem for MPs is the lack of public acknowledgment for these necessary services. With little indication that this situation will change in the near future, it is likely that the gap between what the public wants and what MPs provide will remain large.

Summary

It is a cliché for researchers to conclude their analysis by calling for a new research agenda. Yet the work presented in these pages suggests that, at the very least, new, coordinated studies on representation in Canada are required. Comprehensive social survey data exist on citizens' attitudes and political behaviour in Canada. Thanks to a commitment from dedicated scholars of public participation, we know an awful lot about how Canadians feel towards their political leaders (and followers). That these data are collected at regular intervals (the irregular calling of federal elections) allows us to measure how the views of citizens change over time.

Yet in many ways these comprehensive data sets sit in a vacuum. We know more about how the general population feels towards politicians than we do about how 301 politicians feel about Canadians. The work presented here has relied on a second-best measure – two studies of parliamentarians and candidates taken in isolation from the broader public survey data. We would be well served to think about research that asks politicians and the public the same questions at the same period in time.

Nonetheless, the richness of the public data and availability of the members' surveys have allowed us to begin to draw some conclusions about the problems of representation in Canada. An already sceptical public is becoming increasingly cynical about the motives and style of federal politicians. Politicians, meanwhile, enter office with goals similar to the wants of the public, only to move away from them as their careers progress. Yet the moves are hardly sinister, and in fact are driven by public demands. Members of parliament are helping people who have asked for help. In many ways, this is the real essence of representation. There are lessons for all of us in these findings.

For politicians, one of the lessons is the need for better communication. Members need to better understand what the public wants in a member. Largely, the public wants to know what is happening in Ottawa and what the member of parliament is doing to protect the interests of their district. Among other things, this means that members need to find innovative ways of 'staying in touch,' and this means moving beyond the traditional methods of town-hall meetings, quarterly 'householders,' and regular attendance at those all important local service-organization functions. This paper has not looked at what methods might be appropriate, but in an increasingly computerized world, more extensive use of Internet and web-page technology seems the most direct possibility. It is worth noting here that members of parliament have been slow to develop their own web pages, particularly compared to U.S. members of Congress, who use their web sites as an important means of communication with voters.

Members must also be thoughtful about exactly what type of message they are communicating. Students of representation may have insight into MPs' access to information that is unavailable to the public and therefore might understand decisions based on different criteria. But if voters do not fully understand this reality, they will continue to see politicians as opportunists, promising one thing as candidates only to take a different course of action once they are safely ensconced in office.

Of course a different approach to communications strategies is just a minor solution and one that would unlikely affect public perceptions of politicians. In order to change the views of voters, politicians must be willing to embrace a more substantive change in their representational roles. Such a change of roles will be difficult without the willingness of parliament, and parliamentary leaders in particular, to acquiesce to the calls for reform that come from within the legislative arena. There are a number of reforms, some requiring greater institutional changes than others, that could provide members with an opportunity to build greater links with their constituents, without moving to a complete delegate style of representation that runs counter to the ideals of a Westminster-style system.

One possible change would be a reform of the method we use to elect members. While some papers in this volume call for a move towards proportional representation, there is little evidence that such a reform would create better links between Ottawa and local ridings. If anything, proportional representation – whether an Isreali-style nation-wide system or a German-top-up system – would have the net effect of driving some elected members further away from voters and making them more relient on their relationship with party leaders and others who determine the placement of names on a ballot. A more realistic change would require a move towards a majoritarian system along the lines of France or an alternative-vote system such as is used in Australia.

In these latter cases, members are not elected until they have received the endorsement of at least half of all voters in their district. There are two benefits with such a system. Members are no longer worried that they are representing a riding where more people voted against than for them. Whether they serve in cabinet or on the backbench, members can take some comfort in knowing that their campaign pledges were endorsed by a majority of voters. Further, with a stronger base of support at home, members should be more inclined to take public issue with their party leaders. Such a system should be taken in context. Most MPs will not win with over 50 per cent of first-place votes, but will require a run-off election or make use of alternative ballots. Nonetheless, members will be going into subsequent elections with a stronger margin of victory than would exist in most ridings with our present single-member plurality system.

The second reform would require members to, in the words of Senator Lowell Murray, 'take back parliament' from the cabinet and prime minister.[54] This is really a call for members to step up their accountability function. Whether MPs serve in opposition or on the government backbench, this line of argument suggests that they must set aside personal ambition (and the hope of a cabinet seat) and not be afraid to challenge party discipline and party leaders. Only when members are no longer tempted by the carrot (promotion) will the stick become ineffective.

Such a reform openly calls into question the age-old debate about what constitutes confidence in a parliamentary system. The United Kingdom has been more comfortable with a more liberal interpretation of confidence than has the Canadian parliament. When a piece of legislation is defeated, the government can simply call for a motion of confidence. As long as they clear this hurdle, there is no need to dissolve parliament. There are no constitutional, or even legislative, changes required to move to this more open view of discipline.

Certainly, a larger House of Commons would make any move in this direction easier. When members see a cabinet career as a remote possibility and a parliamentary career as more probable, they will be less enamoured with the carrot. Creating a larger Commons without increasing the size of cabinet would go a long way to making the carrot look smaller and less attainable. In order to be effective, however, the Commons would have to be substantially increased, probably by at least one hundred new members.

Of the recommendations, or ideas, cited above, the larger House of Commons is the least likely. It is hard to imagine, given the evidence presented above, that any serious political party would take to the hustings with a promise of more politicians. Changes to confidence and party discipline are the easiest, but no doubt the lease palatable, to party leaders in general and the prime minister in particular. This leaves changes to the electoral system as the most viable of large-scale reforms.

But changes to parliament and to members' duties alone cannot change the relationship politicians have with voters. Members of the public should also be prepared to appreciate the work that members of parliament currently undertake. Citizens who contact members for assistance are usually satisfied with the work done on their behalf. What evidence we have suggests that contact breeds trust. In this light, politicians may be similar to bankers, doctors, teachers, and other professionals. There is general scepticism regarding the profession and its members, but people like their own bank manager, doctor, and child's teacher.

Much of the work of members of parliament is thankless. The 1993 survey of MPs overwhelmingly found that members claimed the worst aspect of their job was the time away from family and other loved ones. The size of Canada and of many of its constituencies means that many politicians spend hours each week commuting – not just back and forth from Ottawa to their district, but within the district itself each weekend. When members do skip local functions to spend time with their family, it can often be misinterpreted as disinterest in their district.

It is worth reinforcing the fact that the type of local service provided by most members, while thankless to the broader public, is nonetheless important. Members help people who need their assistance. Should we change the type of representative we have in Canada, that work would still need to be done. It is perhaps best left where it is now, in the hands of individuals who have a strong tie to their district, as well as an electoral and personal incentive in solving problems.

And finally, for those of us interested in understanding more about public trust, the role of the representative, and the relationship between voters and politicians, there is a final lesson to be learned. Studies of voting and citizenship participation cannot be done in isolation from studies of representation. It is not enough for us to look from the outside in. We must also recognize that reforms often hold unintended consequences. Offering mechanisms to keep politicians more in touch might make a substantial segment of the population happy, but it may also risk the freedom politicians now enjoy to represent a different, yet no less important, section of the population. Looking from the inside out may help us detect the danger of uninformed reform. Future election and citizenship studies could easily increase our knowledge of the gap between the public and politicians if they included legislators, and would-be legislators, as an integral part of the study cohort.

Notes

This paper was funded by the Social Sciences and Humanities Research Council of Canada and the Policy Research Secretariat. I thank both bodies for their generous support. The funding made it possible to make use of research assistance. I would like to thank Ms. Emily Bain for her able and professional assistance. In addition, I thank Neil Nevitte for advice and comments on earlier drafts. Finally, I thank Herman Bakvis and Senator Lowell Murray for their helpful comments at the June Workshop held in Toronto. Of course, I accept full responsibility for any errors or omissions in the paper.

1 André Blais and Elizabeth Gidengil, *Making Representative Democracy Work: The Views of Canadians*, vol. 17 of Research Studies, Royal Commission on Electoral Reform and Party Financing (Toronto: Dundurn Press, 1991).

2 See Neal Roese, chapter this volume; see also Neil Nevitte, *The Decline of Deference* (Peterborough, ON: Broadview Press, 1996).

3 Maureen Mancuso et al., *A Question of Ethics: Canadians Speak Out* (Toronto: Oxford University Press, 1998), 68.

4 Ibid., 2.

5 See Neil Nevitte, this volume.

6 Gallup kindly provided the author with demographic breakdowns of the respondents on these questions.

7 See, e.g., Alan Kornberg, *Canadian Legislative Behaviour: A Study of the 25th Parliament* (New York: Holt, Rinehart and Winston, 1967). See also P.A. Hall and R.P. Washburn, 'Elites and Representation: A Study of the Attitudes and Perceptions of MP's,' in Jean-Pierre Gaboury and James Ross Hurley, eds, *The Canadian House of Commons Observed: Parliamentary Internship Papers* (Ottawa: University of Ottawa Press, 1979).

8 See Munroe Eagles, 'The Political Ecology of Representation in English Canada: MP's and Their Constituencies,' paper presented at annual meeting of the Canadian Political Science Association, St Johns, Newfoundland, June 1997.

9 David C. Docherty, *Mr. Smith Goes to Ottawa: Life in the House of Commons* (Vancouver: UBC Press, 1997). Some of the questions in these surveys mirror questions raised nationally by Gallup Canada in late 1993.

10 Sharon Sutherland and James Mitchell, 'Ministerial Responsibility: The Submission of Politics and Administration to the Electorate,' in Hugh Mellon and Martin Westmacott, eds, *Public Administration and Policy: Governing in Challenging Times* (Scarborough, ON: Prentice Hall Allyn and Bacon Canada, 1999), 21.

11 Anthony Birch, *Representative and Responsible Government* (Toronto: University of Toronto Press, 1964), 12–17.

12 Docherty, *Mr. Smith Goes to Ottawa*, chap. 7.

13 See, e.g., Hanna Pitkin, *The Concept of Representation* (London: University of California Press, 1967), 81–2.

14 David Smith, 'The Federal Cabinet in Canadian Politics,' in Michael Whittington and Glen Williams, eds, *Canadian Politics in the 1990's* (Toronto: Nelson Canada, 1997), 382–401.

15 Heinz Eulau, *The Politics of Representation* (London: Sage Publications, 1978), 31.

16 Pitkin, *The Concept of Representation*, 168.

17 Taken from 'Speech Previous to the Election, Bristol, 1780,' *The Works of Edmund Burke* (London 1815–27), vol. 3: 360–1.

18 For the framers of the U.S. Constitution, the thought of dominating local interests was an anathema. As a result, they conceived a system of representation that was based on a large number of relatively small ridings, and frequent elections. The theory was that factions would compete against each other, and that any coalitions between interests would be short-lived and issue-specific (see Federalist Papers nos. 10 and 52).

19 W.L. Morton, *The Progressive Party of Canada* (Toronto: University of Toronto Press, 1967).

20 The Reform Party of Canada folded into the Canadian Alliance in spring 2000. It is presumed that the Alliance will continue this approach to representation. However, the data used for the analysis contained herein refer to the party in its earlier incarnation. For this reason, 'Reform party' is sometimes used in this chapter in the present tense.

21 Blais and Gidengil, *Making Representative Democracy Work.*

22 See Docherty, *Mr. Smith Goes to Ottawa.*

23 Ibid., 145 (see also table 6.6 for a similar comparison). The actual question wording in the survey forces members to choose between two near extremes. The question is worded as follows:

Select the statement that most closely reflects your views on representation:
VIEW A: On an issue that is not seen as crucial either locally or nationally, I would vote against the majority of my constituents for the sake of party unity and my relationship with my leader's office.
VIEW B: There is no issue on which I would vote against the wishes of my constituents.

24 Harold Clarke et al., *Absent Mandate: Interpreting Change in Canadian Elections*, 2nd ed. (Toronto: Gage Publishing, 1991).

25 Of all organizations, private, state, or political, public schools consistently rank the highest in terms of public respect and confidence. Of all private organizations, churches and organized religion consistently enjoy higher levels of public respect than do banks, large corporations, and labour unions.

26 All figures in this and the following paragraph are from Gallup Canada. The author thanks Gallup for the use of these data.

27 Keith Spicer (Chair), *Citizens' Forum on Canada's Future: Report to the People and the Government of Canada* (Ottawa: Minister of Supply and Services, 1991), 96–106.

28 Gallup Canada, *Annual Survey of Respect for Institutions*, April 1999.

29 Pierre Lortie (Chair), *Final Report Volume 1: Reforming Electoral Democracy*, Royal Commission on Electoral Reform and Party Financing (Ottawa: Minister of Supply and Services, 1991), 209.

30 Mancuso et al., *A Question of Ethics*.

31 A detailed breakdown of socio-economic and demographic indicators correlated to the question of politicians soon losing touch can be found in appendix A.

32 John Ferejohn and Brian Gaines, 'The Personal Vote in Canada,' in Herman Bakvis, ed., *Representation, Integration and Political Parties in Canada*, vol. 14 of Research Studies, Royal Commission on Electoral Reform and Party Financing (Toronto: Dundurn Press, 1991), 292–4.

33 See Bruce Cain, John Ferejohn, and Morris Fiorina, *The Personal Vote: Constituency Service and Electoral Independence* (London: Harvard University Press, 1987).

34 Ibid., 45–52.

35 See Richard Fenno, *Home Style: House Members in Their Districts* (London: Scott, Foresman and Co., 1978); see also Robert Fleming and J.E. Glenn, *Fleming's Canadian Legislatures 1997*, 11th ed. (Toronto: University of Toronto Press, 1997).

36 See Docherty, *Mr. Smith Goes to Ottawa*; see also C.E.S. Franks, *The Parliament of Canada* (Toronto: University of Toronto Press, 1997).

37 Philip Norton and David Wood, *Back from Westminster: British Members of Parliament and Their Districts* (Lexington: University of Kentucky Press, 1993).

38 See Cain, Ferejohn, and Fiorina, *The Personal Vote*, 39.

39 Donald Searing, *Westminster's World: Understanding Political Roles* (Cambridge: Harvard University Press, 1994), 36.

40 Michael Atkinson, 'What Kind of Democracy Do Canadians Want?' *Canadian Journal of Political Science* 27(4) (1994): 717–46.

41 David Laycock, 'Reforming Canadian Democracy? Institutions and Ideology in the Reform Party Project,' *Canadian Journal of Political Science* 27(2) (1994): 213–47.

42 Respondents were asked to choose between one of the two following statements:

    'On a matter that is not a crucial issue, I have gone [would go] against my

constituents' wishes for the sake of party unity and/or my relationship
with my leader's office.'
'There is no "critical issue" on which I would vote against the wishes of
the majority of my constituents.'

43 The sample of candidates underestimates the number of Bloc Québécois
seeking office. For detailed information on the sample of candidates and
members see Docherty, *Mr. Smith Goes to Ottawa*, xvi–xviii.
44 A more detailed discussion of the importance and enjoyment of representational responsibilities of members of parliament can be found in
Docherty, *Mr. Smith Goes to Ottawa.*
45 Ferejohn and Gaines, 'The Personal Vote in Canada.'
46 See William Irvine, 'Does the Candidate Make a Difference? The Macro-
politics and Micro-politics of Getting Elected in Canada,' *Canadian Journal
of Political Science* 15(4) (1982): 755–85; see also Munroe Eagles, 'The Political Ecology of Representation in English Canada,' paper presented at
annual meeting of the Canadian Political Science Association, St John's,
NF, June 1997.
47 Docherty, *Mr. Smith Goes to Ottawa.*
48 David Docherty, 'Parliamentarians and Government Accountability,' in
Mellon and Westmacott, *Public Administration and Policy*, 38–52; see also
Report of the Liaison Committee on Committee Effectiveness (Ottawa: Minister
of Supply and Services, 1994).
49 Jonathan Malloy, 'Reconciling Expectations with Reality in House of
Commons Committees: The Case of the 1989 GST Inquiry,' *Canadian Public
Administration* 39(3) (1996): 314–35.
50 Much of the analysis and data from this section comes from Docherty, *Mr.
Smith Goes to Ottawa.* Chapters 5 through 7 explore how members adapt to
and change their legislative work world and the effect that this has on
their relationship with their constituency.
51 See Franks, *The Parliament of Canada*, chap. 2; also Sharon Sutherland, 'The
Consequences of Electoral Volatility: Inexperienced Ministers 1949–90,' in
Bakvis, *Representation, Integration and Political Parties in Canada.*
52 The months were chosen at random, using fall in the first two years and
spring in the subsequent years. There was no spring 1993 sitting or fall
1997 sitting of the 35th Parliament.
53 Paul Thomas, 'Caucus and Representation in Canada,' *Parliamentary
Perspectives*, no. 1, May 1998
54 Once again, the author thanks Senator Murray for his comments on an
earlier version of this paper. It is hoped the discussion above does justice
to his thoughtful concerns.

Appendix A
Faith in Politicians and Socio-Demographic Characteristics
1984–1997

	1984	1993	1997
Regions			
Atlantic provinces			
MPs soon lose touch			
Agree	76.7%	80.3%	83.3%
Disagree	23.3	19.7	16.7
N	473	228	402
Quebec			
MPs soon lose touch			
Agree	78.7	82.5	79.6
Disagree	21.3	17.5	20.4
N	697	285	979
Ontario			
MPs soon lose touch			
Agree	77.7	77.2	82.3
Disagree	22.4	22.8	17.7
N	897	307	929
Western Provinces			
MPs soon lose touch			
Agree	77.4	81	86.1
Disagree	23.6	19	13.9
N	1039	609	1315
Gender	1984	1993	1997
Males			
MPs soon lose touch			
Agree	77.9	81.3	82.7
Disagree	22.1	18.7	17.3
N	1364	726	1797
Females			
MPs soon lose touch			
Agree	76.9	79.4	83.3
Disagree	23.1	20.6	16.7
N	1742	703	2014
Income level	1984	1993	1997
>$20,000			
MPs soon lose touch			
Agree	77.7	80.9	78.3
Disagree	22.3	19.1	21.7
N	1907	199	184

Appendix A – *continued*
Faith in Politicians and Socio-Demographic Characteristics
1984–1997

	1984	1993	1997
$20,000–29,000			
MPs soon lose touch			
Agree	77.6	79.7	76.3
Disagree	22.4	20.3	23.7
N	429	207	135
$30,000–39,000			
MPs soon lose touch			
Agree	75	83.8	85.2
Disagree	25	16.2	14.8
N	212	216	115
$40,000–49,000			
MPs soon lose touch			
Agree	72.7	84.2	86
Disagree	27.3	15.8	14
N	110	203	86
$50,000+			
MPs soon lose touch			
Agree	50	76.5	85.7
Disagree	50	23.5	14.3
N	8	510	175
Level of education	**1984**	**1993**	**1997**
Some elementary			
MPs soon lose touch			
Agree	78.2	69.2	73.2
Disagree	21.8	30.8	26.8
N	229	26	82
Completed elementary			
MPs soon lose touch			
Agree	78.6	82.7	70.3
Disagree	21.4	17.3	29.7
N	215	52	138
Some high school			
MPs soon lose touch			
Agree	81.7	81	81.5
Disagree	18.3	19	18.5
N	783	216	639

Appendix A – *concluded*
Faith in Politicians and Socio-Demographic Characteristics
1984–1997

	1984	1993	1997
Completed high school			
MPs soon lose touch			
Agree	77.1	85.6	83.6
Disagree	22.9	14.4	16.4
N	707	326	884
Some technical			
MPs soon lose touch			
Agree	76.8	76.7	85.1
Disagree	23.2	23.3	14.9
N	164	146	302
Completed technical			
MPs soon lose touch			
Agree	76.9	82.4	86
Disagree	23.1	17.6	1
N	346	205	609
Some university			
MPs soon lose touch			
Agree	74.5	80.1	85.4
Disagree	25.5	19.9	14.6
N	235	141	302
Completed university			
MPs soon lose touch			
Agree	70.3	75	83.4
Disagree	29.7	25	16.6
N	408	312	799

Source: 1984 and 1997 Canadian National Election Study; 1993 Political Support in Canada Study.

Appendix B
Questions for Table 6.6

United States

1. Helping people in the district who have personal problems with the government (abbreviated as 'helping people').
2. Making sure the district gets its fair share of government money and projects ('protecting the district').
3. Keeping track of the way government agencies are carrying out laws passed by Congress ('oversight').
4. Keeping in touch with the people about what the government is doing ('keeping in touch').
5. Working in Congress on bills concerning national issues ('policy').

United Kingdom

1. Helping people in the constituency who have personal problems with the government.
2. Protecting the interests of the constituency.
3. Keeping track of civil servants.
4. Keeping in touch with the people about what the government is doing.
5. Debating and voting in Parliament.

Canada

Importance of the following responsibilities of individual members of parliament:

1. Helping people in the constituency who have personal problems with government.
2. Protecting the interests of the constituency.
3. Ensuring that the bureaucracy is administering government policy efficiently and effectively.
4. Keeping in touch with constituents about what the government is doing.
5. Debating issues and voting in the House of Commons.

Note: Questions for the United States and the United Kingdom from B. Cain et al., *The Personal Vote*. Questions for Canada from D.C. Docherty, *Mr. Smith Goes to Ottawa*.

References

Abramson, Paul, and Ronald Inglehart. *Value Change in Global Perspective*. Ann Arbor: University of Michigan Press, 1995.

Almond, Gabriel, and Sidney Verba. *The Civic Culture: Political Attitudes and Democracy in Five Nations*. Princeton: Princeton University Press, 1963.

Anderson, Christopher J., and Christine A. Guillory. 'Political Institutions and Satisfaction with Democracy: A Cross-National Analysis of Consensus and Majoritarian Systems.' *American Political Science Review* 91 (1997): 66–81.

Ansolabehere, Stephen, and Shanto Iyengar. *Going Negative: How Attack Ads Shrink and Polarize the Electorate*. New York: Free Press, 1995.

Apter, D.E., editor. *Ideology and Discontent*. New York: Free Press, 1964.

Atkinson, Michael. 'What Kind of Democracy Do Canadians Want?' *Canadian Journal of Political Science* 27(4) (1994): 717–46.

Bailey, J., editor. *Social Europe*. London: Longman, 1992.

Bakvis, Herman, editor. *Representation, Integration and Political Parties in Canada*. Volume 14 of Research Studies, Royal Commission on Electoral Reform and Party Financing. Toronto: Dundurn Press and Ottawa: Minister of Supply and Services, 1991.

Bandura, Albert. *Self-Efficacy: The Exercise of Control*. New York: W.H. Freeman and Co., 1997.

Barber, Benjamin R. *Strong Democracy: Participatory Politics for a New Age*. Berkeley: University of California Press, 1984.

Barnes, Samuel, and Max Kaase, editors. *Political Action: Mass Participation in Five Western Democracies*. Beverly Hills and London: Sage Publications, 1979.

Bartolini, S., and P. Mair. *Identity, Competition and Electoral Availability: The*

Stabilization of European Electorates 1885–1985. Cambridge: Cambridge University Press, 1990.

Becker, G.S. 'Investment in Human Capital: A Theoretical Analysis.' *Journal of Political Economy*, 70(5) (1962) part 2, supplement: 9–49.

– *Human Capital: A Theoretical and Empirical Analysis, with Special Reference to Education*. 1st and 2nd editions. New York: National Bureau of Economic Research, 1964 and 1975.

Bell, Daniel. *The Coming of Post-Industrial Society*. New York: Basic Books, 1973.

– *The Cultural Contradictions of Capitalism*. New York: Basic Books, 1976.

Berelson, B.R., P.F. Lazarsfeld, and W.N. McPhee. *Voting: A Study of Opinion Formation in a Presidential Campaign*. Chicago: University of Chicago Press, 1954.

Berg-Schlosser, Dirk, and Ralf Rytlewski, editors. *Political Culture in Germany*. New York: St Martin's Press, 1993.

Betz, H.G., and Stefan Immerfall, editors. *The New Politics of the Right: Neo-Populist Parties and Movements in Established Democracies*. New York: St Martin's Press, 1998.

Birch, Anthony. *Representative and Responsible Government*. Toronto: University of Toronto Press, 1964.

Black, Jerome H. 'The Practice of Politics in Two Settings: Political Transferability among Recent Immigrants to Canada.' *Canadian Journal of Political Science* 20 (1987): 731–53.

Blais, André, and Agnieszka Dobrzynska. 'Turnout in Electoral Democracies.' *European Journal of Political Research* 33 (1998): 239–62.

Blais, André, and Elisabeth Gidengil, editors. *La démocratie représentative: Perceptions des Canadiens et Canadiennes / Making Representative Democracy Work: The Views of Canadians*. Volume 17 of Research Studies, Royal Commission on Electoral Reform and Party Financing. Toronto and Oxford: Dundurn Press, 1991.

Blais, André, and Richard Nadeau. 'Measuring Strategic Voting: A Two-Step Procedure.' *Electoral Studies* 15 (1996): 39–52.

Blais, André, Richard Nadeau, Elisabeth Gidengil, and Neil Nevitte. 'Voting Strategically against the Winner: The 1997 Canadian Election.' Prepared for 1998 annual meeting of Midwest Political Science Association, Chicago, 23–26 April 1998.

Bollen, Kenneth A. 'Liberal Democracy: Validity and Method Factors in Cross-National Measures.' *American Journal of Political Science* 37 (1993): 1207–30.

Braithwaite, V.A., and Margaret Levi, *Trust and Governance*. New York: Sage, 1998.

Brann, P., and M. Foddy. 'Trust and the Consumption of a Deteriorating Common Resource.' *Journal of Conflict Resolution* 31 (1987): 615–30.

Brehm, John, and Wendy Rahn. 'Individual Level Evidence for the Causes and Consequences of Social Capital.' *American Journal of Political Science* 41(3) (1997): 999–1023.

Brittan, Samuel. 'The Economic Contradictions of Democracy.' *British Journal of Political Science* 5 (1975): 129–59.

Cadenhead, A.C., and C.L. Richmond. 'The Effects of Interpersonal Trust and Group Status on Prosocial and Aggressive Behaviors.' *Social Behavior and Personality* 24 (1996): 169–84.

Cain, Burce, John Ferejohn, and Morris Fiorina. *The Personal Vote: Constituency Service and Electoral Independence*. London: Harvard University Press, 1987.

Canada West Foundation. *Alternative Service Delivery Project: Research Bulletin*. Calgary: Canada West Foundation, 1999.

Cappella, Joseph N., and Kathleen Hall Jamieson. *Spiral of Cynicism: The Press and the Public Good*. New York: Oxford University Press, 1997.

Carty, R.K., W. Cross, and L. Young. *Rebuilding Canadian Party Politics*. Vancouver, BC: UBC Press, 2000.

Clark, Terry Nichols, and Vincent Hoffman-Martinot, editors. *The New Political Culture*. Boulder, CO: Westview Press, 1998.

Clark, Terry Nichols, and Michael Rempel, editors. *Citizens Politics in Post-Industrial Societies*. Boulder, CO: Westview Press, 1997.

Clarke, Harold D., and Nittish Dutt. 'Measuring Value Change in Western Industrialized Societies: The Impact of Unemployment.' *American Political Science Review* 85(3) (1991): 905–20.

Clarke, Harold D., Nittish Dutt, and Jonathon Rapkin. 'Conversations in Context: The (Mis)Measurement of Value Change in Advanced Industrial Societies.' *Political Behavior* 19 (1997): 19–40.

Clarke, Harold D., Jane Jenson, Lawrence LeDuc, and Jon Pammett. *Political Choice in Canada*. Toronto: McGraw-Hill Ryerson, 1980.

– *Absent Mandate: Interpreting Change in Canadian Elections*. 2nd edition. Toronto: Gage, 1991.

– *Absent Mandate: Canadian Electoral Politics in an Era of Restructuring*. 3rd edition. Toronto: McGraw-Hill Ryerson, 1996.

Clarke, Harold D., and Allan Kornberg. 'Evaluations and Evolution: Public Attitudes toward Canada's Federal Political Parties 1965–1991.' *Canadian Journal of Political Science* 26 (1993): 287–311.

Clarke, Harold D., Allan Kornberg, et al. 'The Effect of Economic Priorities on the Measurement of Value Change: New Experimental Evidence.' *American Political Science Review* (forthcoming).

Clarke, Harold D., and M. Stewart. 'The Decline of Parties in the Minds of Citizens.' *Annual Review of Political Science* 1 (1998): 357–78.

Crewe, I., and D. Denver. *Electoral Change in Western Democracies: Patterns and Sources of Electoral Volatility*. London: Croom Helm, 1985.

Crozier, Michael, Samuel P. Huntington, and Joji Watanuki. *The Crisis of Democracy: Report on the Governability of Democracies to the Trilateral Commission*. New York: New York University Press, 1975.

Dahl, Robert A. *Polyarchy*. New Haven: Yale University Press, 1971.

– *Democracy and Its Critics*. New Haven: Yale University Press, 1990.

Dalton, Russell J. 'Cognitive Mobilization and Partisan Dealignment in Advanced Industrial Democracies.' *Journal of Politics* 46 (February 1984): 264–84.

– *Citizen Politics in Western Democracies: Public Opinion and Political Parties in the United States, Great Britain, West Germany and France*. 1st edition. Chatham, NJ: Chatham House Publishers, 1988.

– *Citizen Politics: Public Opinion and Political Parties in Advanced Democracies*. 1st edition. Irvine: University of California, 1988.

– *Citizen Politics: Public Opinion and Political Parties in Advanced Democracies*, 2nd edition. Irvine: University of California, 1996.

Dalton, Russell J., P.A. Beck, and R. Huckfeldt. 'Partisan Cues and the Media: Information Flows in the 1992 Presidential Election.' *American Political Science Review* 92(1) (1998): 111–26.

Dalton, Russell J., Scott Flanagan, and Paul Allen Beck. *Electoral Change in Advanced Industrial Democracies: Realignment or Dealignment?* Princeton: Princeton University Press, 1984.

Dalton, Russell J., and Manfred Kuechler. *Challenging the Political Order: New Social and Political Movements in Western Democracies*. New York: Oxford University Press, 1990.

Delli Carpini, Michael X., and Scott Keeter. *What Americans Know about Politics and Why It Matters*. New Haven: Yale University Press, 1996.

de Moor, Ruud, editor. *Values in Western Societies*. Tilburg, The Netherlands: Tilburg University Press, 1995.

Dickerson, M., and T. Flanagan. *An Introduction to Government and Politics: A Conceptual Approach*. Scarborough, ON: ITP Nelson, 1998.

Dickinson, P., and J. Ellison. 'Plugged into the Internet.' In *Canadian Social Trends* (Statistics Canada Catalogue no. 11-008), Winter 1999.

Dickinson, P., and G. Sciadas. 'Canadians Connected.' In *Canadian Economic Observer*, February 1999.

Docherty, David C. *Mr. Smith Goes to Ottawa*. Vancouver, BC: UBC Press, 1997.

Dogan, Mattie. 'Erosion of Confidence in Advanced Democracies.' *Studies in Comparative International Development* 32(3) (1997): 3–29.

Downs, A. 'An Economic Theory of Political Action in a Democracy.' *Journal of Political Economy* 65 (1957): 135–50.

Drake, P., and M. McCubbins, editors. *The Origins of Liberty*. Princeton: Princeton University Press, 1998.

Eagles, Munroe. 'The Political Ecology of Representation in English Canada: MPs and Their Constituencies.' Paper presented at annual meeting of the Canadian Political Science Association, St Johns, Newfoundland, June 1997.

Eagly, Alice H., and Shelley Chaiken. *The Psychology of Attitudes*. Orlando, FL: Harcourt Brace Jovanovich, 1993.

Easton, David. *A Systems Analysis of Political Life*. New York: Wiley, 1965.

– 'A Re-Assessment of the Concept of Political Support.' *British Journal of Political Science* 54 (1975): 435–7.

– 'Theoretical Approaches to Political Support.' *Canadian Journal of Political Science* 9 (1976): 431–48.

Edwards, Bob, and Michael W. Foley. 'The Paradox of Civil Society.' *Journal of Democracy* 7(3) (1996): 38–52.

– 'Social Capital and Civil Society Beyond Putnam.' *American Behavioral Scientist* 42(1) (1998): 124–36.

Edwards, S. 'Canada's No. 1, United Nations says anew.' *National Post*, 29 June 2000.

Eliasoph, Nina. *Avoiding Politics: How Americans Produce Apathy in Everyday Life*. Cambridge: Cambridge University Press, 1998.

Ester, Peter, Loek Halman, and Ruud de Moor, editors. *The Individualizing Society: Value Change in Europe and North America*. Tilburg, The Netherlands: Tilburg University Press, 1993.

Eulau, Heinz. *The Politics of Representation*. London: Sage Publications, 1978.

Farrell, David M. *Comparing Electoral Systems*. London: Prentice Hall, 1997.

Fenno, Richard. *Home Style: House Members in Their Districts*. London: Scott, Forseman, and Co., 1978.

Finifter, Ada, editor, *Political Science: The State of the Discipline II*. Washington: American Political Science Association, 1993.

Fleming, Robert, and J.E. Glenn. *Fleming's Canadian Legislatures 1997*, 11th edition. Toronto: University of Toronto Press, 1997.

Fletcher, Frederick J., and Robert Everett. 'Mass Media and Elections in Canada.' In *Media, Elections and Democracy*, vol. 19 of Research Studies, Royal Commission on Electoral Reform and Party Financing. Toronto and Oxford: Dundurn Press, 1991.

Franklin, M., T. Mackie, and H. Valen. *Electoral Change: Responses to Evolving Social and Attitudinal Structures in Western Countries*. New York: Cambridge University Press, 1992.

Franks, C.E.S. *The Parliament of Canada*. Toronto: University of Toronto Press, 1997.

Frizzell, Alan, Jon H. Pammett, and Anthony Westell. *The Canadian General Election of 1988*. Ottawa: Carleton University Press, 1989.

– *The Canadian General Election of 1993*. Ottawa: Carleton University Press, 1994.

– *The Canadian General Election of 1997*. Toronto: Dundurn Press, 1997.

Gaboury, Jean-Pierre, and James Ross Hurley, editors. *The Canadian House of Commons Observed: Parliamentary Internship Papers*. Ottawa: University of Ottawa Press, 1979.

Gallup Canada. *Annual Survey of Respect for Institutions*. April 1999.

Galston, William A. 'Won't You Be My Neighbor?' *The American Prospect*, no. 26 (May/June 1996): 16–18.

Gidengil, Elisabeth, André Blais, Richard Nadeau, and Neil Nevitte. 'Exit, Voice and Loyalty: Anti-Party Parties.' Paper presented at annual meeting of the Atlantic Provinces Political Science Association, Sackville, NB, 15–17 October 1999.

Gidengil, Elisabeth, and Neil Nevitte. 'Know More: Information, Interest and the Constitutional Proposals.' Paper delivered at Canadian Political Science meetings, Ottawa, 1993.

Goertzel, T. 'Belief in Conspiracy Theories.' *Political Psychology* 15 (1994): 731–42.

Guppy, N., and S. Davies. *Education in Canada: Recent Trends and Future Challenges*. Government of Canada: Minister of Industry, 1998.

Habermas, Jürgen. *Legitimation Crisis*. Boston: Beacon Press, 1975.

Hedges, Alan, et al. *New Electoral Systems: What Voters Need to Know*. London: The Publications Officer, 1999.

Held, David. *Models of Democracy*. Cambridge: Polity Press, 1987.

Hofstetter, C.R., D. Barker, et al. 'Information, Misinformation, and Political Talk Radio.' *Political Research Quarterly* 52(2) (1999): 353–69.

Howe, Paul, and David Northup. *Strengthening Canadian Democracy: The View of Canadians*. 'Policy Matters' Collection. Montreal: Institute for Research on Public Policy, 2000.

Huntington, Samuel. 'Post-Industrial Politics: How Benign Will It Be?' *Comparative Politics* 6 (1974): 147–77.

ICORE. *Comparative Study of Electoral Systems, 1996–2000*. Version 1. Ann Arbor: Center for Political Studies, February 1999.

Ignazi, Pierro. 'The Silent Counter-Revolution: Hypotheses on the Emergence of Extreme Right-Wing Parties in Europe.' *European Journal of Political Research* 22 (1992): 3–34.

Inglehart, Ronald. 'Cognitive Mobilization and European Identity.' *Comparative Politics* (October 1970): 45–70.
- *The Silent Revolution: Changing Values and Political Styles among Western Publics*. Princeton: Princeton University Press, 1977.
- *Culture Shift in Advanced Industrial Society*. Princeton: Princeton University Press, 1990.
- *Modernization and Postmodernization: Cultural, Economic, and Political Change in 43 Societies*. Princeton: Princeton University Press, 1997.
Inglehart, Ronald, and Paul R. Abramson. 'Economic Security and Value Change.' *American Political Science Review* 88 (1994): 336–54.
- 'Measuring Postmaterialism.' *American Political Science eview* (forthcoming).
Irvine, William. 'Does the Candidate Make a Difference? The Macro-Politics and Micro-Politics of Getting Elected in Canada.' *Canadian Journal of Political Science* 15(4) (1982): 755–85.
Jackman, Robert W., and Ross A. Miller. 'A Renaissance of Political Culture?' *American Journal of Political Science* 40 (1996): 632–59.
Janoski, Thomas. *Citizenship and Civil Society: A Framework of Rights and Obligations in Liberal, Traditional and Social Democratic Regimes*. Cambridge: Cambridge University Press, 1998.
Jennings, M. Kent. 'Political Knowledge over Time and across Generations.' *Public Opinion Quarterly* 60 (1996): 228–52.
Jennings, M. Kent, and Jan van Deth. *Continuities in Political Action*. New York: Walter de Gruyter, 1989.
Johnston, Richard, André Blais, Henry E. Brady, and Jean Crête. *Letting the People Decide: Dynamics of a Canadian Election*. Montreal: McGill-Queen's University Press, 1992.
Johnston, Richard, André Blais, E. Gidengil, and Neil Nevitte. *The Challenge of Direct Democracy*. Montreal and Kingston: McGill-Queen's University Press, 1996.
Johnston, Richard, André Blais, et al. 'The Collapse of a Party System? The 1993 Canadian General Election.' Paper presented at 1994 annual meeting of the American Political Science Association, New York.
Kaase, Max, and Kenneth Newton. *Beliefs in Government*. Oxford and New York: Oxford University Press, 1995.
King, Anthony. 'Overload: Problems of Governing in the 1970's.' *Political Studies* 23 (1975): 284–96.
Klingemann, H., and D. Fuchs, editors. *Citizens and the State*. New York: Oxford University Press, 1995.
Kornberg, Allan. *Canadian Legislative Behaviour: A Study of the 25th Parliament*. New York: Hold, Rienhart and Winston, 1967.

Kornberg, Allan, and Harold D. Clarke. *Citizens and Community: Political Support in a Representative Democracy*. New York: Cambridge University Press, 1992.

Kornberg, Allan, and Harold D. Clarke. 'Beliefs about Democracy and Satisfaction with Democratic Government: The Canadian Case.' *Political Research Quarterly* 47 (1994): 540.

Kumar, P., and R. Ghadially. 'Organizational Politics and Its Effects on Members of Organizations.' *Human Relations* 42 (1989): 305–14.

Lane, Jan-Erik, and Sven Ersson. *Politics and Society in Western Europe*. 2nd edition. London: Sage Publications, 1991.

Lane, Jan-Erik, D. McKay, and K. Newton. *Political Data Handbook: OECD Countries*. Oxford: Oxford University Press, 1991.

Laroche, M., M. Merette, and G.C. Ruggeri. 'On the Concept and Dimensions of Human Capital in a Knowledge-Based Economy Context.' *Canadian Public Policy* 25(1): (1999).

Laycock, David. 'Reforming Canadian Democracy? Institutions and Ideology in the Reform Party Project.' *Canadian Journal of Political Science* 27(2) (1994): 213–47.

LeDuc, Lawrence, Richard G. Niemi, and Pippa Norris, editors. *Comparing Democracies: Elections and Voting in Global Perspective*. Thousand Oaks, CA: Sage Publications, 1996.

Levi, Margaret. 'Social and Unsocial Capital: A Review Essay of Robert Putnam's *Making Democracy Work*.' *Politics and Society* 24 (1996): 45–55.

Lewis-Beck, Michael S. *Economics and Elections: The Major Western Democracies*. Ann Arbor: University of Michigan Press, 1988.

Lijphart, Arend. *Democracies*. New Haven: Yale University Press, 1984.

– 'Democracies: Forms, Performance, and Constitutional Engineering.' *European Journal of Political Science* 25 (1994): 1–17.

Lind, E. Allan, and Tom R. Tyler. *The Social Psychology of Procedural Justice*. New York: Plenum, 1988.

Lipset, Seymour Martin, and Stein Rokkan, editors. *Party Systems and Voter Alignments: Cross-National Perspectives*. New York: Free Press, 1967.

Lipset, Seymour Martin, and William C. Schneider. *The Confidence Gap: Business, Labor, and Government in the Public Mind*. New York: Free Press, 1983.

– *The Confidence Gap: Business, Labor, and Government in the Public Mind*. Revised edition. Baltimore: Johns Hopkins University Press, 1987.

Lockerbie, Brad. 'Economic Dissatisfaction and Political Alienation in Western Europe.' *European Journal of Political Science* 23 (1993): 281–93.

Lortie, Pierre (Chair). *Final Report Volume 1: Reforming Electoral Democracy*.

The Royal Commission on Electoral Reform and Party Financing. Ottawa: Minister of Supply and Services, 1991.

Malloy, Jonathon. 'Reconciling Expectations with Reality in House of Commons Committees: The Case of the 1989 GST Inquiry.' *Canadian Public Administration* 39(3) (1996): 314–35.

Mancuso, Maureen, Michael Atkinson, André Blais, and Neil Nevitte. *A Question of Ethics: Canadians Speak Out*. Toronto and London: Oxford University Press, 1998.

Mayer, William G. 'The Polls-Poll Trends: The Rise of the New Media.' *Public Opinion Quarterly* 58 (1994): 124–46.

McClosky, H. 'Consensus and Ideology in American Politics.' *American Political Science Review* 58(2) (1964): 361–82.

Mellon, Hugh, and Martin Westmacott, editors. *Public Administration and Policy: Governing in Challenging Times*. Scarborough, ON: Prentice Hall Allyn and Bacon Canada, 1999.

Mendelsohn, Matthew, and Richard Nadeau. 'The Rise and Fall of Candidates in Canadian Election Campaigns.' *Harvard International Journal of Press and Politics* 4 (1999): 63–76.

Miller, Arthur H., and Ola Listhaug. 'Political Parties and Confidence in Government: A Comparison of Norway, Sweden and the United States.' *British Journal of Political Science* 29 (1990): 357–86.

Montgomery, S.M., D.G. Cook, M.J. Bartley, and M.E.J. Wadsworth. 'Unemployment Pre-dates Symptoms of Depression and Anxiety Resulting in Medical Consultation in Young Men.' *International Journal of Epidemiology* 28 (1999): 95–100.

Morton, W.L. *The Progressive Party of Canada*. Toronto: University of Toronto Press, 1967.

Muller, Edward, and Mitchell A. Seligson. 'Civic Culture and Democracy: The Question of Causal Relationships.' *American Political Science Review* 88(3) (1994): 635–52.

Nadeau, Richard, and André Blais. 'Accepting the Election Outcome: The Effect of Participation on Losers' Consent.' *British Journal of Political Science* 23 (1993): 553–63.

Nadeau, Richard, and Richard G. Niemi. 'Educated Guesses: The Process of Answering Factual Knowledge Questions in Surveys.' *Public Opinion Quarterly* 59 (1995): 323–46.

Nadeau, Richard, Richard G. Niemi, and Jeffrey Levine. 'Innumeracy about Minority Populations.' *Public Opinion Quarterly* 57 (1993): 332–47.

Neuman, Russell W. *The Paradox of Mass Politics: Knowledge and Opinion in the American Electorate*. Cambridge, MA: Harvard University Press, 1986.

Nevitte, Neil. *The Decline of Deference: Canadian Value Change in Cross-National Perspective*. Peterborough, ON: Broadview Press, 1996.

Nevitte, Neil, André Blais, Elisabeth Gidengil, and Richard Nadeau. *Unsteady State: The 1997 Canadian Federal Election*. Toronto and New York: Oxford University Press, 2000.

Newton, Kenneth. 'Social Capital and Democracy.' *American Behavioral Scientist* 40(5) (1997): 575–86.

Nie, Norman H., Jane Junn, and Kenneth Stehlik-Barry. *Education and Democratic Citizenship in America*. Chicago: University of Chicago Press, 1996.

Nie, Norman, J. Mueller, and T.W. Smith. *Trends in Public Opinion*. New York: Greenwood, 1989.

Norris, Pippa. *Electoral Change since 1945*. Cambridge, MA: Blackwell Publishers Ltd., 1997.

Norris, Pippa, editor. *Critical Citizens: Global Support for Democratic Governance*. Oxford: Oxford University Press, 1999.

Northrup, David, and Anne Oram. *The 1993 Canadian Election Study, Incorporating the 1992 Referendum Survey on the Charlottetown Accord: Technical Documentation*. Toronto: Institute for Social Research, York University, 1994.

Norton, Philip, and David Wood. *Back from Westminster: British Members of Parliament and Their Districts*. Lexington: University of Kentucky Press, 1993.

Nye, Joseph S., Jr. 'In Government We Don't Trust.' *Foreign Policy* 108 (1997): 99–111.

Nye, Joseph S., Jr., P.D. Zelikow, and D.C. King, editors. *Why People Don't Trust Government*. Cambridge, MA: Harvard University Press, 1997.

O'Connor, Pauleen. *Mapping Social Cohesion*. CPRN Discussion Paper no. F.01. 1998. Available at http://www.cprn.ca.

Paletz, David L. 'Advanced Information Technology and Political Communication.' *Social Science Computer Review* 14(1) (1996): 75–7.

Pateman, Carole. *Participation and Democratic Theory*. Cambridge: Cambridge University Press, 1970.

Patterson, Thomas E. *Out of Order*. New York: Knopf, 1994.

Patterson, Thomas E. 'Bad News, Bad Governance.' *Annals of the American Academy of Political and Social Science* 546 (1996): 97–108.

Pitkin, Hanna. *The Concept of Representation*. London: University of California Press, 1967.

Popkin, S. *The Reasoning Voter: Communication and Persuasion in Presidential Campaigns*. Chicago: University of Chicago Press, 1991.

Putnam, Robert. *Making Democracy Work: Civic Traditions in Modern Italy*. Princeton: Princeton University Press, 1993.

– 'Tuning In, Tuning Out: The Strange Disappearance of Social Capital in America.' *PS: Political Science and Politics* 28(4) (December 1995): 664–83.

– 'Bowling Alone : America's Declining Social Capital.' *Journal of Democracy* 6(1) (1995): 65–78.

Putnam, Robert D. *Bowling Alone: The Collapse and Revival of American Community.* New York: Simon and Schuster, 2000.

Reif, Karlheinz, and Ronald Inglehart, editors. *Eurobarometer: The Dynamic of European Public Opinion – Essays in Honor of Jacques-René Rabier.* New York: St Martin's Press, 1991.

Report of the Liaison Committee on Committee Effectiveness. Ottawa: Minister of Supply and Services, 1994.

Rogowski, Ronald. 'Eckstein and the Study of Private Governments: An Appreciation, Critique, and Proposal.' *Comparative Political Studies* 31(4) (1998): 444–63.

Rose, Richard. *Survey Measures of Democracy.* Glasgow: University of Strathclyde Studies in Public Policy no. 294, 1997.

Rosenstone, S., and J. Hansen. *Mobilization, Participation, and Democracy in America.* New York: Macmillan Publishing Co., 1993.

Ross, W.H., and C. Wieland. 'Effects of Interpersonal Trust and Time Pressure on Managerial Mediation Strategy in a Simulated Organizational Dispute.' *Journal of Applied Psychology* 81 (1996): 228–48.

Rucht, Dieter, editor. *Research on Social Movements: The State of the Art in Western Europe and the USA.* Boulder, CO: Westview Press, 1991.

Sartori, Giovanni. *The Theory of Democracy Revisited.* Chatham, NJ: Chatham House Publishers, 1987.

Schultz, T.W. 'Investment in Human Capital.' *American Economic Review* 51(1) (1961): 1–17.

– 'Reflections on Investment in Man.' *Journal of Political Economy* 70(5) (1962), part 2, supplement: 1–8.

Searing, Donald. *Westminster's World: Understanding Political Roles.* Cambridge, MA: Harvard University Press, 1994.

Secretary of State for Home Department. *The Report of the Independent Commission on the Voting System.* London: The Stationery Office, 1998.

Semetko, H., and P. Valkenberg. 'The Impact of Attentiveness on Political Efficacy: Evidence from a Three-Year German Panel Study.' *International Journal of Public Opinion Research* 10(3) (1998): 195–210.

Shaw, Daron R., and Bartholomew H. Sparrow. 'From the Inner Ring Out: News Congruence, Cue-Taking, and Campaign Coverage).' *Political Research Quarterly* 52(2) (1999): 323–51.

Sniderman, Paul M. *A Question of Loyalty.* Berkeley: University of California Press, 1981.

Sniderman, P., R. Brody, and P. Tetlock. *Reasoning and Choice: Explorations in Political Psychology.* New York: Cambridge University Press, 1991.

Spicer, Keith (Chair). *Citizens' Forum on Canada's Future: Report to the People and the Government of Canada.* Ottawa: Minister of Supply and Services, 1991.

Statistics Canada. *Caring Canadians, Involved Canadians: Highlights from the 1997 National Survey of Giving, Volunteering and Participating.* Ottawa: Minister Responsible for Statistics Canada, 1998.

Steel, J.L. 'Interpersonal Correlates of Trust and Self-Disclosure.' *Psychological Reports* 68 (1996): 1319–20.

Stewart, M., and H. Clarke. 'The Dynamics of Party Identification in Federal Systems: The Canadian Case.' *American Journal of Political Science* 42 (1998): 197–216.

Thomas, Paul. 'Caucus and Representation in Canada.' *Parliamentary Perspectives,* no. 1, May 1998.

Thorburn, Hugh G., editor. *Party Politics in Canada.* Scarborough, ON: Prentice Hall Canada Inc., 1996.

Tyler, Tom, and Roderick Moreland Kramer, editors. *Trust in Organizations: Frontiers of Theory and Research.* Thousand Oaks, CA: Sage, 1996.

United Kingdom. *Compact on Relations between Government and the Voluntary and Community Sector in England.* London: Queen's Printer, 1998.

United Nations Development Programme. *Human Development Report.* New York: Oxford University Press, 1994–9.

van Deth, Jan. 'Interesting but Irrelevant: Social Capital and the Saliency of Politics in Western Europe.' *European Journal of Political Research* 37 (2000): 115–47.

van Deth, Jan, and Elinor Scarborough, editors. *The Impact of Values.* New York: Oxford University Press, 1995.

Verba, Sidney, Kay Lehman Schlozman, and Henry E. Brady. *Voice and Equality: Civic Voluntarism in American Politics.* Cambridge, MA: Harvard University Press, 1995.

Wattenberg, M. *The Decline of American Political Parties: 1952–1988.* Cambridge, MA: Harvard University Press, 1990.

White, Charles S. 'Citizen Participation and the Internet: Prospects for Civic Deliberation in the Information Age.' *The Social Studies* Jan./Feb. 1997: 23–8.

Whittington, Michael, and Glen Williams, editors. *Canadian Politics in the 1990's.* Toronto: Nelson Canada, 1997.

Wills, Garry. *A Necessary Evil: A History of American Distrust of Government.* New York: Simon and Schuster, 1999.

Zaller, J. *The Nature and Origins of Mass Opinion.* New York: Cambridge University Press, 1992.

Zhao, Xinshu, and Steven H. Chaffee. 'Campaign Advertisements versus Television News as Sources of Political Issue Information.' *Public Opinion Quarterly* 59 (1995): 41–65.